The Art of Digital Branding

Ian Cocoran

ALLWORTH PRESS
NEW YORK

For Kate & Lucy

11   10   09   08   07   5   4   3   2   1

Published by Allworth Press
An imprint of Allworth Communications, Inc.
10 East 23rd Street, New York, NY 10010

Cover design by Derek Bacchus
Interior design by SR Desktop Services, Ridge, NY
Page composition/typography by SR Desktop Services, Ridge, NY

Library of Congress Cataloging-in-Publication Data
    Cocoran, Ian.
    The art of digital branding / Ian Cocoran.
        p.   cm.
    Includes index.
    ISBN-13: 978-1-58115-488-7 (hardcover)
    ISBN-10: 1-58115-488-7 (hardcover)
    1. Internet marketing.   2. Web sites—Design.   3. Brand name products.
4. Electronic commerce.   I. Title.
HF5415.1265.C6364   2007
658.8'2702854678—dc22

                                                        2007011449

Printed in Canada

Contents

Foreword

WHAT CAUSES A FLASHY AUTOMOTIVE BRAND TO CHOOSE a demure online presence? Why would a business obscure half its product line beneath a complicated navigation system? How can a fan visit a Web site and conclude he's more passionate about the brand than the company itself? This may sound exaggerated, but it can all come horribly to life in a couple of browser clicks.

Lack of cohesion between brand position and brand identity, messages at cross-purposes with the business model, brand architecture that resembles a plate of noodles, absent customer service: none of these issues gains clarity in migrating to the Web. Certainly businesses that are not completely in sync offline can quickly unravel online, but there are a staggering number of businesses that ace offline branding and still go on to commit serious online blunders.

So what's the secret? Pointing out the obvious probably doesn't help dissipate the anxiety generated by every medium that proclaims the alarming speed of advancement and scope of the Internet. But stepping back and considering the "obvious" with a clear head and purpose can only help focus your online venture toward a strategic and tactical plan.

The dilemma in trying to codify digital branding is that what's written today risks being obsolete by the time it hits ink. However, there are some universal best practices for operating online. When you run out of ideas or courage, there are unlimited opportunities to browse the Net and see what works and what doesn't work. Ian's best practice suggestions, illustrated by site reviews, will help take the mystery out of the mix while leaving the magic in place.

—Robin Rusch
Founding Editor, brandchannel.com
New York, January 2007

A Note from the Author

IF YOU ARE READING THIS BOOK, THEN YOU ARE PROBABLY *a marketer or an executive with an interest in online branding. You could also be a student who's looking to pick up some extra information before submitting a particular paper or just seeking to improve your knowledge of branding on the Web. Alternatively, you may have grabbed this title from the shelf of a bookstore in an airport or a railway station in the hope that it will pass the time on some long journey or other. Either way, thank you very much for buying this book.*

The subject of digital branding has long been held as an esoteric process—after all, there's so much to consider, what with the design of a Web site, the choice of technology and imagery, and, of course, the decision as to whether or not the host organization should be selling its wares online. Add to that the complexity surrounding such extravagant concepts as search engine optimization and then throw in a couple of buzz words such as "Java" and "Flash" and it's probably little wonder that the management of company Web sites is frequently delegated out to the techies and the Net nerds that reside within IT.

Despite all of the fearsome rhetoric, however, I passionately believe that the subject of digital branding is anything but rocket science and that, provided that you follow a set of simple rules, it should be no more difficult or complex than your average marketing plan. Indeed, setting the science aside, digital branding is as much of an art as it is a technical skill, so creativity and innovation are key to making it work.

To that end, what I have tried to do within the pages of this book is break down the digital branding process into a series of simple modules, which, when put together, can help anyone with an open mind address the subject with confidence. In writing the conclusion, I have also attempted to articulate my belief that in today's world of ever improving technology and chaotic corporate change, Web sites can represent an emotionally intelligent medium from which businesses and organizations can reach out to their customers. When managed correctly, these sites can considerably enhance the brands they represent.

I sincerely hope that you find this book informative and useful; I also hope that it measures up to your level of expectations. Above all, however, I would hope that you will find it a light and entertaining read—in the way that all good business books should be.

Acknowledgments

IN WRITING THIS BOOK, I WOULD LIKE TO ACKNOWLEDGE the help, advice, and guidance of a number of people, without whose contributions this publication would never have seen the light of day.

First, I would like to say thanks to the following—Helen Whitfield, Steve Jones, David Burgess, Scott Crighton, James Clarke, Kevin Parker, Nigel Hayes, Derek Mitchell, and Phil Hockaday, for keeping me gainfully preoccupied with business in the real world when it would have so often been easier for me to drift off into cyberspace instead. Likewise, I would like to thank Tony Corrigan for his continual humor and candor in an environment where I quite often behaved like a kid in a sweet shop and (to use his words) "just couldn't help myself."

Thanks also to Mike Latham, Steve Smith, and David Jukes, for both their stoic comments and their steadfast advice, without which I probably would never have embarked on the journey of writing this book at all.

A special thank-you also goes to James Clark at *Voxego.com*, whose feedback on the more technical aspects of Internet design and SEO was invaluable during the early stages of writing.

Next, I would like to say a very big thank-you to my father-in-law, Dr. Gordon Ker. A founder of the Scottish Hypnosis Society and an undoubted expert in "affairs of the mind," Gordon has helped ensure that this book actually progressed within the desired timescales and in keeping me motivated from conception to conclusion. He is indeed a special man and someone I will always hold in the very highest regard.

Thanks also go to my father, Paul Mann, and to his long-standing Australian confidant, Margaret O'Sullivan, who, as published authors, have been both influential in their guidance and invaluable in their advice. In the same regard, I would also like to thank the team at Allworth Press and, in particular, Nicole Potter-Talling, without whom this publication would never have been possible. Likewise, I would like to thank Robin Rusch, who has been tireless in her pursuit of great things for brandchannel.com and an absolute rock for all of its contributors.

Finally, I have reserved perhaps the biggest thank-you of all to my family, without whose love and blessing I would have stayed well away from this foray into authorship and, instead, would have probably just gone fishing: To my mother Maureen, for her love and best wishes, to my step-father, Doug, for his constant goodwill, and to my wife Kate and my daughter Lucy, who are always in my thoughts.

Introduction

THE INTERNET HAS CHANGED OUR LIVES. THE PORTAL once known as the Information Superhighway became a necessity long ago and is now the most influential medium to human behavior since television.

There is very little that cannot be achieved on the Internet—for good or for bad. With a few taps on a keyboard and the simple click of a mouse, users can find a date; play games; chat with friends; purchase goods and services; download audio and video; take part in virtual tours of museums, houses, auditoriums, and cruise liners; manage their finances; and, of course, carry out as much research as they could possibly need on subjects that range from the building of bombs to recipes for apple pie.

In the corporate world, the Internet represents an unparalleled opportunity for businesses of every size and description to globalize in an instant. The rules for market penetration have been twisted in such a way that companies no longer need to invest in bricks and mortar, labor, or even stock in order to ply their wares in a specific country or geography. They don't need to bother with advertising or market research, nor is there a need to pay for an army of consultants to come and present Boston Grids, Porter's 5 Forces, or SWOT analyses. Indeed, these days, if a business wants to sell its goods and services overseas, all it needs to do is evangelize its capabilities in cyberspace and badge itself as a "virtual organization"—its initial investment can therefore be miniscule.

Now if you're reading this as a traditional marketer, you may well be laughing your socks off by now and could probably be forgiven for thinking that instead of paying good money for this book, you would have been much better off with a copy of *Men's Health, Vogue,* or *Forbes Magazine.*

"What nonsense," I can hear you saying. "Surely everyone needs to undertake a viable evaluation of risk before entering a new market. Otherwise, we'd all be doing it and the bank managers and venture capitalists among us would never see a day off."

Well, just close your eyes for a second and consider the successes of eBay, Paypal, and Amazon—all very different businesses but all with a myriad of virtual subdistribution networks that have driven up their brand equity by providing a reach and depth that in the past was simply unimaginable. Now consider file sharing via P2P networks and the global recognition achieved by Napster and Kazaa. Then there's Google, one of the most valuable stocks on Wall Street—now are you getting the picture?

Love it or hate it, the Web is a truly global gateway. It's open all hours, easily accessible, and as Paris Hilton, Pamela Anderson, and the entire "You Tube" (1) community will testify, capable of inflicting global ignominy on the most unsuspecting people with breathtaking alacrity.

As a communications medium, the Web is second to none. Al Qaeda, for example, has regularly used the World Wide Web to both spread its message and communicate with potential new recruits and members scattered right across the planet, while in 1997 the Heaven's Gate religious cult created a sensation when it was discovered that it had used the Web to attract new associates before organizing a mass suicide in San Diego, California.

During 9\11, Web sites such as CNN and Reuters buckled under the sheer weight of traffic as millions of people around the globe scrambled to watch events unfold, while in April 2006 "Crazy" by Gnarls Barkley became the first ever song to top the UK charts based on download sales alone.

The Internet can be anything you want it to be. It can be overt or discreet, a learning tool or a platform for preaching. It is a haven for the shy and a stage for those who seem hell-bent on the pursuit of self-publicity. It can be molded to suit both our habits and our lifestyles, and within environments such as those created by online communities like "Second Life" (2) it can make all of your dreams come true.

The paradigm created by the World Wide Web is changing before our very eyes and global multinationals are frantically trying to change with it. Organizations have spent millions of dollars developing their e-marketing concepts to attract, retain, and grow their business—and with somewhere in the region of 16 percent of the world's population now Web-enabled (3), it's a worthwhile course of action. Never before has the Internet represented such an opportunity for companies large and small to exploit their online presence by clearly defining their Web proposition and adding value to their brands.

As an example of the Web's fluidity and its ability to manifest debate, the billionaire investor and Internet entrepreneur Mark Cuban said on September 28, 2006 (4), that only a "moron" would buy You Tube, the Internet site that's dedicated to the publication and sharing of videos. Just a few days later, on October 10, Google, one of the world's most valuable brands, agreed to pay $1.65 billion for it (5) and in the process of doing so catapulted its CEO, Eric Schmidt, to the status of a muttonhead in the eyes of Cuban.

So with all of this opinion and the prolific rate of change that pervades the World Wide Web, not to mention, of course, the billions of dollars that were wiped from investors' portfolios during the last dotcom crash, is it any wonder that many organizations still struggle with what is expected of them online and are they really trying hard enough with regard to their propositions and content?

Within the pages of *The Art of Digital Branding*, I have attempted to answer as much of that question as possible by evaluating the dos and don'ts of building and enhancing a brand on the Internet. In using some of the real-life examples of the good, the bad, and the just plain ugly that I have regularly come across during my time spent writing for *brandchannel.com* (the world's only dedicated online branding Web site), I want to share my findings with you.

In this book, I have considered the types of material that organizations should publish and what they probably shouldn't. I've also looked at technology in terms of the bare essentials, the extra gimmicks and gizmos that are designed to keep the hit counter spinning, and of course some of the stuff that you wouldn't want to go near without a radiation suit. I've covered the luxury brand debate, cause-related marketing, and, of course, the traditional brand-building concepts of awareness, positioning, and segmentation. Finally, and in closing, I have attempted to pull everything together to present my view of how the perfect brand should look on the Web, by way of articulating my theory of the emotionally intelligent Web site.

This is not a book on Web design, although that concept is covered in various chapters due to its impact on navigation, culture, and emotional intelligence. I'm also afraid that this book is unlikely to help you devise the perfect brand strategy or, indeed, prevent you from blowing your marketing budget on expensive technological paraphernalia—that, I'm afraid, will be up to you. This is a book on digital branding, for better or for worse. As such, and if you use it correctly, it should help you steer clear of a lot of the basic pitfalls that are associated with the digital branding concept and also help you identify some of the real added value stuff that's around on the Web today.

I've been reviewing corporate Web sites for brandchannel since January 2001, and during that time I've seen some fantastic online representations of intrinsic brand value. I've also seen some things that you wouldn't go near with a cattle prod, and others where you would swear that the Web designers and content editors had either been high on Pink Floyd or a cocktail of illicit substances before setting off for work. I've reviewed brands from Asia, Australia, Europe, and North America and from both the public and private sectors. I've even reviewed some countries as they attempt to seduce the tourist dollar and also the odd soccer club during their search for worldwide appeal.

Hopefully, my experiences of reviewing these Web sites and the work I have done for brandchannel.com will help you during your quest to identify the perfect online brand. I also hope that after reading this book, you will come to the same conclusions as I have with regard to the concept of branding on the World Wide Web.

It is not an esoteric process. Nor is it surrounded in a cloud of myth that falls beyond the realm of comprehension for anyone without a degree in IT or a master's in marketing. It can be as simple as following a few basic rules—and within the pages of this book I will endeavor to show you, brick by brick, just exactly what they are.

ENDNOTES

1. *www.youtube.com/*
2. *http://secondlife.com/*
3. *www.Internetworldstats.com/stats.htm*
4. *http://today.reuters.com/news/articlenews.aspx?type=InternetNews&story ID=2006-09-29T115658Z_01_N28230044_RTRUKOC_0_US-MEDIA-YOUTUBE.xml&WTmodLoc=InternetNewsHome_C1_%5bFeed%5d-2*
5. *www.smh.com.au/news/biztech/apple—google-v-microsoft/2006/08/ 30/1156816939604.html*

1

What's in a Name?

The beginning of wisdom is to call things by their right names
—CHINESE PROVERB

THE WORLD WIDE WEB IS, WITHOUT DOUBT, THE MOST popular constituent of the global Internet. Its growth since inception has been nothing short of phenomenal, and already billions of dollars have been made and lost as a succession of corporate enterprises have launched themselves into cyberspace with little more than a well-conceived idea and a book from the Gideon Society. Seeking to boldly go where no brand has boldly gone before, many of these companies are now suspended in the ether, wondering exactly where their money went, while others have come crashing back to Earth with all the grace and humility of an asteroid. A few, however, have been extremely successful—and are now plotting their trajectories well beyond their original estimates and across that final frontier.

As far as individuals are concerned, the Web has proven to be a magical place with ever increasing boundaries and a depth of capability that would appear to be as limitless as the depths of one's imagination. It's also as addictive as crack cocaine, as the millions of Net nerds and Web heads who constantly trawl the pages of this vast ocean of information will testify. Blessed with global coverage and unaware of class, the Web is an environment for all ages, all cultures, and all levels of ability, regardless of whether you consider yourself an accomplished two-handed tapper or a flaccid-fingered failure who's experience of a keyboard runs no further than the nearest Bontempi.

For brand managers and owners alike, the advent of the World Wide Web has brought unparalleled opportunities in regions and geographies that have historically proved inaccessible because of limited resources and short-range communications. This is largely due to the fact that over the past ten years or so, the cyber-mechanics that make the Internet tick have become increasingly sophisticated, while bandwidth and download speeds have been improved dramatically, in turn affording Net users a richer and more interactive Web-driven experience.

In addition to the improvements in technology, the number of available sites on the Web has multiplied exponentially, and most have adapted to the improving technology with ease, bringing intense competition to an ever changing and ever crowded marketplace. As a result, most Net surfers spend only a few seconds in any given place—unless someone or something really grabs their attention.

With so much content to choose from, haven't you ever stopped and wondered just why you feel suddenly drawn to a Web site? What does it do for you? What floats your boat? What is it that gets your curiosity aroused and stimulates your neurons to the extent that you're encouraged to rev up someone's hit counter?

In this first chapter, we will try to answer some of those questions by covering the basics of how the Internet works, and we will attempt to put into place the absolute cornerstones of the digital branding concept.

We will focus on the importance of choosing the right domain name and making the correct association between that and the brand it represents. We will also look at the importance of search engines and how they can help to ensure that your brand gets some well-deserved attention, as well as taking a little peek at some of the more opportunistic approaches to branding on the Internet.

IP Addresses

If you're not too familiar with some of the terminology that's covered in this chapter, please try not to worry, as I have endeavored to keep the technical stuff to an absolute minimum. I have also tried to analogize whenever I've found it possible, in order to stop ourselves from drowning in the type of techno-babble that can usually be heard coming from the room that's next to the water cooler and behind the door marked "IT."

The use of the Internet is predicated on IP (Internet protocol) addresses that are subsequently used to identify either individual devices (computers, phones, blackberries, etc.), or individual domain names. Quite simply, they are very similar to phone numbers, but instead of identifying an individual's phone, they are used to identify either a device that's accessing the Internet, the site that a person is looking at, and/or the ISP (Internet service provider) that's hosting a particular session.

IP addresses look boring, as they're really nothing more than a series of four numbers that are separated by periods (for example, 012.345.67.89). Given their powers of navigation and traceability, however, you should try and think of them as either digital identities or individual hallmarks that provide instant recognition between two communicating machines (one being the server that's hosting the Web site you are looking at and the other being the machine that you are using to surf the Net). If you know the IP address of a Web site you are after, you can key it straight into your Internet browser rather than carrying out a search for the site's actual domain name and, all things being equal, the Information Superhighway should lead you straight to it.

The IP address in figure 1.1, for example, is that of the Internet Corporation for Assigned Names and Numbers, or ICANN for short (we will learn more about the ICANN organization later but for the moment, let's just concentrate on the process behind Web site location). If you key this IP address into your browser, you will be taken directly to the ICANN Web site:

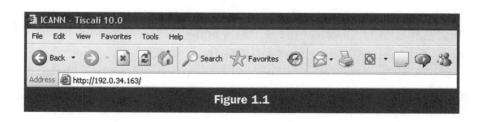

Figure 1.1

The key thing to remember with IP addresses is that by and large they are just like opinions—everyone has one. If they didn't, you wouldn't be able to surf the Web at all, as the server of the Web site that you were trying to locate and the machine that was physically surfing the net (your PC, for example) wouldn't be able to talk to each other, and your wonderfully interactive Web experience would be about as lively and entertaining as a night on the town with a bunch of Trappist Monks.

The consequences of this point (the fact that everyone has an IP address, not a night out with the friars) should be very extremely obvious to you. Be aware, therefore, that IP addresses are a critical component of surfing the Web and by their very nature create a tangible record of who's been where and what they looked at—as a certain Paul Gad (1) will testify. In other words, every time you visit a Web site, your PC recognizes and logs the IP address of the content you are viewing and the Web site does the same thing in order to find out a little bit more about you. So the next time that you find yourself ever so "accidentally" logged onto something that's quite obviously innocent, like *swedishnymphetsonrollerskates.com*, you may want to bear in mind that there's a very good chance that the host server knows quite a bit more about you than you might like to think!

Characteristics of IP Addresses

IP addresses can be either static or dynamic. If they are static, they are permanent and can always be used to identify a specific location—servers predominantly use static IP addresses as, in general, they can be found in the same place and seldom have a need to change their protocols. Internet users such as you and I, however, are a completely different proposition, as we may often log on wirelessly from a variety of different locations or, indeed, while partaking of the odd Chai Latte when visiting an Internet café and checking our e-mails via a fixed PC. So how does that work?

Well, because the popularity of the Internet has generated a somewhat exponential demand for the online facilitation of more and more users and content providers, it became clear sometime ago that there just wouldn't be enough static IP addresses to go around and that ISPs would need to find a solution to that particular problem if the Net's growth rate were to be sustained.

By way of resolving their quandary, the techies and the geeks devised a very clever way of allocating dynamic or temporary IP addresses from an ISP's individual pool, which could simply be loaned to a user for the duration of his online session and returned to the pool when he was finished. In many ways, this is very similar to renting a mobile phone. You get the use of the number and the device for the duration of the rental period and when you're done, you return it to the hire company, who then rents it to somebody else.

Thanks to this development, it is now common practice for ISPs to restrict the allocation of static IP addresses to fixed servers only and subsequently use their pool of dynamic IP addresses for the majority of their domestic customers, who use their PCs or mobile devices just to surf the Web. This is particularly the case in high-traffic areas and, of course, for wireless connections, such as airports and "hot spots," where multiple users often connect and disconnect.

I am sure that by now all of this talk of traceability has made you somewhat curious and you are probably keen to know just exactly what it is that you are transmitting whenever you go online. Should you ever wish to check your IP address, therefore, there are plenty of sites on the Web that will do it for you, such as *www.showmyip.com* or *www.whatismyipaddress.com*.

Alternatively, if the converse of the above is true and you are one of those individuals who take exception to Big Brother, you can download some software to conceal your IP address in order to inhibit the amount of information that others can see or, indeed, should you wish to disguise the location from which you are accessing the Internet. Examples of Web sites where such software is available are prevalent on the Internet, with *www.unknownip.com* or *www.netconceal.com* constituting just two of them. Please be aware, however, that I have named these Web sites only to illustrate the particular case in point and that neither I nor the publishers recommend or endorse the downloading of software from any Internet site. With that in mind, any such software that you choose to install on your machine is done so entirely at your own risk!

Uses of IP Addresses

If you're a typical marketer with an attention span similar to mine, you're probably starting to get a little bit bored with the technical stuff and are also probably wondering just what it's all got to do with the concept of digital branding. Well, first and foremost, and as you now know, your IP address can provide almost as much information as your credit card or tax file number to a Web server and, as such, it can be used to great effect within businesses that carry out extensive data mining and CRM (customer relationship management) activity. Indeed, because an IP address can tell an organization everything from the time that you logged on until the time that you logged off, the location of the PC you used, and the ISP that facilitated the session, the Web-savvy businesses just love them to bits and subsequently treat the software they use to monitor them as the equivalent of a first-class market researcher.

The Coca-Cola Company sums up the entire concept rather nicely within its Web site privacy policy (2) by stating:

> *Your Internet Protocol (IP) address is an identifying number that is automatically assigned to your computer by your Internet Service Provider (ISP). This number is identified and logged automatically in our server log files whenever you visit the Site, along with the time(s) of your visit(s) and the page(s) that you visited. We use the IP addresses of all Visitors to calculate Site usage levels, to help diagnose problems with the Site's servers, and to administer the Site. We may also use IP addresses to communicate or to block access by Visitors who fail to comply with our Terms of Service. Collecting IP addresses is standard practice on the Internet and is carried out automatically by many Web sites.*

If all of this Big Brother stuff has got you slightly worried, please try to remember that, aside from being used for marketing purposes, IP addresses also form an integral part of the Web's policing activity and they have often been used to identify and prosecute a number of criminals. Consider, for example, the findings of the 2005 Digital Terrorism and Hate Report (3), which revealed a 25 percent increase in Internet hate sites and the fact that the police have been forced to patrol Internet chat rooms in order to monitor the behavior of pedophiles (4), and I am sure you will agree that there is a need to exercise caution. To that very end, I wish the governing authorities well in their quest to make the Internet a much safer place for us and our children and would hope that they only use the information they recover for the purposes of improving society.

Because IP addresses are an excellent way of identifying the specific geographies associated with a Web site's inbound traffic, it is possible to use them not just for the purposes of data collation but also to block the amount of content they can access. Imagine, for example, that you are hosting a Web site that's been tailored to meet the exclusive demands of the North American market and that you have posted some material that you would prefer residents of those countries outside of that geography not to see. By monitoring and filtering your IP addresses, you can do exactly that and effectively create a "Backstage Pass" for residents of your preferred geography, while keeping users from elsewhere firmly located within the auditorium.

In the UK, the BBC (British Broadcasting Corporation) and several commercial radio stations, such as the London-based Capitol, have been forced down this track as a result of a wrangle over performing rights royalties and, as a consequence, no longer allow residents of overseas countries to listen to their live radio content (5).

The dispute started when various audio licensing bodies such as PPL (Phonographic Performance Limited) realized that there were numerous UK radio stations broadcasting content over the Internet, which was subsequently being listened to by thousands of people who lived well away from the original fee-payers' domestic area of jurisdiction. Upset by the perceived loss of revenue (or motivated by the desire to gain some more), PPL argued that if radio stations that were indigenous to the UK were going to broadcast material to residents of overseas countries, both it and the artists that it represents should be entitled to additional royalties. As a direct response, many radio stations simply switched off the audio streams they were previously broadcasting on the Net, while others such as the BBC elected to filter the inbound traffic.

The crazy thing about all of this is that despite the somewhat zealous controls that exist for the broadcast of outbound content, the UK is currently powerless to stop the reception of inbound material from Web sites based beyond its shores—so it cops a double whammy. The Brits should fear not, however, as dialogue has started between PPL and its counterparts in several overseas countries to restrict some of the inbound broadcasts received. If successful, this will ensure that the UK will become the only developed country on the planet, with the exception, of course, of China, to actively prohibit its residents from accessing foreign media!

Thankfully, and despite the best efforts of the self-appointed "fun police," the Internet community is not as dumb as people think and it is possible to get around the filtering of traffic by downloading some of the software that is readily available online and disguising one's IP address as that from another geography—not that I would endorse such behavior, of course. That issue aside, I hope that as we move on through the concept of digital branding that this little cameo has helped you understand the Web's unparalleled ability to cross both cultures and borders with a depth of penetration and a speed of execution that has been hitherto unheard of—and I also hope that you've improved your knowledge of IP addresses.

Domain Names

Now that you know that the Internet is fundamentally driven by the concept of IP addresses, you will probably be starting to wonder where domain names come in to the equation. The short answer to this is that they evolved over time as an alternative to keying in numbers and subsequently ran parallel to the growth of the World Wide Web. The more detailed answer is as follows:

In the beginning, not long after the Internet was born, all registered IP addresses and their associated host names were kept on a single file named hosts.txt, which was managed and maintained by an organization that is known today as SRI International, which was originally founded in 1946 as the Stanford Research Institute. In those early days, people navigated the Internet by simply logging on to the hosts.txt file and retrieving the IP address of the site that they wanted to visit.

For years this system fulfilled its purpose, and the majority of the Internet's small number of users found that they could both orient themselves and carry out basic searches with a minimum of effort. As the Web's popularity surged and network use increased, however, it soon became clear that the host.txt system had some major limitations, not least of which was keeping pace with the many changes in IP addresses that its growing band of users seemed hell-bent on initiating.

By way of counteracting this problem without stifling the Internet's growth, Paul Mockapetris invented a system called the "domain name server" (DNS) in 1983 (6), which was predicated on the assignation of information belonging to a domain to a series of zones, which could then be delegated out for further management.

The DNS works by starting with a series of top-level domains, which are then subdivided via a hierarchy into a series of sub-zones. Each sub-zone can then be managed by a series of different authorities and each level of the hierarchy can relate to Web address of each name. In many ways, it's just like a structure for pyramid selling, where each level of the pyramid contributes to the profit streams of those directly above it until such time as the guy at the top either makes his mega millions or is arrested for malpractice.

Now don't worry if this is not sinking in, as the nuances of the DNS are difficult to follow, but try and stick with it as we run through an example of how domain names are structured. Before that, however, let's start with a diagram of the DNS hierarchy in theory, which should help clarify exactly how the system works.

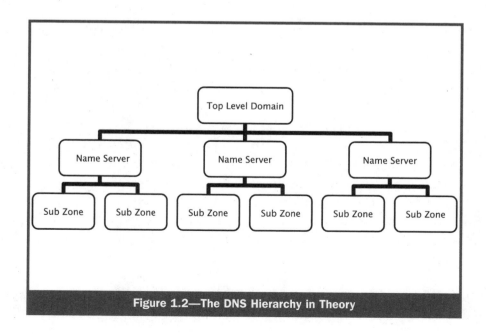

Figure 1.2—The DNS Hierarchy in Theory

Top-level domains are managed by registrars and are generally used to specify either the type of activity or the geographic location with which a Web site may be associated. Because of their level of influence, they reside at the pinnacle of the DNS hierarchy and everything else hangs off them. Examples of some of the more common top-level domains can be listed as:

- Com—Commercial Business
- Gov—Government agency
- Org—Non-profit organization
- co.uk—United Kingdom
- ca—Canada

Once a top-level domain has been established, it then becomes possible for a number of name servers and subdomains to be added simply by naming them as a prefix to the top-level domain and separating them with periods. Obviously, the more prefixes that are associated with a domain, the more subdomains it has; for example:

www.news.bbc.co.uk

In this instance, .co.uk (United Kingdom) is the top level domain, bbc (the British Broadcasting Corporation) is the name server, and news is the final subdomain. Theoretically, it is possible to continue adding subdomains up to a maximum of either 127 levels or 255 characters, whichever comes first, although in practice, of course, this would be highly unusual.

Perhaps the most important thing to remember when dealing with subdomains is that they should not be confused with directories, because although they may appear to be quite similar, they are in fact fundamentally different. For instance, where domains are cited as prefixes to a top-level domain and are separated by periods, directories are sited as suffixes to the top level domain and are separated by slashes. Quite apart from their physical appearance, however, directories differ from subdomains because they don't need to be managed by independent third parties and, more often than not, their creation and upkeep is, directly controlled by the hosting organization.

With all of that in mind and given the notoriously short attention spans of most marketers, you will now be somewhat relieved to hear that I don't intend to delve any further into the murky world of DNS hierarchies, subdomains, or directories for fear of boring most readers rigid. From a branding perspective, however, it is important that you understand just exactly what makes the Internet tick and, as a result, what buttons you should push in order to get the most out of it.

On the other hand, if you were one of those kids who spent hours playing with a Meccano set when everyone else was playing with a ball and all of this talk of technical stuff has simply whetted your appetite about the intricate machinations of the World Wide Web, there are plenty of Web sites that will be happy to indulge you with all of the necessary detail. In terms of pointing you in the right direction, I have generally found the level of granulation provided on the subject by one of the Web's most prominent online encyclopedias, *Wikipedia.com* (7), to be a sure-fire cure for insomnia!

Brands as Domain Names

As previously discussed, the introduction of the DNS was a monumental breakthrough in terms of making the Internet more user-friendly and ratcheting up the adoption rate yet another level. The principal reason for this is that humans find remembering names much easier than remembering numbers, with the exception perhaps of Akira Haraguchi, who in 2005 recalled the first 83,431 decimal places of pi (8).

Unfortunately, most of us are not blessed with Mr. Haraguchi's powers of recall or, indeed, would prefer to do something with our spare time other than reciting numerical incantations. As a direct consequence, we tend to rely on the powers of association and memory to find what we are looking for on the Web, and therein lies the major advantage of the DNS, as it enables us to search the Internet by key word instead of IP address—and this has proven to been nothing short of an absolute revelation for those with a mercantile mind.

As everyone knows, brands are a considerable part of any organization's asset portfolio and as such, they need to be maintained and protected. Consider the value of the Coca-Cola brand, for example, which experts believe is currently worth somewhere in the region of $70 billion (9). Imagine if you owned it—what lengths would you go to in order to protect it from being either abused or misrepresented?

When the DNS was invented almost twenty-five years ago, Paul Mockapetris must have had little idea as to the global phenomenon the Internet would become or that, from a digital branding perspective, he had just ignited a slow-burning fuse. Indeed, he was only interested in making the World Wide Web a lot more user-friendly and simplifying the process of search and navigation.

Of course, what Mockapetris hadn't foreseen was the dramatic surge in Internet growth rates that would precede the millennium and the fact that, thereafter, millions of people would turn to it each day when either looking for information or managing their lives. He also hadn't foreseen the magnitude of the impact that the DNS would have on the corporate world and the fact that some domain names would be worth a virtual fortune.

As a direct consequence of the Internet's surge in popularity during the 1990s and because it was now possible to use brands as domain names due to the development of the DNS, many companies and corporations tripped over each other in a mad stampede to protect their prize assets and prevent them from being misused. Unfortunately, not all of them were as quick off the mark as some aspiring entrepreneurs who also saw the registration of domain names as something of a gold rush and in many cases had already registered a number of big brand domains before the corporations themselves.

Perhaps not surprisingly, the upshot of all this activity was nothing short of chaos, with both individuals and businesses frantically competing against each other in order to register some of the more lucrative domains. In the midst of all this confusion, the lawyers just couldn't believe their luck and started rubbing their palms with glee.

A great example of the current case in point is a man named Jeff Burgar.

A resident of Alberta, Canada, Jeff snapped up a multitude of domain names throughout the mid-1990s and as a result of his erstwhile activities, earned himself the somewhat notorious reputation of being the Web's most preeminent "cybersquatter." During his prime, Jeff registered quite literally thousands of domain names that more or less represented anything and everything that was likely to be of value.

Indeed, if a domain showed even the remotest chance of being popular in the future, the likelihood was that Jeff wasn't very far behind it—regardless of whether it represented a business, a celebrity, or a well-known sports team.

In many cases, the legal consequences of what Jeff did more than a decade ago are still rumbling on today. Since the turn of the millennium, Jeff has frequently found himself defending his position in front of the World Intellectual Property Organization (WIPO) with regard to registering the domain names of such well-known entities as *HewlettPackard.com*, *CelineDion.com*, and *TomCruise.com*.

In total, Jeff now owns around 1,500 domain names and is determined to hold on to as many as he can by continuing his battles in court. Although he lost the rights to the Hewlett-Packard domain in 2000 (10) and then lost Celine Dion's to a very uptight Sony Music in 2001 (11), he actually won the battle to keep *BruceSpringsteen.com* in the same year (12).

Given the nature of Burgar's legal battles, exactly what the future may hold for *TomCruise.com* is anyone's guess, particularly when considering that the world-famous actor and renowned scientologist only embarked upon his quest to own the rights to the domain as recently as May 2006—even though Burgar, the Canadian entrepreneur, first registered it a full decade earlier!

If I were Tom Cruise, however, I would probably spend less time worrying about Jeff Burgar and more time either trying to renew the fourteen-year relationship I'd just blown with Paramount Pictures in August 2006 due to my off-screen antics or attempting to get a grip on the Tom Cruise anti-site, *tomcruiseisnuts.com*, as both issues look as though they are capable of presenting the vertically challenged thespian with a series of more pressing problems.

By way of illustrating this fact and perhaps in pointing Thomas Mapother IV in a suitably relevant direction, I have included a screenshot of *tomcruiseisnuts.com* in figure 1.3 on the following page.

Domain Name Management

Notwithstanding the Jeff Burgars of this world, for most people the registration of a domain name should prove to be a very straightforward process and, in many cases, has resulted in the birth of a whole

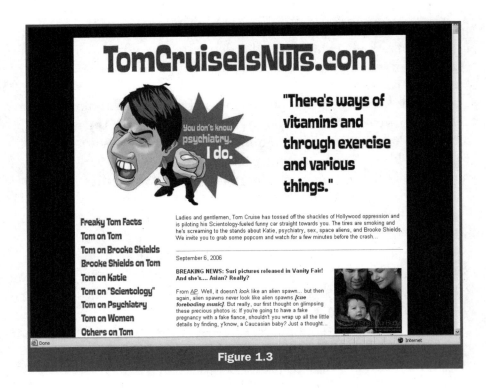

Figure 1.3

new brand. For example, eBay, Yahoo, Google, and Amazon are all great examples of multimillion dollar brands that wouldn't exist today had it not been for the explosion in Internet growth that was catalyzed by the birth of the DNS.

Before you go rushing out to register the next Yahoo, however, you may wish to bear in mind that just like anything else in life, it pays to do your research before selecting your domain name registrar, because the type of deal you get can often vary greatly depending upon your provider. For instance, apart from the upfront fees and charges that normally apply to registration and hosting, most providers stipulate a finite timescale that will subsequently apply to the domain name in question, and these can be almost anything—although somewhere between one to three years tends to be the most prevalent.

A belt-and-braces approach to choosing the right partner is to select a registrar from ICANN's accredited database (13), which contains a list of organizations that specialize in the management of top-level domains. ICANN now plays a pivotal role in the assignation of domain names right across the world and, thankfully, is a not-for-profit organization. ICANN states its role as being:

> *Responsible for coordinating the management of the technical elements of the DNS to ensure universal resolvability so that all users of the Internet can find all valid addresses. It does this by overseeing the distribution of unique technical identifiers used in the Internet's operations, and delegation of Top-Level Domain names (such as .com, .info, etc.).*

Aside from managing the technical elements that relate to the DNS, ICANN operates the Uniform Domain Names Dispute Resolution Policy, or UDRP for short, which is largely designed to resolve trademark disputes. Upon visiting the policy's homepage (14), interested parties can indulge themselves with a comprehensive list of proceedings that have been opened as a result of the UDRP coming into force. Consequently, it's well worth a visit for anyone with an interest in corporate hijacking.

If you have ever visited the ICANN Web site and its accredited database, you will not have wasted much time before coming across a company called Verisign, which is a provider and operator of the central data base for the top-level domains of .com, .net, .cc, and .tv. In 2002, Verisign conducted a study of the world's top twenty-five brands as defined by Interbrand and evaluated their digital presence across three main categories before publishing the results in the "Verisign Digital Brand Index Report" (15).

By applying some simple criteria, the report focused on:

- How the brands in question were representing and protecting their names on the Internet
- How often a brand was damaged by a third party (such as a cybersquatter or a hijacker)
- How often a Web address that was owned by a company physically led to a branded site

Although by no means perfect, the Verisign study became an excellent early indicator of a business's level of efficiency with regard to the digital branding concept. If nothing else, it certainly highlighted the organizations that were keen to invest at the concept's bleeding edge (16).

Perhaps somewhat strangely, the results of the Verisign report showed that four out of the top five brands were correlated across the automotive companies of BMW, Mercedes, Ford, and Toyota, although the overall winner at that time was American Express (the IT industry didn't feature within the top five). As an aside, I actually had the pleasure of reviewing the Web sites of both BMW and American Express on behalf of brandchannel long before the Verisign report was released. Should you ever wish to see my conclusions, you can do so via the brandchannel Web site.

Since producing the first Digital Brand Index Report in 2002, Verisign has moved forward substantially in terms of evangelizing its digital brand management capability as a result of having identified a major opportunity in the marketplace. Today, the company has a stand-alone business unit that specializes in the concept (17) and, as one would expect, is only too pleased to be of service.

One of the cornerstones of Verisign's digital brand management strategy is that, by its very nature, the company is capable of registering and maintaining a series of domain names for a single IP address, which can be a major benefit for businesses that are frequently referred to by more than one designation or brand. The functionality that makes the assignation of multiple domains to one IP address possible is also a major plus that has come out of the development of the DNS. Perhaps somewhat perversely, however, it also presents a rather large loophole for corporate hijackers and cyber-squatters to exploit. It is exactly this concept that has provided the Jeff Burgars of this world with the opportunity to take advantage of any visible weakness that exists within a major brand's Net management strategy.

Thankfully, during the course of the last few years, most multinationals have become increasingly cognizant of the problem and more vigilant in their approach to managing their online brands. As a direct consequence, many have since bought up almost every conceivable configuration of their brand's association with a top-level domain in order to keep the agent provocateurs at bay.

A good example of what I am talking about with regard to multiple domain name association can be found by keying either *Cocacola.com*, *Coca-cola.com*, or *coke.com* into your Web browser, as all of these entries will take you to Big Red's homepage. Likewise, *bmw.com* or *bmw.net* will achieve exactly the same result and guide you, as if by magic, to the home of "Bayerische Motoren Werke."

Although these are just two very small examples of the types of domain names that are physically owned by some of the world's most valuable brands (as hundreds of registered domain names never actually see the light of day), the principle of preclusion is there for all to see. This is why many of the world's large organizations have recognized the need to register multiple domains. If they didn't, the chances of some irksome cybersquatter or would-be corporate hijacker getting their mitts on some hard-earned brand value would escalate considerably and that just wouldn't sit well in the corridors of power. So with the mad scramble for domain name registration and the subsequent need to manage the outputs still very much alive and kicking, it is perhaps not surprising that companies such as Verisign have attempted to carve a niche for themselves in the domain portfolio market.

Despite Verisign positioning itself at the forefront of the digital brand management concept, it has not all been smooth sailing for the company; in 2003 another ICANN-approved registrar, Go Daddy, initiated a lawsuit against the business as a result of its ubiquitous "Site Finder" service.

The legal argument was predicated on Go Daddy's assertion that Verisign was abusing its position as a top-level database operator, by diverting Web users who had inadvertently mis-keyed an address or entered a nonexistent Web site into the address bar of their Web browsers to the company's "Site Finder" facility, thereby subjecting them to advertising. Needless to say, after something of a hullabaloo and subsequent intervention by ICANN, Verisign was forced to shut down its "Site Finder" service, but not before it had filed a lawsuit against ICANN in order to gain some clarification as to what its terms of operation were, citing ICANN's perceived procrastination at decision-making and the resultant stagnation of Internet growth as the major issues involved. Eventually both sides reached a settlement, but not before receiving widespread criticism over the terms that were agreed upon.

Perhaps this interesting sequence of events really does highlight the value of what's at stake with regard to the value of domain names and the brands they represent across a medium that by its very nature refuses to be monopolized. It is also a pivotal point of consideration in the digital branding concept, as it's no longer good enough for a company to be *online*, it's also got to be *in line*. The starting point for this is to obviously ensure that anyone wishing to locate a brand on the Web can do so with consummate ease.

Since the simplest way to achieve this is by naming the domain in question after the brand or corporation that owns it, thereby enabling users to make a direct association between the Web location and the brand itself, one would think that organizations would have adopted such a policy long before now. Sadly this just hasn't been the case and although it is getting better with the passage of time, organizations such as WIPO are still laden with schedules that are attempting to resolve catfights over who owns what—and more are being added each week.

Search Engines

These days, almost everybody who has ever been exposed to the Internet will have at least some familiarity with the medium's major search engines, such as Google and Yahoo. Over time, they have proven to be fantastic tools by which to navigate the World Wide Web and great ways of locating those difficult-to-find Web sites. In this section, we will attempt to cover the basics of what search engines do as well as trying to identify the ways in which they are often manipulated in order to drive up the amount of inbound traffic to a specific Web site or portal.

Historically there have been three types of search engines, which can be described as follows:

- Spiders, otherwise known as crawlers
- Directories, which are usually driven by human submissions
- Hybrids, which are a blend of the above

Spiders—These engines work by sending some crawler-based software to a Web site, which then clambers all over it like an amphetamine-powered arachnid in order to retrieve essential information such as keywords, links, and meta tags (more on these later), before returning to base and depositing the data it has acquired in an index file. Spiders can visit a Web site with any degree of frequency, and they can also be empowered to carry out specific tasks, although they usually follow a preset pattern of activity as defined by the controlling search engine's administrators.

Directories—These are essentially index files, which store information about a Web site after collating a predetermined amount of data that has been submitted by individuals. This process usually occurs as a result of people filling in a series of online forms that are designed to identify the major characteristics of the Web site in question, such as the industry in which it operates and what its core activities are. Because the online forms are regimented in order to produce a guaranteed standard of data, all of the information pertaining to a site can easily be catalogued in order to simplify the process of retrieval.

Hybrids—Strangely enough, these types of search engines are driven by a combination of data that has been indexed and catalogued after having been acquired by a combination of spiders and human submission. While this process doesn't necessarily make them any more accurate than their counterparts, it does give them some flexibility and latitude in terms of data collation.

Without a shadow of doubt, the most critical thing to remember when dealing with search engines is that when you key your search terms into the engine's dialogue box and subsequently press "go," it doesn't actually search the Web. Instead, it rattles through its index files and catalogues at breakneck speed to hurriedly retrieve the most relevant responses it can find and present you with the responses that it feels are best suited to the search criteria you entered.

Based on this system, you could probably be forgiven for wondering why most search engines on the Web don't retrieve exactly the same responses to a given set of search terms you have entered. It's because there are a number of variables at play within the search engine's working parameters, such as the type of algorithms that they have used to generate the responses in the first place, the type of directory-based information that has been submitted by humans, and, of course, the viability of the meta tags and links that the spiders have found on their travels.

Notwithstanding the commonality that exists between search engines, the Web's biggest players, such as Google and Yahoo, have spent years defining, developing, and perfecting their systems to ensure that they continue to attract the majority of traffic to their sites and thereby grow their revenue streams. As a result of their investments, both of these search engines operate extremely sophisticated software systems to ensure that they can produce accurate, timely, and relevant results for every available user. Perhaps not surprisingly then, both now inhabit commanding positions within the Internet community and are constantly used as reference points for many of the average Joes who innocently surf the Web.

Search Engine Optimization (SEO)

Now that you have a basic understanding as to how search engines work, it's time to have a look at how they can be manipulated in order to improve the level of prominence that a Web site can achieve as a result of being highlighted in response to some search terms.

Unfortunately, there is no single panacea for improving a Web site's ranking, so most of the sites that you will repeatedly find at the top of the page in response to having entered a particular set of search terms are there for a very good reason—either they have invested very heavily in their SEO programs or they have bought their way to the top.

The size and scope of the search engine debate is so lateral and holistic that entire books have already been written on the subject. Forgive me, therefore, if I do not cover the concept in any great depth during the remainder of this chapter. If at the end of this section, however, you are still thirsty for knowledge on the subject of SEO and would like to get your hands on a particular publication, I would readily suggest a visit to Google Book Search and the entering of the keywords, "search engine optimization" as a more than worthwhile starting point.

Although SEO can look like an absolute minefield to most of us mere mortals, there are some basic rules to follow in promoting a Web site. It can usually raise a site's ranking when it is subsequently returned in a search engine's response list or the list created in response to a given search term. In order to identify some of the rules of promotion and their associated protocols, I have attempted to cover the basics as follows:

Paid Inclusions—First of all, there is a very strong argument for those who are short on patience but long on cash to save themselves a lot of grief by simply getting their wallets out and paying for a position. This method of SEO is known as a "paid inclusion" and is driven by companies paying a search engine to carry a particular site within its index or catalogue. Quite obviously, the more a company is willing to pay, the higher the profile its Web site receives and the higher its ranking will be on the response list.

At the time of writing, most search engines on the Internet operate a paid inclusion policy, with the most notable exception being Google. The fees involved for paid inclusions can vary significantly and can be either annual or charged on a "per-click" basis, with the latter being determined by the amount of visits a site receives as a result of the search engine's recommendations. Critics of the paid inclusion system quite often state that it is fundamentally wrong to match the relevance of a Web site to an individual's search terms based on the depth of a company's pockets rather than the quality of the content. Advocates of the paid inclusion policy would obviously beg to differ—provided they can find the time to stop playing with their yachts or driving their Ferraris.

Pay Per Click Advertising—Hot on the heels of paid inclusions is "pay per click advertising." This process, in my view, is rapidly becoming something of a menace on the Internet today and concerns the practice of search engines positioning advertisements for fee-paying Web sites right next to a set of search results. As with the paid inclusion policy, companies are then charged a fee every time someone clicks on the participating Web page. The major drawback of this system, if you are an innocent surfer, is that you can quite often find yourself distracted by the advertising and subsequently drawn to a Web site that is not necessarily the most relevant to the search terms you entered. The upside of this system is that it most definitely works.

Costs for pay per click advertising are largely dependent upon the search engine provider and the popularity of the search terms entered. As a guide, however, the Google Adwords system (18) charges a one-off activation fee followed by a pay per click structure that can range from a penny to $100.

Outside of the fee-paying methods of improving a brand's exposure are what can best be termed organic, or natural, search results. This is probably the most complex area of SEO and quite often involves a range of technological hocus pocus that, more often than not, makes the more corporate techies simply salivate with excitement. Perhaps not surprisingly then, it would be an absolute impossibility for me to cover all of the options and configurations available to practitioners of organic SEO within the scope of this chapter, so I have simply attempted to identify the major areas as follows:

Essentially, organic or natural SEO falls into two basic categories, the white hat approach and—you've guessed it—the black hat approach. While the former attempts to manipulate a search engine by employing a number of basic techniques that can quite easily be incorporated within a site, the latter relies almost entirely on a technological approach to climbing up the rankings lists and, as such, is out of the scope of this book. So if we just focus on the white hat approach, we can probably classify the most commonly used methods associated with natural SEO as keyword optimization, keyword inclusion, content writing, and link inclusion.

Keyword Optimization—This method of SEO floods a Web page with the terms and buzzwords that are naturally associated with the industry in which the site is operating, and, by their very nature, are likely to reflect the search terms that a user will plug into an engine. An old trick here used to be to fill an entire page with keywords, but to color the font to match the background so that they couldn't be seen with the naked eye. When an unsuspecting spider turned up, it would then be distracted by the number of keywords on the page and automatically flag the site with a high index ranking. These days, however, and by way of introducing a viable set of countermeasures, most search engines have equipped their spiders and associated software with spam detectors. Now, if they come across a Web page with too many keywords, it is automatically labeled as spam.

Similarly, Web designers formerly used meta tags, which are simply HTML (hyper text markup language) tags that appear in the header section of a Web page to provide information about the site, to flood unsuspecting search engines with as many keywords as possible. Today, however, very few search engines continue to use meta tags for indexing since they are wide open to abuse and subsequently downgrade a Web site's ranking.

Keyword Inclusion—Another method of natural SEO, this involves the placing of keywords in as many obvious locations as possible, such as within a Web site's URL (uniform resource locator) titles, images, and links, to gain maximum exposure from a search engine. Quite often, keywords can be set in bold text or italics in order to add extra gravity to their meaning. As with keyword optimization, however, it is important not to over-egg the pudding. Otherwise, the smarter search engines' spam detectors will simply flag a site as not worthy and it will be forever consigned to a nondescript existence—a bit like Scorsese's *Gangs of New York*!

Content Writing—A more subtle way of including keywords within your site is to employ a natural approach to content writing and only use the relevant words where they fit within the context of the actual script. This may prove to be a somewhat labor-intensive exercise, but it has been known to achieve some very good results. Because the key-words have been used within context, the results should be unlikely to alert any spam detectors.

Link Inclusion—Yet another way of bumping a site up the rankings lists is to ensure that it has as many inbound links to it as possible. This can be done in a variety of ways such as using industry or business directories, partnership sites, reciprocal linking, and generally just being open to some good old-fashioned collaboration whenever the opportunity presents itself. When used correctly, inbound links have proven to be a very successful way of improving a Web site's ranking and will usually enhance traffic flow. When used inappropriately, however, they can be seen to devalue a brand by portraying the Web site's owners as nothing more than a participant in one of the many "link farms" that are currently cultivating themselves on the Web.

Finally, and if all of this DIY stuff has started to give you a headache, a quick five minutes on any of the major search engines is guaranteed to produce a myriad of firms and consultancies just itching to help you with SEO, all of which can probably be likened to an eighteenth-century salesman traveling the West with a wagon load of life-changing elixir. Indeed, the Internet has never had a shortage of companies and organizations willing to supply a range of products and services in exchange for cold hard cash, so think about what you want carefully before parting with any money.

Before spending any money, however, it always pays to try and find out just exactly what it is that people are actually looking for. If one understands this fact, it then becomes possible to tailor the content of a Web site in order to meet the particular needs of a specific market segment. The Clickz Network (19) can certainly help with that because it regularly publishes a list of the top search terms by category, which can then be built into a dynamic SEO strategy to hopefully improve a Web site's hit rate.

Perhaps the key thing to remember when evaluating SEO is that there is no panacea or magic bullet for success and that building a quality Web site that will be picked up by the search engines is very much like building a brand. It takes persistence, patience, commitment, time, or, if all else fails, an endless supply of money from an extremely charitable donor.

If you would like more information on search engines, how they work and what they do, I would recommend the dedicated search engine site of *www.searchenginewatch.com.*

RSS—In completing this last section on search engines, I felt that it would be well worth looking at the new kid on the block—or the concept known as RSS. The acronym stands for really simple syndication, and the system works by your browser, or RSS reader, pulling content from all over the Web based on your selection of RSS feeds. While not strictly a search engine, an RSS feed is an excellent way of staying up to date with news reports and new content from Web sites that have equipped themselves with RSS technology. Its major advantage is that it can provide you with updates from your favorite Web sites without you having to visit them first, so instead of constantly visiting a range of sites you can pick and choose those you wish to look at based on the level of appeal within the updated RSS feeds.

There is practically no limit to the amount of RSS feeds that you can receive, and you can set them for a variety of subject matter and across a whole host of providers. Before you can use RSS, however, you will need to ensure that your browser is equipped with a built-in RSS reader or you will have to download one separately from another software provider. Microsoft is currently equipping its latest version of Explorer with a built-in RSS reader, while others such as Safari and Mozilla Firefox have them already.

• • •

Key Points

The key points to remember from this chapter are as follows:

- The Internet is predicated on IP addresses, which are subsequently associated with domain names.
- It is possible to associate multiple domain names with a single IP address.
- Great care should be taken when registering domain names to ensure that they reflect the most popular configurations of a brand or corporation.
- Brands and corporations should register domain names against as many top level domains as possible to prevent or deter both cybersquatting and hijacking.
- Search engines define their rankings lists on either a fee-paying basis or the relevance of a Web site's content to a given set of search terms.
- Brands and corporations should attempt to incorporate their most recognizable names within their domains and URLs to improve visibility.
- There is no single panacea to improving a Web site's ranking, and a combination of strategies will need to be used if an organization is intent on improving its position

ENDNOTES

1. Paul Gad is "Garry Glitter's" real name. Jailed for child molestation and child pornography in the UK, he has also had similar brushes with the law in Southeast Asia.
2. *www2.coca-cola.com/privacy.html*
3. *www.hardware-depot-online.com/digital_terrorism_hate_2005_report_shows_25_per_cent_increase_in_hate_hif.jspx*
4. *http://society.guardian.co.uk/children/story/0,,1235016,00.html*
5. *http://technology.guardian.co.uk/weekly/story/0,,1766532,00.html*
6. *http://en.wikipedia.org/wiki/Paul_Mockapetris*
7. *http://en.wikipedia.org/wiki/Domain_name_system*
8. *http://news.bbc.co.uk/1/hi/world/asia-pacific/4644103.stm*
9. *http://news.bbc.co.uk/1/hi/business/4706275.stm*
10. *www.arb-forum.com/domains/decisions/93564.htm*

11. *http://arbiter.wipo.int/domains/decisions/html/2000/d2000-1838.html*
12. *http://arbiter.wipo.int/domains/decisions/html/2000/d2000-1532.html*
13. *www.icann.org/registrars/accredited-list.html*
14. *www.icann.org/udrp/udrp.htm*
15. *www.verisign.com/verisign-inc/news-and-events/news-archive/us-news-2002/page_000783.html*
16. *http://en.wikipedia.org/wiki/Bleeding_edge*
17. *www.verisign.com/information-services/digital-brand-management/page_001210.html*
18. *https://adwords.google.com./select/*
19. *www.clickz.com/showPage.html?page=3623623*

2
First Impressions Last

There is only one pretty child in the world and every mother has it.
—CHINESE PROVERB

WHEN MARGARET THATCHER, BRITAIN'S FIRST FEMALE
prime minister, said, "I make my mind up about someone within the
first ten seconds and I very seldom change it," she was probably only
stating how the majority of human beings behave. Indeed, according to
recent research carried out by psychologist Alexander Todorov (1),
most people actually make a judgment about someone based on his
facial appearance within one-tenth of a second—which makes Maggie
look positively tolerant! The fact is, we all have emotional triggers that
respond to different sensory signals, and what some people find attractive, others will avoid like the plague.

Throughout history, individuals such as fashion designers, artists,
musicians, architects, and numerous other types of trend-setting vision-
aries have been influential in dictating popular culture. At exactly the
same time, brand managers and owners have attempted to tailor their
strategies to take advantage of each evolutionary shift to either steal a
march on the competition or avoid being seen as out of date. Hugh
Davidson, in his book *Offensive Marketing* (2), has historically summed
this up rather well by stating, "a brand is a constantly changing mental
inventory inside the customer's mind."

This recognition of a brand as a progressively developing entity is an important observation for a number of different reasons, not least of which is because just like their human counterparts, their perceived value can both rise and fall depending on the experiences they encounter during their respective life cycles. Consider, for example, the effect that the Bhopal disaster had on the chemical company Union Carbide or the ways in which both Nike and Adidas were treated as a result of the sweatshop scandals that followed them around during the mid- to late 1990s. Given these circumstances, the need for a brand to communicate the right messages is of paramount importance, as is the need to make good use of the platforms it chooses from which to evangelize itself.

People can find brands attractive for a variety of reasons, many of which are dictated to us as a result of a particular brand's positioning and segmentation strategy. For instance, some individuals are attracted to luxury brands or those that demonstrate a set of charitable or phil-anthropic values because they see them as a positive and value-enhancing reflection of their own self-image. Likewise, people can mentally give a brand a preferred level of status because of the synergies that brand has evoked with a person's lifestyle or attitude. Others are attracted to brands because they have bought into the functional qualities associated with them and believe that they will receive the extrinsic rewards of security of purchase and value for money. The list goes on and on.

As with any art or science, the principles of brand development have evolved over time and while there is always space in the market for an innovative new approach, the larger corporations now tend to follow a predetermined flight path when attempting to attract new business or stoke up brand value. Because of the global nature of the World Wide Web and the interactive nature of its content, however, this somewhat methodical approach to improving brand awareness has presented a series of challenges to both Web designers and corporate brand stakeholders, as millions of people around the world now have instant access to both brands and businesses of which they'd previously never heard.

In many ways, the advent of the World Wide Web as both a com-munications medium and an information portal (not to mention its strengths around functionality) has raised the bar considerably with regard to how brands tackle the concept of immediacy and of course, recognition. To that end, a brand's primary messages must be totally synchronized with those of its offline counterpart and continually strike the right emotional connections within the minds of both potential and existing consumers.

Following on from the fundamentals of the digital branding concept that were discussed in chapter 1, we will use this chapter to try and identify just what attracts people to a brand on the Internet and why a site's homepage is so crucially important to the enhancement of brand value. By building on the constructs of the last chapter, we will also attempt to explore the primary elements of a brand's Web experience and seek to identify some of the basic associations that people can draw from a Web site, based on their impressions of its initial presentation, its content, and its culture.

How the Human Brain Works

Before we can even begin to understand the primary sensory factors that influence our opinion on such things as people, structures, images, and events, we first need to undertake a very short biology lesson in order to ascertain just how our gray matter processes the information it is given in order to reach its conclusions.

The brain is the most complex and powerful piece of machinery that inhabits the human body. Reaching far beyond the body's basic functions of heartbeat and respiration, the brain controls both conscious and unconscious thought processes, is instrumental in developing personality, and hosts a constantly changing library of memories based on the many associations it has made with millions of sensory inputs.

Essentially, the brain is divided into two cerebral hemispheres that are joined at the *corpus colossum*—an organ consisting of thick white tissue that is used to carry messages from one side of the brain to the other. The left cerebral hemisphere controls the right side of the body, and the right cerebral hemisphere looks after the left side of the body. In humans, the brain's neocortex, which is basically the top layer of the two cerebral hemispheres, represents somewhere in the region of 76 percent of the organ's total volume, thereby making it unique within the great variety of creatures on planet Earth. Because of this characteristic, the human brain is capable of processing quite literally billions of neuron-driven synaptic connections, which makes it one of the most advanced and complex pieces of biological machinery that we're ever likely to encounter.

Despite the brain's convoluted architecture, scientists have, over time, significantly improved their knowledge as to how it works and have managed to attribute certain types of behavior to corresponding regions within its structure. Before one or two of you go reaching for your medical dictionaries, however, you should sit back and relax, because, for the purposes of this book, we are simply going to focus on the main characteristics of the left and right cerebral hemispheres and the types of sensory activity that are often used to stimulate them.

Although by no means entirely conclusive (3), many studies on brain activity have revealed that the left side of the brain is geared to process information that is presented in a linear, logical, and sequential way, whereas the right side of the brain is more at home with intuitive, creative, and perception-driven reasoning.

As a general rule of thumb, people who are left-brain dominant tend to be good at analytical problem-solving, strong with words and numbers, and are attracted to process. Conversely, people who are right-brain dominant tend to be creative, color sensitive, and not fazed by ambiguity. As a result of the ways in which it is believed that the brain processes information, it is now widely accepted that new experiences or sensations are processed via the right side of the brain, while anything that the brain already recognizes is processed via the left side.

Given the advancements in neurological research and the parallel teachings associated with the psychological aspects of the marketing process, it probably won't surprise you to learn that the more clued-in corporate entities (which already place a large degree of emphasis on the psychosomatics of branding) have been well aware for some time of the dynamics associated with the process of human reasoning. As a direct consequence, they have developed their branding strategies to appeal to those demographics that they believe will add the greatest value to their businesses. At the top end of the scale, the largest and most valuable brands spend almost enough cash to run an impover-ished African nation on attempting to ensure that their products and services will stimulate your emotional G-spot. Further down the scale, however, many companies and marketers are still fumbling around like nervous teenagers in search of the magic button—and this is particularly evident when exposing their brands to the Internet. The results of these respective approaches are often plainly evident in the way a brand drives its online positioning and segmentation strategies. They will be covered in more detail as you read through this book.

Whole-Brain Branding

Now that we have a very basic understanding as to how the human brain both processes information and reacts to sensory inputs, let's have a look at some of the marketing theories that pervade the concept of brand awareness and how they are put into practice:

According to Dibb and Simpkin et al. (4), the concept of brand awareness concerns the increasing amount of recognition and recall that a potential consumer can associate with a brand, based on a range of product experiences that are supported by promotional activity.

This common academic belief is supported by Dave Dolak, a self-styled branding expert and author of several E-books, who states on his Web site that brand awareness is (5):

. . . when people recognize your brand as yours. This does not necessarily mean they prefer your brand (brand preference), attach a high value to, or associate any superior attributes to your brand, it just means they recognize your brand and can identify it under different conditions.

Embellishing his theory, Dolak goes on to state that:

Brand awareness consists of both brand recognition, which is the ability of consumers to confirm that they have previously been exposed to your brand, and brand recall, which reflects the ability of consumers to name your brand when given the product category, category need, or some other similar cue.

Given these points, one doesn't need to be a rocket scientist to identify with the fact that a major contributing element to the concept of brand awareness is advertising, but how do marketers actually use their knowledge of how the brain works to mount successful campaigns?

Well, according to Rapp and Collins (6), the concept of left and right brain advertising has been in existence since the late nineteenth century and in their book, *Maxi Marketing*, they have cited a number of arguments to that effect.

They quote Jon O. Powers of Wannamaker's department store, for example, as being one of the early advocates of left-brain advertising when he stated back in 1895:

> *Print the news of the store. No catchy headlines, no catches, no headlines, no smartness, no brag, no fooling, no foolery, no attempt at advertising, no anxiety to sell, no mercenary admiration. . . .*

Needless to say, Jon O. Powers must have been an absolute joy to work for and one could easily be forgiven for assuming that he subsequently sired an entire generation of traffic cops!

Early supporters of right brain advertising, on the other hand, are believed to contain, among others, the co-founder of Calkins and Holden, Ernest Elmo Calkins, who said in 1907:

> *Copy is not just the words, but that combination of text and design which produces a complete advertisement.*

When building on the elements that are connected to both left- and right-brain behavior and in recognizing that the associated methods of advertising still have a role to play in the modern world of marketing, Rapp and Collins go on to extend their theories by describing some of the key characteristics that one would expect to encounter when working with "whole-brain" advertising as "building awareness and motivating a response." They then summarize their thoughts on the concept by stating:

> *Whole-brain communication that combines the dream image and the persuasive argument is the secret ingredient that is so often missing in brand-building awareness advertising, and that can do so much to increase its effectiveness.*

They cite Helen Lansdowne Resor, who was creative director at J. Walter Thompson around seventy-five years ago, as one of the pioneers of the "whole-brain" approach and credit this strategy as being instrumental in increasing the sales of Woodbury facial soap by over 1,000 percent during the course of an eight-year period.

Although we should be careful not to confuse the protocols associated with advertising and branding, the two concepts have many synergies on the Web, not least of which is the perception of predominantly working within a limited medium that is incapable of providing customers with the associated touches, tastes, and smells that would normally arouse curiosity and stimulate emotion. That said, the Web (as with television) still has sight and sound to play with, and these two sensory qualities should never be underestimated in terms of their ability to manifest opinion.

The importance of a Web site's homepage and its ability to strike a connection between itself and its target audience from the very first click of the mouse should now be abundantly clear to everyone. Indeed, I simply cannot stress strongly enough the gravity of ensuring that a brand's home portal is completely designed around conveying the fundamentals of brand value that may or may not already exist within a customer's mind.

To that end, a person who visits the Web site of a brand with which he has already built an association must be rewarded by receiving the relevant intrinsic stimuli that led him there in the first place. If a Web site fails at this primary juncture, the consequences for the brand that it represents could prove extremely damaging, as individuals will not just walk away from the brand in cyberspace. They will also be carrying seeds of doubt that relate to the brand's credibility. Over time and with enough momentum behind it, the combined effect could be continual erosion in brand loyalty, which more often than not leads to a reduction in overall brand value. When that happens, it becomes an uphill task to restore consumer confidence.

Examples of fundamentally associating a Web site with a brand can be listed as seeing the color red at *coca-cola.com*, the three stripes at *Adidas.com*, or indeed expecting to come across a vodka-toting pilot or a fifteen-year old boy at the controls of an Asia-bound Airbus at *Aeroflot.com* (7).

Getting the visual basics right is important on the Internet, because it usually represents the first of the sensory inputs experienced by the brain. It is therefore critical to ensure that a brand can instantaneously establish the fundamental attributes that have served to accumulate value. If managed correctly, these visuals should then drive the associated and required emotions of recall and recognition within a visitor's mind, leaving site designers and marketers free to develop the ensuing Web experience with confidence. They can focus on enhancing and enriching the user's perception of the brand through informative, expressive, and interactive content.

This last point is important because whereas recall and recognition is certainly relevant for brands that have already established themselves within a particular market or industry sector, thought also needs to be given to the type of Web experience that will speak to new visitors to a site whose initial click on a homepage may well represent their very first exposure to a brand that they've previously never come into contact with. After all, it would be a shame to waste all that hard work, time, and effort that's been spent on SEO, wouldn't it?

In demonstrating the need to produce an engaging and captivating homepage, many studies have shown that more than half of the visitors to a particular Web site will stay less than sixty seconds before hopping off elsewhere. At the most punitive end of the scale, the figures can be so harsh that they border on the incredible. For example, according to Gitte Lindgaard, the director of the Human-Oriented Technology Lab at Ottawa's Carleton University and lead researcher of a study regarding the initial appeal of Web sites (8), people can make an instinctive decision as to whether a Web site is good or bad in 1/20th of a second. In articulating the results of her study, Lindgaard said:

> The bit (of the Web site) that's based on aesthetics is really just my body telling me whether this feels good or bad. Biologically and genetically, we are hard-wired to make snap decisions.

Lindgaard also believes that if, as her study shows, people take only a fraction of a second to identify with the appeal of a Web site and they end up unimpressed, they won't even look at a company's products and services, regardless of whether or not it's competitive.

Notwithstanding Lindgaard's research, Internet shoppers are known to be critical. Research carried out by Clickz (9) in the first quarter of 2006 revealed that, on average, a prospective online shopper will make the decision to buy online from a Web site within the first forty seconds of turning up at the door. Quite obviously, these statistics compound the theory that a first-time visitor's initial impressions of a brand's homepage will be instrumental in helping him decide whether or not he should spend time on a company's Web site or indeed return in the future. In the real world, traditional marketers would simply refer to this process as attracting and retaining customers—and the Internet is no different.

With this in mind, the perception of an online brand is absolutely time critical. If a site is to make good use of its hard-earned traffic flow, it needs to have some captivating content or pivotal points of engagement in order to nail down a user's attention. Some companies do this extremely well and have introduced animation, audio, and video to their homepages in order to focus a user's level of concentration. Other sites simply rely on reputation and use subtle design work to constantly reinforce and underpin the predetermined values that they believe should already exist within a customer's mind.

In the next section we will look at the actual homepages of several online brands. You can decide for yourself just how good, bad, or indifferent they are based on what you have learned so far from this book and, of course, from whatever your existing impressions of the brands in question may be.

The Good, The Bad, and the Largely Indifferent

By developing the concepts discussed so far within this chapter, we will now attempt to draw some parallels with what excites the human brain and the basic associations that one would expect to see on the homepages of some of the world's most popular brands. In doing so, I will try and relate much of what we have learned to a number of the Web sites that I have previously reviewed for brandchannel, in order to provide you with some real-life examples of what goes on in cyberspace.

Sega

Let's start with Sega, the multinational games developer and owner of Sonic the Hedgehog.

In March 2006, I wrote a less-than-complimentary review of Sega's online offering (10). The extract below should give you a feel for what the major discussion points were, starting first with the company in general and then moving on to the Web site.

To understand Sega's Web proposition, one should first seek to understand Sega: A business with American roots that made it big in Japan. The company lost its shirt on the appallingly marketed Dreamcast games console—a product which, when launched in the US on 9/9/99 was deemed by many to be far superior to the Sony PlayStation or the Nintendo N64.

Despite receiving many plaudits, enjoying promising early sales, and being almost three years ahead of the Xbox, the Dreamcast failed to gain a sustainable hold on the market due to such issues as not being backwards compatible with its predecessor and an inability to play DVDs. Sony, upon recognizing the Dreamcast's shortfalls, let rip with a tirade of guerrilla-style marketing ahead of the launch of its PS2 (PlayStation 2), whilst Nintendo and Microsoft pushed on with the GameCube and Xbox, respectively.

All of this commotion proved too much for Sega, who terminally retired the Dreamcast less than two years after its launch and rapidly ran for cover in the software market. Now, Sega specializes in making games for the consoles with which it once competed, and its subsequent Web proposition is an apologetic attempt at covering its tracks.

When commenting on Sega's homepage, I remarked:

Sega's global homepage is a dull and disappointing portal that subsequently leads to an enigmatic pastiche of culturally biased activity. Upon arrival, you are rapidly encouraged by Sonic himself to move to the European site (which is available in all of four different languages), the Japanese site, or the home of Sega of America—which actually resides at Sega.com. Confused? You will be.

A screenshot of Sega's global homepage, taken in July 2006, is shown overleaf in figure 2.1:

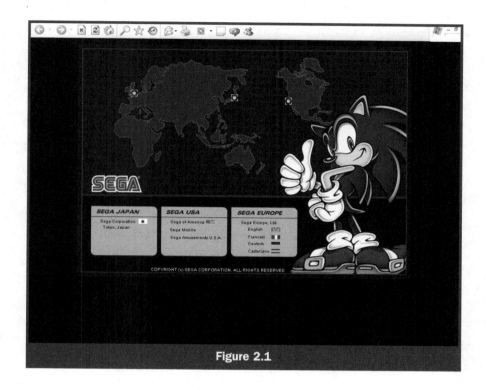

Figure 2.1

As you will no doubt have deduced from my comments, my difficulties with Sega's Web proposition started from the very first click, as I found it somewhat difficult to get a fix on what was being used as Sega's global portal due to the responses that had been returned from Google. For instance, when the search term of "Sega" is entered into the search engine, it dutifully responds by listing *www.sega.com* as "the official Sega Web site." It also lists exactly the same Web address as "the online home of Sega of America, providing news and information on Sega video games for all platforms."

Slightly confused by the above results, I did some further digging around on Google and discovered that if I entered the word "global" as a suffix to Sega, I could generate a primary response from the search engine that actually lists the company's worldwide homepage as *www.sega.com/global.php*.

Now, if you cast your mind back to what was discussed in chapter 1 with regard to domains and directories, you will have worked out that Sega's "global homepage" is actually a subdirectory of *Sega.com—*

the official Sega site and the home of Sega of America, so let's consider the implications of that for a minute:

Is the company trying to play down the fact that it has a global directory concealed within the confines of Sega of America, or should we as Internet users simply accept the fact that its preferred point of primary contact is actually *Sega.com* and therefore discount the prominence of both its Japanese and European sites? My opinion, for what it's worth, is that Sega's global homepage is either *Sega.com* or it isn't. What's the point of sticking a global portal at the back end of the primary domain? That is anyone's guess. Answers on a postcard please.

In attempting to resolve the issue, I decided to try and evaluate the navigational qualities of each site on its own merits in order to ascertain which did the better job in terms of acting as a gateway. Unfortunately, I found that this just added to the confusion, as the content contained within each page was radically different from its counterpart.

For instance, it is clear from the animated graphics that reside on the global homepage (as illustrated in figure 2.1) that Sega is attempting to segment its proposition on the Web by both geography and business group. To this end, it has listed its relevant subsites in a clear and unambiguous way in order to allow users the freedom of navigation that should come as a prerequisite when attempting to locate data within a multisite environment. *Sega.com*, on the other hand, only carries direct links to the European and Japanese sites, both of which are somewhat sheepishly represented by a couple of miniscule flags that can easily be overlooked given the size, scope, and depth of the content that pervades the space beneath them.

In order to fully articulate the case in point, a screenshot of the "Sega of America homepage," also taken in July 2006, is illustrated in figure 2.2 on the next page.

As I am sure you can imagine, having repeatedly found myself running around in ever decreasing circles and spending an inordinate amount of time trying to resolve just exactly which site represented Sega's global gateway, my frustrations eventually boiled over and I subsequently decided to park the issue in favor of reviewing *Sega.com*. Far from making me feel any better, however, my problems with the company's Web proposition continued once I got stuck in the portal's content. I went on to write of *Sega.com*:

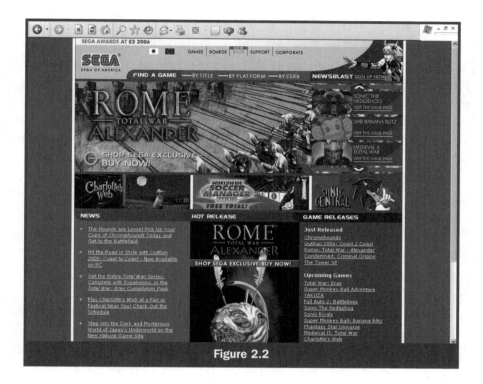

Figure 2.2

Every one of the Sega sites lacks passion and energy and they all have the feel of a third-rate games developer.

When describing Sega's online offering as having "the feel of a third-rate games developer," I was referring to the fact that the homepage looked extremely "busy" on the eye and seemed to be lacking in terms of quality content. In essence, I found that the amount of material on show, coupled with the somewhat excessive and unstructured use of copy, meant that I was struggling to see the wood for the trees. The net effect of all of this, of course, was to overload my brain with a series of confusing signals as to what I should and shouldn't be looking at, while my subconscious mind was simultaneously attempting to locate the previous associations that I had already developed with the Sega brand.

Perplexed by the layout of the homepage and frustrated by the complexity of the references to Sega's rapid rodent, Sonic (not to mention my previous experiences with trying to resolve the location of

Sega's global portal), it wasn't long before I found myself completely unclear as to just what Sega actually stood for and what I should be gaining by spending time on its Web site. As a result of my emotional state, I went on to write an unflattering review of a brand that I had previously held in very high regard.

To make matters worse and as if to rub salt into what was an already irritable wound, upon carrying out further research within the second-tier areas of *Sega.com* I discovered that there were several individual Web sites of titles within Sega's games portfolio that were very good indeed. They were lively, vibrant, brimming with animated and interactive content, and a pleasure to peruse.

Quite the opposite of encouraging me to soften my stance, however, this annoying dichotomy only served to give me the lasting impression of Sega as a brand that was very capable of marketing its subproducts and services but at the very top was disparate and confused, lacking in direction, and quite possibly struggling to communicate with itself.

Notwithstanding these observations, perhaps the most important thing to remember when reflecting upon the example of *Sega.com* is that regardless of whether I'm right or wrong, what I *think* is most important. Indeed, having originally set out to review Sega's Web proposition with nothing but enthusiasm and respect for the brand, I had subsequently discovered that Maggie's ten-second rule had prevailed yet again and that as a result of the emotional experiences I had encountered online, I left the company's digital offering feeling decidedly disappointed. The moral of this story, therefore, and as any marketer will testify, is that perception is reality in the mind of the consumer—and as a consequence of the problems I had encountered on its Web site, my perception of Sega's place within the World Wide Web had suddenly become quite unflattering.

Aston Martin

Moving on from the example of Sega, let's now take a look at a luxury brand that, by its very nature, predicates its success on its ability to stir the emotions by evoking a range of sensory and psychological stimuli—the brand of Aston Martin.

Although Aston Martin is currently owned by Ford, there is still no mistaking its profoundly British roots or, indeed, denying the appeal of its sartorial range of automobiles.

Aston Martin Lagonda Limited was originally founded in 1913 by two automotive enthusiasts, Lionel Martin and Robert Bamford, who joined forces the previous year to sell cars manufactured by Singer. The first Aston Martin essentially consisted of an Isotta-Fraschini chassis loaded with a Coventry Simplex engine and came about as a result of Lionel Martin racing cars along the famous Aston climb—a competition where drivers raced their vehicles up a steep hill against the clock.

Throughout the next five decades and after surviving two world wars, Aston Martin went on to become a more-than-reputable brand in its own right before enhancing its image considerably when, in 1964, it joined forces with James Bond to star in the movie *Goldfinger*. Notwithstanding the fact that the coupling was somewhat fortuitous (as according to the urban legend, the movie executives only approached Aston Martin after they were turned down by Jaguar), the marriage between the quintessential British spy and one of the world's most prominent premium automotive brands has continued irrepressibly and is still going strong today—despite the former's occasional dalliances with the offspring of some other European manufacturers. As a consequence of its enduring appeal and its undoubted character, the cars that now bear the Aston Martin brand are driven by the privileged and the influential, not to mention reportedly being the preferred modes of transport for the likes of Nicholas Cage, David Beckham, and HRH the Prince of Wales.

With sophistication, style, and a price ticket that would choke a donkey, Aston Martin is a luxury brand at the very top end of the scale. As such, it relies heavily on its ability to associate lifestyle with exclusivity and desire with demand in order to keep its order books perpetually full. Not surprisingly, qualities like these are notoriously difficult to convey on the Web as, like all luxury brands, there is an air of expectation that precedes any sort of encounter with it, which, if not met in full, can leave the recipient feeling somewhat shortchanged.

When reviewing the Aston Martin Web site for brandchannel, I was particularly interested in discovering how the brand was addressing the challenge of marketing itself on the Web, given its level of dependence on emotive and sensory contact. As a result, I had this to say about its presence online (11):

A visit to Astonmartin.com is an experience full of anticipation. After all, nothing drives demand in luxury goods like a feeling of inimitable exclusivity, and with its cars selling at price points between US$110,000 to 260,000, Aston Martin can be confident that it's attracting the elite.

The homepage is a treat for the self-indulgent as you get to start your own engine before the excursion begins (a click of the mouse, not a turn of the key), but not without feeling mildly disconcerted by the low-resolution graphics and the relatively short trip to HQ.

What Aston Martin did really well was slowly build excitement in much the same way that an experienced pole dancer will titillate the audience (not that I have ever had any experience of that sort of thing!) before finally unleashing the goods in a climatic but tasteful crescendo. To that end, *Astonmartin.com* went to a lot of effort to avoid the embarrassing act of premature exhilaration, by making it clear that it was putting the brakes on new visitors' excitement by encouraging them to take a dignified journey to the organization's homepage where, only then, would they be allowed to do whatever their hearts desired. The audio track of an Aston Martin DB9 starting its engine as a response to clicking the starter button underpinned this concept, as users of the Web site could then close their eyes and imagine themselves behind the wheel of one of the world's most expensive production-driven cars, before learning more about what the company and the brand has to offer its prospective clients.

Figure 2.3 is a screenshot of *Astonmartin.com* taken in July 2006.

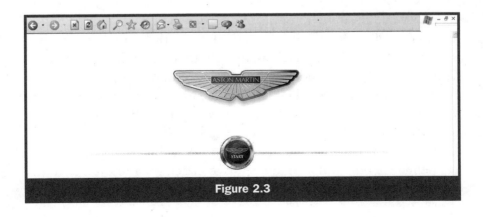

Figure 2.3

The drawback of this strategy as far as I was concerned was that because Aston Martin had taken the time to build visitors' expectations before letting them view the homepage, the subsequent Web site then had little option but to exceed most users' expectations by presenting itself as a vibrant and dynamic environment that was completely representative of the brand. Unfortunately, I felt that Aston Martin had fallen short of the mark in this regard and I went on to write:

> *Upon arrival at the main portal visitors can immediately start to access the action, although the Web design is rather one-dimensional and doesn't do enough to complement the Aston Martin brand. Sure, the "Company" section is interesting, as it provides a comprehensive backdrop to the business's history as well as attempting to capture the spirit and edify visitors as to just what makes Aston Martin unique. However, there's just not enough excitement or justification of the kudos to match a product that is represented by a price tag way beyond most people's reach.*

Figure 2.4, taken in July 2006, carries a screenshot of Aston Martin's homepage.

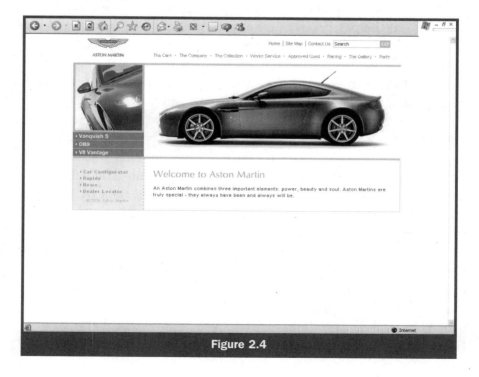

Figure 2.4

Although in terms of its basic design work Aston Martin had most certainly gotten the fundamentals right and appealed to both sides of my brain, I just didn't feel turned on enough to go and open up the new mortgage required to buy one of its cars based on what I thought the brand would deliver. Naturally, this came as something of a disappointment, as Aston Martin really does have a well-presented Web proposition that so nearly gets it spot on the button. For instance, the layout and design is remarkably easy to follow, the color scheme is in keeping with the dignified and sophisticated culture that Aston Martin represents, and the sleek lines of the images spoke volumes for the cars. All things considered, though, I just felt that the homepage needed a bit more dynamism and vitality to get it past the checkered flag. Consequently, what had begun so well had gone on to deliver much less than I had originally anticipated, and I left Aston Martin's Internet offering with both a sense of unfulfilled curiosity and a bit of a downer on the brand.

Bratz

Having looked at the two contrasting examples of Sega and Aston Martin from the perspective of Net presentation, let's now have a look at Bratz—the brand that's rewriting the codes of conduct and consumerism for today's teenagers.

The Bratz brand is owned by MGA entertainment, an American-based manufacturer and wholesaler of dolls and toys. Emerging as a serious threat to Barbie shortly after they went into production in 2001, the Bratz range of dolls has spread like an epidemic and has become the must-have accessory for prepubescent girls who reside in every Westernized economy from Adelaide to Zurich. The dolls are instantly recognizable due to their extra large heads, pouting lips, and wide-eyed expressions—and they also have a fashion sense that would make Barbie run a mile.

In just five years, the Bratz brand has become so successful that it has spawned a TV series, a movie, a host of interactive DVDs, and, of course, a video game. The Bratz range of dolls has also proliferated dramatically and, having originally been launched with only four major protagonists, the portfolio has grown to such an extent that it now boasts more than thirty models, including Boyz and Babyz. With each clutch of characters seemingly fixated on the merits of materialism, Bratz has ignited a fierce debate that questions the changing morals of youth and challenges the very direction that society is headed.

Due to the explosion in Bratz's popularity, it was only a matter of time before the brand fell under the gaze of brandchannel. As a result, I was lucky enough to get the gig of reviewing its Web site in June 2006 and, in doing so, I said of the brand in general (12):

> Few could have predicted that Barbie's nemesis would prove to be her exact antithesis. Born of the baby boomers, for decades Barbie evangelized the credo that the path to adolescence is as easy as eating apple pie, partaking in the odd bit of equestrianism, and getting a good dose of the Partridge Family.
>
> That hypothesis was shattered in 2001 when the first Bratz dolls exploded onto the scene like a miniature version of the Sex Pistols. Clad in crop-tops and hipster jeans, the dolls have proven to be more than just brazen babes with brattitude.
>
> Bratz is a millennium brand—make no mistake about it. Wonderfully positioned by its owners, MGA entertainment, the brand is riding roughshod over the competition like a linebacker on speed.

Because of the way Bratz has carved up the doll market, it's difficult not to develop any preconceived ideas when evaluating the brand and, if you're at all like me, prior to coming into contact with it, you'll have found yourself wondering whether it really is that good. Notwithstanding any initial concerns I may have had, I found that my questions were answered with great alacrity as I discovered that *Bratz.com* had an overwhelming sense of compatibility with the offline brand that's a credit to those behind it. Indeed, such was the quality and depth of the content on show that I became increasingly convinced of the quality and sustainability of Bratz with almost every single click of the mouse.

Figure 2.5 (on the following page) is a screenshot of the *Bratz.com* homepage that was taken in July 2006.

In terms of first impressions, it was great to find Bratz on the Web without the use of Google and Yahoo because, as with Aston Martin, the company had named its home portal directly after the brand. What

Figure 2.5

the company also did well was to underpin the "brattitude" concept from the absolute outset by displaying a colorful message while the homepage was loading that read, "Please wait . . . it takes time to look this GOOD." (This message is displayed throughout the site whenever a page with animated content is loading.)

The positive reaction that was generated by being greeted with such an upbeat and dynamic proposition continued throughout the Bratz homepage. As totally in keeping with the offline brand, the imagery and design was vivacious and bright while the layout was easy to navigate.

Aside from immediately seeking to match my offline perceptions of the Bratz brand in general to those of its online proposition, *Bratz.com* set about ensuring that I was both captivated and entertained by engaging me with an energetic video of its latest TV campaign, simultaneously using animation to continually shift the graphics in the primary viewing area. This enabled the Web site to bombard me with messages in support of the brand by constantly showing me samples of the material that was available elsewhere on the site and rein-forcing its mantra with audio. As a direct consequence, my curiosity became aroused and I felt compelled to keep clicking on the links that presented themselves.

All in all, I couldn't fail to be impressed. The site was easy to locate, matched my perceptions of the offline brand, built value with its content, and appealed to both sides of my brain by being both linear and logical in terms of its layout and also displaying enough col-orful imagery to keep me entertained. The built-in audio streams added another sensory dimension that extended the associations I already had and, as a result, further embedded the brand in my mind.

Section Summary

In choosing the three examples—Sega, Aston Martin, and Bratz—I wanted to try and give you as much of a feel as possible for the pri-mary aspects of the digital branding concept. Hopefully, therefore, during this first course of material we have reviewed you will have developed both your understanding of branding on the Web to the point that you will now realize that as far as online branding is con-cerned, nothing ever happens by accident. Indeed, whether it's the allocation of the domain name, the designing of the homepage, or the establishment of the content and color scheme, every compo-nent represents a deliberate act of choice and, as a result, will regu-larly be measured and compared against the characteristics of the offline brand.

Web sites can be good, bad, or indifferent. They may have cost mil-lions or they may have been done on the cheap. They may be the result of one man's work or, indeed, the output of a series of collabo-rating focus groups that contain an organization's finest minds. No matter how they came into existence, however, the second that they hit the Web is the second that they impact the brand—and that is an absolute fact.

Who Has the Prettiest Child?

Obviously, the normal answer to this sort of question is the smart-assed retort of "beauty is in the eye of the beholder." Unfortunately, however, businesses just don't have the luxury of *hoping* that some philanthropic soul will see them for what they truly are, pull them onto the dance floor, and immediately start getting jiggy with it as a result of their associated reputation.

Because they have stakeholders to satisfy, profits to deliver, and many bills to pay, businesses and corporations need to ensure that they have cash flows that are sustainable enough to keep the proverbial wolf from the door not just today, but tomorrow as well. To facilitate their survival, they need to perpetuate the cycle of customer attraction and retention by continually improving brand awareness and, of course, living up to their expectations.

As we now know, a company's Web offering can play a pivotal part in this cycle by adding value to the brand or brands in question. Conversely, a poor proposition can erode brand value and leave potential customers in a more negative and less flattering state of mind.

By pulling together the elements of what we have discussed so far within this chapter and learning from the examples of Sega, Aston Martin, and Bratz, it is possible to identify a number of common denominators between the Web sites we have looked at and what, at least in theory, should constitute a homepage that's not just pleasing to the eye, but worth exploring further.

So without further ado, let's start breaking down the beliefs that digital branding is an esoteric process that is best left to the Web-heads and the ego-driven high flyers.

Color Scheme

One of the first things that will hit you when you sign on to a Web page is the colors that have been used in its design. What are they saying to you? Are they bright, brash and "in your face," or are they graceful hues that complement the construction of the site? Colors appeal to the right side of the brain because, by nature, they're creative. Bright colors will scream at you (Bratz and Sega), whereas gentle shades and pastels can be used to highlight certain facets of a Web page's layout such as links, headers, or images (Aston Martin). Because colors can be used to draw the eye of the visitor and either add emphasis or, indeed, take one's attention away from something else, they need to be applied with care.

A critical point to bear in mind when choosing a site's color pallet is that it should be completely empathetic toward the brand's existing artwork. Imagine, for example, what the homepage of *Coca-Cola.com* would look like if it were set against a bright blue background (either to the delight or consternation of Pepsi) or what the public would think of *McDonalds.com* if the home page were festooned in green and white stripes (albeit that might look good on St. Patrick's Day)?

Another key point to consider is how colors can be used to intuitively draw attention to the graphics, links, or headers that the host company wants us to see as a priority. By way of examining the two extremes, have a look at the homepages of both Sega and Aston Martin in figures 2.2 and 2.4 and then sign on to the respective Web sites before asking yourself which one does a better job of guiding an ignorant user to the areas of the site that will add the most value to the brand.

In Sega's case, it is difficult to make out the forest for the trees because the boldness of the colors that are used to depict the links are lost within a carnival of text and images that put a strain on one's eyes. Aston Martin, on the other hand, has a much more open feel, which means that the links and headers that they want us to see are every bit as noticeable in monochrome as they are in color.

Layout

Along with the color scheme, the layout of a homepage is another critical factor in site-based aesthetics and is probably *the* most influential dynamic in terms of navigation. When designed correctly, a strong layout will dictate to users just where they should be going and what they should be looking at—in other words, it will quite literally point to a path. Research into this particular area of Web site design, although still relatively embryonic, has identified a number of ways in which the process of site navigation can be made more intuitive for users, with perhaps one of the more popular techniques becoming known as "information scent."

First defined by Xerox at its Palo Alto Research Center and subsequently employed by Intranet designers such as Step Two (13), information scent was established as a concept after having identified a number of similarities between the ways in which human beings search for information and the ways in which animals hunt. As far as Web site design is concerned, exponents of the information scent technique, such as Step Two, believe that:

Most research into the way users navigate a site reveals that people follow one path and then, when that doesn't provide the information they require, they retrace their steps using the back button, until they find another suitable path to follow. Users can find this process frustrating and after following a couple of unsuccessful attempts, give up on a site. Sites with strong information scents are good at guiding users to content. Conversely, sites with weak information scents cause users to spend longer evaluating the options they have and increase the chance that they will select the wrong option, forcing the user to employ the back button.

Because of the degrees of linearity employed during the design of a homepage, the layout will most likely appeal to the left side of the brain because it constitutes a set of directions that a user can instinctively process before deciding where to go next—unless, of course, you're someone who inherently has trouble with maps!

The best types of layout are those that are in tune with the brand, complementary to the color scheme, and have enough information scent available on the homepage to suggest that navigation is a breeze. If these three criteria are met, visitors to a Web site should easily be able to emotionally connect their online preconceptions with the existing associations they have made with the offline brand, engage their whole brain, and be relaxed at the prospect of finding what they're after.

Have another look at the three examples we have covered and decide for yourself just how good, bad, or indifferent each of the homepages are at satisfying those criteria. In my opinion, Sega is too noisy. It's not only too full of content, but the size and prominence of the images are so visually demanding that they detract from the script at the bottom of the page. Now imagine what it would look like if Sega scrapped the link-driven subtitles beneath the "News" and "Game Release" headers. How much more logical and organized would it look?

Aston Martin, on the other hand, is more or less the polarized version of Sega. There's lots of empty space and a light and expansive background that's reminiscent of a car showroom. While all of the links are easy to see, those that lead to the Vanquish S, the DB9, and the V8 Advantage are highlighted in bold, just asking to be clicked. There is also a nice little welcome note, which takes a step towards defining the Aston Martin culture and a prominent search engine for those in a hurry.

Bratz on the other hand, powerfully combines these two methods to actively engage its users, effectively lay information sent, and drive home brand association. The links are easy to spot, the layout is most definitely linear, and the liberal use of imagery helps to add depth, allowing the principal viewing areas to scroll through their animated repertoire in order to give the homepage a holistic and dynamic feel. Despite its intensity, however, the Web site isn't too crowded, and its overall presentation is complimentary to the brand.

When designed correctly, an easily navigable and understandable layout that goes along with the color scheme will enhance brand value by instantly putting a user at ease. Conversely, a confusing layout that is difficult to navigate and obtrusive in its presentation is likely to result in a user becoming a sub-sixty-second statistic and a frustrated critic of the brand per se.

Images

Pictures can speak louder than words, and the appropriate use of imagery on a homepage can be an invaluable component of enhancing brand value. Although each of the examples that we have discussed so far in this chapter contains extensive artwork of one type or another, some are more complimentary to their Web sites than others.

While Sega uses a sequence of screenshots and advertisements from its games to underpin its core business, Aston Martin chooses to give center stage to a series of photographs of its HQ and its cars, which gently merge into one another like a PowerPoint slide show. Bratz, on the other hand, utilizes a combination of these two methods, with both animated artwork and the occasional photograph combining with each other to drive association with the brand, draw attention to its links, and engage the user where possible.

Although it could be argued that each of the images depicted in our examples are relevant representations of each company's basic activities, do they really enhance the brands in question? The answer to this will be yes and no. Some images work well, like the sequence of automobiles that glide through the center of the Aston Martin homepage, but others lose their impact due to being surrounded by clutter—Sega.

Images are important because they give life to a proposition that would otherwise be dominated by copy (*a la* Rapp and Collins). When used correctly, they can ignite the desired emotions within potential customers' minds by activating the subconscious triggers that subsequently result in a positive impression of the brand. When used incorrectly, their messages can be confusing and their impact will be lost or misread.

Bells and Whistles

As technology has moved on, so has the level of trickery that can be used to augment a Web site and subsequently engage an innocent user. In the early days of the Internet when bandwidth and download speeds were positively archaic compared with what we have today, we were lucky if a Web site contained a photograph, a static cartoon, or a very basic GIF (graphic interchange format). Nowadays, however, we can look forward to streaming video, real-time audio, and a host of other gadgets that bedazzle and bemuse.

From a digital branding perspective, technological advancement has been an absolute revelation because it moves the concept forward from a passive two-dimensional era to one of dynamic interactivity. In the past, for example, users could simply read, listen, and hopefully absorb. Now, they can participate and connect with live and vibrant content to such an extent that the potential for organizations to emotionally attach an individual to a brand has multiplied considerably.

Although all of the Web sites we have looked at in this chapter have used one form of advanced Web marketing or another, the one that really stands out in this department is Bratz. This isn't just because it's the only homepage with video but because it appeals to a number of our senses in a variety of ways.

From a top level perspective, the homepage uses its layout and its color scheme to focus our concentration while simultaneously using a parade of moving images that are designed to attract our attention. On top of all this, it rattles through a video of its latest TV campaign, which, although we might not be watching, is playing away in our sub-conscious and aligning its music and messages to the existing associa-tions that reside within our minds—it's almost sensory overload!

Although the improvements in Web technology have certainly opened up more possibilities with regard to digital branding, they must be used *appropriately* if they are to have maximum effect. In many cases, less is more, so try not to get too carried away in the stampede and consider what you are trying to achieve before blowing your cash on the latest toys. If, on the other hand, you can't wait to see what the latest developments are, feel free to read ahead because within the pages of this book, there are plenty of examples of what's just around the corner.

Culture

In many cases (unless you actually work for, sell to, or are a stakeholder in the business in question), a brush with a company's homepage is the first exposure that most individuals will have with an organization's cul-ture. It is therefore imperative when designing a homepage to consider the combined effect that everything we have talked about so far within this chapter will have on the unsuspecting visitor.

How will he see the organization and the brand or brands it repre-sents? Will he view it as a professional outfit with philanthropic values that takes pride in its work and looks after its employees and cus-tomers, or will he see it as a fly-by-night cowboy firm with all the credibility of a double-glazing salesman?

Web culture is important. Not only does it reflect the subtle nuances in an organization's makeup and behavior (remember the example of Sega's global portal), but it will also convey subliminal messages to a user about the quality of the brand. Thinking again of the examples that we have discussed within this chapter, what are your impressions of Sega, Aston Martin, and Bratz and the companies they represent?

Culture is a fascinating and engaging subject, and many books have been written about it. Indeed, those written by Fons Trompenaars and Geert Hofstede have carried considerable weight in academic circles over the past decade or so and are now widely quoted throughout organizational corridors of power.

In closing this chapter and by way of articulating just how important the cultural feel of a Web site actually is, I would like to relay a piece of advice that was given to me by a mentor of mine, a business consultant and trained psychologist named Duncan Richards.

When I was working on the board of a good-sized company within the UK, Duncan would go to great lengths to tell me that as directors, "we were watched by our people more than we would ever know."

Although Duncan's advice was fundamentally aimed at both me and my colleagues, I can categorically assure you that exactly the same principles apply to brands and brand management, regardless of whether they are presented on the Internet, discussed on the radio, watched on TV, or passively referred to within movies and video games. Bear in mind, therefore, that whatever content is displayed on a company's homepage, inclusive of its images, layout, color scheme, language, and terminology, it will have an instantaneous effect on whoever is exposed to it—for better or for worse.

• • •

Key Points

The key points to remember from this chapter are as follows:

- The brain creates associations based on information and experiences that can be recognized and recalled when triggered.
- For the sake of satisfying a global audience, homepages should be designed to appeal to the whole brain and not just focus on one side or the other.
- Homepages should complement and enhance a brand's value by associating themselves with as many of the brand's characteristics as possible, including straplines (slogans), buzzwords, images, and audio.
- Layouts, color schemes, images, and technology should be used appropriately and in keeping with the qualities of the brand in question.

A homepage is a starting point for organizational culture. It is therefore imperative that its content and presentation reflect the types of messages that an organization would wish to publicize with consistency.

ENDNOTES

1. *www.blackwell-synergy.com/doi/abs/10.1111/j.1467-9280.2006.01750.x*

2. Davidson, Hugh. *Offensive Marketing*. London: Penguin, 1987.

3. *www.rense.com/general2/rb.htm*

4. Dibb, Sally, et al. *Marketing: Concepts and Strategies*. Boston: Houghton Mifflin, 1994.

5. *www.davedolak.com/articles/dolak4.htm*

6. *www.canada.com/saskatoonstarphoenix/story.html?id=864ebd16-2d70-4c77-ac3d-105c5a4892f3&k=96169*

7. *http://travel.guardian.co.uk/article/2004/jul/22/travelnews1*

8. Rapp, Stan, and Thomas Collins. *Maxi Marketing*. New York: McGraw Hill, 1995.

9. *www.merchandizer.com/Ecommerce-Articles/2006/04/you-have-46-seconds-to-sell-to-your.html*

10. *www.brandchannel.com/features_Webwatch.asp?ww_id=271*

11. *www.brandchannel.com/features_Webwatch.asp?ww_id=272*

12. *www.brandchannel.com/features_Webwatch.asp?ww_id=284*

13. *www.steptwo.com.au/papers/kmc_informationscent/index.html*

3
Say What You Mean and Mean What You Say

Words are just words, and without heart they have no meaning.
—CHINESE PROVERB

BY NOW YOU SHOULD BE ACUTELY AWARE OF THE IMPORtance of providing an engaging and value-added Web proposition that is completely in tune with an offline brand. You will also be mindful of some of the consequences of getting it badly wrong. Since we have reconciled the domain name, discussed the types of attributes that constitute an appealing homepage, and touched on some of the technological aids available (more on these later) to help retain a user's attention, it's now time to start evaluating the types of content and configuration that, when applied correctly, can infuse a site with culture, underpin a brand's positioning strategy, and provide potential visitors with all they need to know about a business and its portfolio.

Edward R. Murrow, the famous American journalist and radio broadcaster who came to prominence during World War II, once said:

The newest computer can merely compound, at speed, the oldest problem in the relations between human beings, and in the end the communicator will be confronted with the old problem, of what to say and how to say it.

As far as digital branding is concerned, Murrow's words can quite literally be used as a mantra by which to stay "on message" when developing the structure and content for a corporate or organizational Web offering. What exactly should a Web site be trying to say, how should it be trying to say it, and how should it be looking to connect with people?

The best corporate Web sites communicate with clarity and without ambiguity. They also focus on the messages that the host organization wants to impart to the general public, without drawing attention to those that it doesn't. In addition, they strive to keep a viewer entertained by delivering a compelling composition of traditional copy, backed up by a range of interactive and value-added material. In many ways, they are "emotionally intelligent" portals that easily connect with a global audience and are capable of both representing and adding value to the organizations they stand for.

The Internet's power as a communications medium is predicated on a number of different attributes—not least of which is its multifunctional capability. Because of this, it can be used as either a galvanizing tool, a database, a self-help facility, or a good old-fashioned advertising platform.

To affirm this point, I would like to refer to an article from *News.com* that is dated as far back as 2002, regarding the use of the Internet as an integrating tool for marketing communications programs (1) and its potential for influencing the brand building process. Upon alluding to the concept of digital branding, the article stated that:

> *Brand building is an area in which the Internet could change everything. Indeed, the real transforming power of the Internet derives from its ability to serve as the central organizing platform for integrated marketing communications programs—the glue that holds disparate channels and executions together, making them a cohesive force. Turning the Internet into the medium that rationalizes a firm's multiplicity of brand-building programs has the potential to change both perception and (the resulting) reality for the brand marketer.*

It could now easily be argued that as time has moved on, the observations made within that *News.com* article have also moved closer to reality as more and more businesses actively pursue the acquisition of a skill set that will enable them to harness the power of the Internet to perpetuate and grow the sustainability of their brands. In doing so, they are creating virtual organizations in cyberspace, complete with communications flows, levels of functionality, and cultures of interactivity, which, by their nature, reflect the very image of their real-world counterparts.

In chapters 1 and 2, we focused on the bare necessities of the digital branding concept by working through such basic elements as domain name resolution and homepage design. In this chapter, we are going to start looking at the essential subject matter and integral types of content that Web sites need to associate with in order to drive their respective brand propositions. As in chapter 2, by critiquing some real-world examples of brands that I have previously reviewed on the Web for brandchannel, we will also attempt to uncover and define the messages and themes (both transparent and subliminal) that organizations convey through the design and application of their Web sites. Finally, we will explore some elements of a Web site's communications policy which, when used correctly, can induce some real momentum to any brand awareness campaign.

About Us

Scott Bedbury is a genuine expert on branding and is inextricably linked to the growth of businesses such as Nike and Starbucks. He is also the author of a book called *A New Brand World: Eight Principles for Achieving Brand Leadership in the Twenty-first Century* (2). In his book, one of the points that Bedbury makes is that for a brand to be successful, it should carry its own "genetic code" that has been developed from the unique qualities that the brand represents. He also believes that a strong and successful brand should be instantaneously associable with the positive emotional attributes that a company or organization has worked hard to establish within the hearts and minds of its stakeholders. In applying the basic principles of established brand awareness strategies, Bedbury believes that businesses should really drive hard to enhance the favorable, intrinsic characteristics of a brand in order to make them more durable and endearing over the long term.

With Bedbury's comments in mind, what better platform could a company possibly have to emotionally connect with its public than a dedicated portal on the Internet? In cyberspace, almost anything is possible, and the opportunities to develop a positive and lasting impression of a brand or a business on a truly global scale are unparalleled. But where do you start?

In my view (and this is always something that I watch for when carrying out a Web review), a link to an "About Us" section is an absolutely fundamental component of any organization's online offering. When accessing a branded portal, a visitor to a Web site should subsequently be able to completely satisfy his curiosity with regard to what a company actually does, where it sits within its market, and also what it stands for. The location of the link should also be so prominently positioned on the homepage that a one-eyed man on a galloping mare in the middle of a pea-soup fog should still be able to see it with minimal effort.

Now, I am certain that at this particular moment, most of you are thinking "eh, isn't that just common sense—who in his right mind wouldn't identify with putting a link to 'company history' or something like that on the homepage?" Well you would be surprised, because at companies such as Nabisco, this particular penny still has a long way to drop.

Nabisco

Nabisco is a world leader in the manufacturing and distribution of cereals, snacks, and convenience foods. The company, owned by Kraft, boasts among its brand portfolio such well-known names as Oreo, Ritz, and Honey Maid. In June 2006, I reviewed the Web site of *Nabisco.com* for brandchannel and said of Nabisco in general (3):

> *Nabisco, a business with a rich and colorful history, is able to trace its founding back to the late 1800s. In the next century, the company experienced a sustained period of growth and became no stranger to the process of mergers and acquisitions, before finally coming to rest under the considerable umbrella of Kraft at the turn of the millennium.*

Regrettably, I didn't find any of the above information at *Nabisco.com*, as nowhere on the site was there a dedicated area that could provide potential customers with the company's background. To Nabisco's credit, there was a direct link to a section that detailed the company's brand portfolio and a scrolling set of images at the bottom of the page that when clicked performed the same function, but I was at a loss to find a concisely written account of Nabisco as a business. While Kraft, Nabisco's parent company, did have some information on Nabisco within the annals of *Kraft.com*, it wasn't particularly easy to find, as *Nabisco.com* didn't carry a direct link to *Kraft.com* on its homepage.

Figure 3.1 is screenshot of Nabisco's homepage taken in July 2006.

Figure 3.1

The implications of Nabisco's actions are pretty obvious to decipher. But how on earth Joe Blow is supposed to identify with Nabisco's heritage, quality, and expertise in the field of manufacturing and wholesaling convenience foods appears destined to remain as much of a mystery as the location of the Holy Grail.

Perhaps the Nabisco brand is so profusely huge in terms of its appeal that everyone should be familiar with it already. Then again, perhaps it's a tragic oversight in terms of the company's understanding of what it is trying to achieve on the Web.

The more I looked at Nabisco's site, the more the paradox deepened and I then went on to write:

> *There seldom has been a stranger Web proposition than Nabisco's. So strange in fact that it demands a double take. On one side of the page the user is invited to take part in such classics as Texas Hold'em Poker, 3D Billiards, and Ping Pong; the other side invites those with a culinary bent to try some new and inviting recipes from Nabisco's extensive library. And the brands that support this bizarre proposition? Well, they're left to wander across the bottom of the screen in a weak-minded html marquee, like a bedraggled bunch of second-class citizens. Don't be fooled by the claim that the games are designed to be played on the "Nabisco World" site either, as the portals for Nabisco World and Nabisco are simply one and the same.*

By now, the words of Edward R. Murrow should be ringing in your ears and swinging around your cerebellum with all the urgency and prowess of Charles Laughton in his prime. Just what exactly is it that Nabisco is trying to tell us? I have no idea.

While there might well be some synergy between playing arcade games and munching through a catering pack of carbohydrate-laden potato chips, I fail to see the fundamental point that *Nabisco.com* is trying to communicate. Give some thought to this one, put your answers on a postcard, and send them to Nabisco!

Accenture

By way of comparison and at the absolute opposite end of the scale in terms of clarity of message, the homepage of Accenture (formerly known as Andersen Consulting) is always well worth a visit, because just as one would expect from a firm of accountants and management consultants, nothing is left to chance.

Figure 3.2 is a screenshot of the Accenture homepage taken in July 2006.

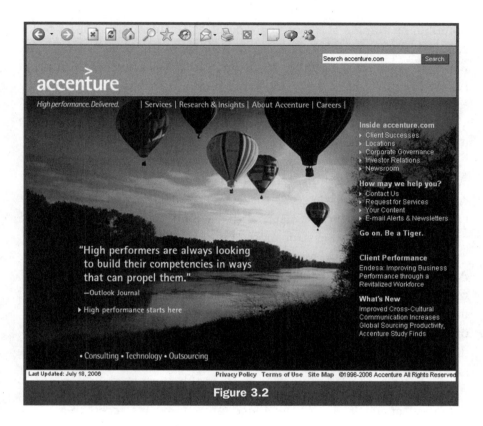

Figure 3.2

Aside from having a color scheme that's full of tranquil pastels so it's easy on the eye and an uncomplicated layout that makes navigation simple, the homepage of *Accenture.com* identifies with the company as a brand by ensuring that all of its key site areas are easily and quickly accessible. From the outset, it is clear that Accenture is an organized outfit priding itself on professionalism and having no intention whatsoever of settling for second-best—including, of course, the price tag for its services. The reasons for this are simple.

Operating within the B2B field, Accenture makes its living by providing a host of outsourced services that are based purely upon the provision of knowledge and skill—regardless of whether it's performing a role based on the regular undertaking of the accounting processes of a business or indulging a team of consultants geared to performing some detailed and complex analytical task. To be successful in this area, Accenture *must* build immediate credibility with all of its potential customers at every single point of engagement in order to convince its future clients that it can help them improve the ways in which they currently manage their operations. With this point in mind, Accenture obviously recognized some time ago that the presentation and provision of a clear and professional Web proposition would form a pivotal point of contact between it and its customer base and set out its stall accordingly.

Unlike visitors to the Nabisco site, visitors to the homepage of Accenture are quickly directed to a wealth of information about the company and its operations, as the "About Accenture" link acts as a gateway to a repository of material that would probably keep even the most avid of readers busy for most of a fortnight.

Aside from facilitating access to a message from Bill Green, Accenture's CEO, which details the company's proactive corporate citizenship, there is a series of links to other important site areas including investor relations, core values, sponsorship activity, and a list of the company's locations around the world. In addition, there are direct links to the latest company report and an overview of Accenture as a business.

In true detailed fashion, Accenture has also strived to ensure that when visitors click each of the above links, they have access to a wealth of subtopical information that should leave them under no illusion as to the compendious amount of knowledge and experience that resides behind Accenture as a brand. Indeed, the entire site just bristles with class and efficiency, and by committing so much material to the most superficial levels of the site (i.e., within one or two clicks of the homepage), Accenture can be almost guaranteed that it's going to get noticed.

As with the examples of Sega and Aston Martin that were discussed in chapter 1, Nabisco and Accenture are quite literally polarized versions of each other. While the former seems unclear as to the direction that its online proposition should be taking, the latter delivers its message with a concise and decisive cutting edge. Nabisco and Accenture are in totally different fields, but given that the Internet is a pivotal point of engagement and a direct reflection of organizational culture, which business would you rather deal with?

Products and Services

The "About Us" section ensures that even the most uninformed of users can furnish themselves with as much information about a business or a company as is realistically necessary, but it's important to understand that this only represents one wheel on the bicycle. The other wheel, therefore, should fundamentally consist of the products, services, and/or brands that are most easily associated with the organizations that they readily represent.

As with a Web site's "About Us" section, a dedicated link from the homepage is nothing short of imperative if users are to familiarize themselves with the products and services of a business. If obvious enough, it should ensure that visitors to the site can continue to extend their knowledge of a company or organization in an erudite and positive way instead of sitting in front of the screen transfixed with a thousand-yard stare. When used together, the "About Us" and "Products and Services" sections should combine in a logical and complementary manner to evangelize the strengths of an organization and evoke a favorable series of emotions for viewers.

L'Oreal

An example of a Web site that does this well is figure 3.3, *Loreal.com*, a screenshot of which was taken in July 2006 (see next page).

In delivering the plaudits to L'Oreal during my brandchannel review of its Web site in March 2006, I had this to say (4):

> *The decadent days of French history may well have ended in revolution, but thanks to L'Oreal's success at mass marketing the concept of exclusivity, discerning owners of brand-conscious boudoirs can still start the day with an aristocratic edge, regardless of whether they live in Baltimore or Beijing.*
>
> *L'Oreal's Web proposition has clearly been designed to create an experience and at first glance screams "Vive la Difference!" with all of the relevant touchstones being both visible and navigable without ambiguity.*
>
> *At the sharp end, the opulence of L'Oreal's brand portfolio comes across strongly without being overpowering and brash and*

Figure 3.3

links blue-chip names such as Cacharel, Garnier, Lancôme, and Maybelline with a lavish sense of luxury that is unmistakably associated with premium priced products. Great care has also been taken to retain the individual characteristics of each brand's personality, so rather than trying to crowd everything into a tight little corner, L'Oreal passively encourages visitors to move directly to the Web site of the brand that they are interested in by providing limited information through the homepage.

As with all good Web sites, *Loreal.com* gets its point across quickly and, as a result of its layout and synergy with the brand, leaves little room for misinterpretation. By arranging its links in a linear way, L'Oreal ensures that visitors to its Web proposition can easily make a selection from a choice of preset menus and, as such, are naturally guided to the areas of the site that are most appropriate for their needs. At the same time, L'Oreal's rich but subtle use of imagery becomes instrumental in evoking a range of emotions synergistic with a brand that holds court at the premium end of the beauty and personal care market.

At the top of the page, the link to the "Our Company" section is very clearly visible and resides alongside a small but poignant selection of other named portals that L'Oreal obviously feels will add most value to a visitor's online experience. For the purposes of this review, however, we will concentrate on the action that's located on the right-hand side of the page entitled "Discover our Brand Portfolio," because what L'Oreal has done in terms of promoting its products and services is very smart indeed.

Far from just providing a series of basic gateways to each of the brands in question, L'Oreal has engineered its homepage in such a way that when a user clicks on a name like "Garnier" or "Cacharel," the content in the main viewing area immediately transforms itself to become a reflection of the targeted brand. The net effect of this is the creation of an impression of synergy between L'Oreal and its brand portfolio that is very nearly seamless. That's not all, however, as rather than being tempted to behave like an oracle and restrict each visiting user to the confines of *Loreal.com*, the content is so limited that it merely serves as an appetizer and subsequently encourages visitors to go directly to the Web site of the brand in which they are interested. Once there, he can fully familiarize himself with each product range in question.

Quite simply, this is a superb bit of branding because it promotes the flow of traffic to a series of different Web sites, each of which is designed to enhance the value and credibility of the brands they represent. L'Oreal does this without imposing its own personality on them in a controlling and domineering way. In other words, L'Oreal is telling us that its brands have their own unique DNAs and individual personalities, while still acknowledging that they're part of the same family.

As an alternative to using the main viewing area to identify with L'Oreal's brands, the homepage also carries a link entitled "brands," which is located at the top of the page, to the right of "Our Company." When clicking on this link, users are treated to the "extended version" of the content that can be accessed via the "Discover our Brand Portfolio" section and can also segment their viewing preferences by either "Luxury, Professional" or "Consumer" products. The combined effect of both this technique and of that mentioned above fulfils the prediction by *News.com* way back in 2002: L'Oreal has begun to capitalize on the benefits of using the Internet as an integrated plat-form from which to evangelize its marketing strategy and bind its com-munications together. As a result, it looks completely in tune with itself and is a pleasure to peruse.

L'Oreal has clearly put considerable time and effort into its online proposition and, in terms of the basics, has set a trail-blazing example of how digital branding should work. The Web design, subject matter, and technological symmetry combine to great effect and, as a direct consequence, reward visitors with an enriching Web experience that they can then directly associate with both the L'Oreal brand and its subsequent portfolio. Nice.

Unfortunately, not every organization has yet reached the standards achieved by L'Oreal, and although some are actively challenging the way they appear on the Web, others are still looking for a sense of direction. With that in mind and having just seen an example of how it should be done, let's now look at an example of a brand, which, if its online proposition is anything to go by, appears to struggle to under-stand what it actually does to make money—it's that well-honed Italian stallion itself, Ferrari.

Ferrari

When reviewing the Ferrari Web site in May 2006 (5), I was really excited by the prospect of looking at a branded Web site that is so openly associated with opulence and whose products are the prerequi-site playthings of the enormously rich and famous. Unfortunately, upon writing the article, I found that Ferrari was stuck in the slow lane as far as the Web was concerned and I went on to write:

> There are very few brands with the raw, intrinsic power of Ferrari. The very mention of the name evokes images of affluence, speed, glamour, and success. Translating such emotion to the Web however can be a process fraught with difficulty, and Ferrariworld.com suf-fered a blow out along the way.
>
> Yes, the homepage is festooned in scarlet and its commitment to the brand's Italian heritage is without question. But where's the rush of adrenalin and the unbridled sense of anticipation that one expects upon ignition? Even the flash technology appears to misfire

as it fails to facilitate the high-octane ride that one expects from Ferrari.

The disappointment from a visit to Ferrari's Web portal is positively palpable and can best be analogized by taking a GTB Fiorano for a test drive only for the gear shift to come off in your hand. So much anticipation, so much expectation and, unfortunately, so much consternation.

A screenshot of *Ferrari.com* (also *ferrariworld.com*) taken in July 2006 is shown below in figure 3.4.

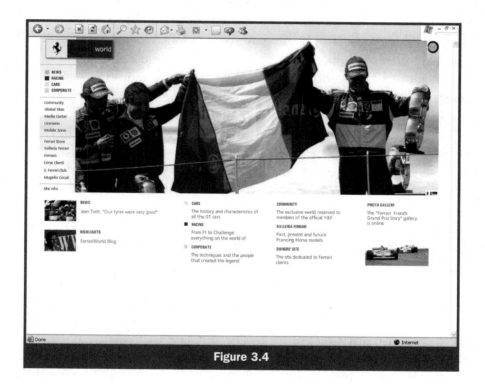

Figure 3.4

Before we begin the process of dissecting Ferrari's homepage for the purposes of science and learning, let's just pause in order to reacquaint ourselves with the words of Edward R. Murrow and ask just what it is that Ferrari is trying to say to us.

My understanding of Ferrari's operations (and please forgive me if I'm wrong) is that the company is in the business of making (and racing) seriously expensive motor cars that go like the proverbial bolt of greased lightning and have an instantly magnetic effect on the planet's fairer sex.

Given such a narrow channel of operating activity, I would have thought that pulling together and presenting Web-enabled material for one of the world's most recognizable and sought-after automotive brands would be a simple and straightforward exercise. Unfortunately, however, it appears as though I've misjudged that one!

The problems at *Ferrari.com* are blatantly apparent from the outset. Nothing stands out, nothing grabs the attention, and nothing draws the eye. Some of the obvious reasons for this are that all of the links are almost exactly the same size and that the primary photograph is somewhat overbearing, but what about the factors that are harder to see—so much so, in fact, that their meaning is almost subliminal.

In addressing this point, let's come back to the question of "what does Ferrari want to say and how is it trying to say it?" The answer, quite simply, is anyone's guess.

If you look closely at the "News, Racing, Cars, Corporate" and "Community" links in the top left of the page, you will see that they're repeated from left to right across the bottom. Perhaps Ferrari did this to try and guide users to specific areas of the site, or perhaps the duplication is the result of a shortfall in content and the need to fill a space—starting with the one between the content provider's ears!

In addition to the duplication, the remaining links on the homepage bear no categorical classification so it isn't very clear whether they apply to both production cars and racing cars or, for that matter, Ferrari as a brand.

Exactly the same criticisms can be made when trying to get a fix on Ferrari's products and services. There is simply no clarity of message other than some indirect links to a partnership with Vodafone and a small selection of merchandise that's available through the online shop. Ferrari is a brand that's at the absolute premium end of its range, so this is nothing much short of a crime and someone, somewhere, needs to take a long hard look at himself.

Because of these issues and the resulting perception of vagueness that pervades *Ferrrari.com*, the output is that of a confusing nonentity that does little to inspire one's confidence in the engineering of the company's vehicles—even though in reality, that couldn't be further from the truth. Ferrari is a magnificent brand with a rich and vivid history, and its cars are not just the playthings of the privileged. They're also the envy of everyone involved in the world of Formula 1 racing.

The glaring weaknesses that appear in Ferrari online, therefore, are absolute testimony to the need to deliver a message with clarity. Instead of getting itself stuck between two stools, Ferrari should be concisely defining the differences between its production portfolio and its participation in Formula 1 and ensuring that access to each site area is much more obvious on the homepage. It should also be evangelizing its heritage instead of sticking it under its "Corporate" banner and proudly aligning its success on the racetrack with the development of its production cars. In short, it should be passionate, dynamic, and driven by precision engineering, just like the cars themselves.

Section Summary

During the first two sections of this chapter, I hope to have developed your understanding of just what it takes to not only build positive brand awareness through the appropriate positioning of some basic online content but to also take the first steps toward invoking the right types of emotional responses from an audience. A brand cannot stand on its logo alone. These days, the public is much too smart for that and they want to understand just what type of business is behind the image and whether its rhetoric is real or just promotional blurb.

To that end, many organizations try and expedite the process of culturally aligning a brand on the Web by augmenting the prerequisite touchstones of "About Us" and "Products and Services" with a number of other points of engagement to which visitors to their sites can relate. Between now and the end of this chapter, we will have a look at some of them.

Contact Us

In 1983, when I was seventeen years old, I was living in a small coal-mining town in Northumberland, England, and like everyone else my age, because there was little else to do, I had an avid interest in the UK music scene. At the time, artists such as David Bowie, Depeche Mode, the Police, and Duran Duran were dominating the charts and synthesized sounds were the order of the day. So it was a refreshing change when a little-known band called Big Country first entered the fray with their instantly recognizable sound that was predicated purely on guitars.

As an apprentice guitarist myself, I instantly became hooked on the rhythms and the melodies that symbolized Big Country's image, and when they announced that they were coming to play in Newcastle-upon-Tyne, which was only a thirty-minute bus ride away from my home town, I made sure I was getting a ticket. I also decided that as I had bought every single record that Big Country had ever put out, I would take the sleeves and covers through to Newcastle in the hope that the band would sign them when they turned up at the venue, which was Newcastle City Hall.

When the big day arrived, I eagerly collected all my record covers and put them in a plastic bag before hopping on the bus to Newcastle with some friends. When we arrived at Newcastle City Hall, we weren't surprised to see that something of a crowd had developed out-side the stage door, so we dutifully took our place before waiting for the band to arrive.

As I remember it, the weather was bitterly cold and we stood around for hours before the tour bus eventually arrived and the band stepped onto the pavement. I had also never done anything like that before, so I wasn't quite sure what to expect; after all, the musicians of Big Country were huge stars and had developed a large following throughout the UK.

The first person off the bus was the band's charismatic front man, singer, and lead guitarist, Stuart Adamson, who was then followed by the other band members, Tony Butler, Mark Brzezicki, and Bruce Watson.

Far from behaving like a bunch of prima donnas, the entire band just smiled and shook hands before signing what seemed like an end-less stream of autographs and posing with fans for photographs. From what I remember, they were outside with us in the freezing cold for well over an hour before leaving for the sound check.

When it came my turn, I asked Stuart Adamson somewhat sheep-ishly if he would have time to sign all of the covers that I'd brought as I was conscious of the demands of his entourage, who were keen to press on with the technical precursors to the show. His answer was something that will stay with me forever, and it went along these lines:

"When I was a kid, I waited all day to meet bands outside of concert halls, usually after the gig in the rain. What really used to upset me was that after I had paid good money to see them and they'd wound me up to fever pitch with their performance during the show, they would pretend to be bloody rock stars and shoot off to their hotels. So I swore that if I ever got famous that I would never behave like that. So I'll sign as many things as you like, no matter how long it takes."

Sadly, Stuart is no longer with us, having committed suicide just before Christmas 2001 as a result of his battle with alcoholism. But the memory of what he said that day is as real and vivid to me now as it was at the time that it happened, and within his words, there's a message for us all.

The world's best companies openly solicit feedback from their stakeholders and treat their responses as a gift. They don't pout, preen, or patronize their public by portraying themselves as arrogant and aloof. They go out of their way to communicate with their customers and consistently treat them with respect, because they understand the importance of meeting and exceeding the expectations of people who have helped them develop their brands.

The advent of the Internet presents many businesses with an unbridled opportunity to control communications flows with any given audience by both pushing and pulling the exchange of information. In addition, and thanks to the perpetual developments in terms of Internet technology, there are now many ways in which this can be done—although some are infinitely better than others.

Phone Numbers and Addresses

The minimum requirement for organizations to consider is the traditional publishing of a list of offices, locations, outlets, and dealerships complete with addresses and phone and fax numbers. The very least that this will achieve is negation of the need for someone to go leafing through a phone book—unless, of course, the host organization doesn't actually want to talk to anyone, in which case its failure to provide such information may actually be quite deliberate.

Needless to say, the consequences of being evasive with regard to the provision of contact details can be quite interesting, as Ryanair, Ireland's low-cost carrier, recently found out.

One disenfranchised patron of Ryanair, spurred on by what was perceived as a complete lack of ethics and a distinct unwillingness by the airline to take responsibility for its actions during a spat over an ill-fated flight, decided to mount a concerted campaign against the company's customer service policies by launching an anti-site at the domain of *www.ryanair.org.uk*. Perhaps not surprisingly, Ryanair soon became hopping mad with the customer's enterprising little initiative and after pursuing the matter, managed to get control of the domain name in August 2006. Not to be outdone, however, the customer simply moved his site to another domain titled *www.ryanaircampaign.org*, from which he continues to extol the weaknesses associated with the Irish carrier's level of care for those who pay for its services.

The key issue behind the customer's seemingly infinite source of motivation appears to be that Ryanair makes it extremely difficult to contact or indeed be challenged on its customer service policies, offering only a premium rate telephone number for those in need of support. By way of addressing this shortfall in knowledge, the Web site above has very considerately published a list of telephone numbers and e-mail addresses to ensure that anyone signing onto its site can therefore contact the airline directly. In addition, the site has embellished its content to include news reports, press releases, exchanges of letters, and an online forum, where people with similar experiences of Ryanair's level of care can exchange their points of view.

Hopefully, Ryanair will wake up and smell the coffee soon and understand that the cost of disenfranchising customers and losing their business for good will at some point far outweigh the revenues generated by premium rate phone lines and the salaries of qualified and empathetic customer service personnel—no matter what the churn numbers might say. Until that day comes, however, we can sit back and watch the rise in popularity of *ryanaircampaign.org*.

E-mail

If e-mail is a preferred mode of communication, some forethought needs to go into the general distribution of inbound mail in order to make sure that enquiries are dealt with both promptly and professionally. Some companies do this by listing a generic e-mail address (such as *enquiry@ . . . com*) which is subsequently picked up by a sales or customer services team. Others publish e-mail addresses for specific geographical or departmental locations, and some actually publish the addresses of named individuals. Whatever route is chosen, great care needs to be taken to afford inbound mail the necessary attention to facilitate a quick response, which will preferably be hours, not days. With that in mind, stick your hand up now if you have ever sent an e-mail to a Web site and never received a reply—it irritated you no end, didn't it?

Online Forms

A method used by many businesses in their attempts to control the quality of inbound information submitted via their Web sites is the mandatory completion of an online form. The quality and consistency of these documents can vary and range from a simple one-page design to a detailed questionnaire. While forms can be useful for organizations wishing to classify and categorize their inbound communications in order to generate an efficient and speedy response, they can also be interpreted as a Web-enabled version of a touch-tone phone, where users are required to press 1 if they have an enquiry, press 2 if they are losing the will to live, and press 3 if they would like to warn someone that they are in danger of going postal. Over the years, I have developed an increasing dislike for the completion of online forms because they very rarely seem to include an option that's relevant to my query—or is that just me?

Live Chat

Far from being the preserve of messenger systems such as those at Yahoo, Microsoft, and, of course, several late-night adult entertainment companies, live chat is increasingly finding a home within the outbound services and help desk departments of several large organizations. One of the best examples of this is eBay, which carries a "live help" button on several of its more prominent pages and enables those who are having problems with certain types of functionality to connect to an eBay representative via a private chat room. In choosing this method of communication, companies can portray themselves as both empathetic in their approach and innovative in terms of their technology. They can also control the workload of inbound queries and ensure that their responses are categorized and scheduled via qualified personnel.

VOIP

VOIP, the acronym for voice over Internet protocol, enables anyone with a PC complete with a microphone and speakers and, of course, an Internet connection to speak to anyone in the world with the corresponding software—for free. A major player in this arena is Skype, which was recently acquired by eBay for $4.1 billion. The growth of VOIP as a communications tool has been nothing short of exponential, and millions of people are now hooking up to chat for hours at the expense of the traditional telecom providers.

In the corporate world, VOIP has presented organizations with a great opportunity to communicate with customers and stakeholders alike at a nominal level of cost. Although companies such as Skype are a relatively recent augmentation in terms of taking the concept to consumers, companies such as Hilton have been using VOIP for years as part of their customer contact system.

For instance, when making a reservation at *Hilton.com*, users can either book online directly or make use of a button titled "push to talk," which when pressed will result in a representative from Hilton calling them back on their land line or via a direct VOIP connection—whichever is the customers' preference. Once contact is made, Hilton can then inject a personal touch into the process of customer contact and, as a result, appear much more empathetic in terms of meeting its clients' needs.

As you can see, there are many different ways in which organizations can communicate with people as a direct result of the Internet, and a visitor to a site can learn a great deal about the culture of a company based upon its method of choice. As I said at the beginning of this section, the best companies openly solicit feedback and are proactive in their attempts to communicate. They are transparent and welcoming and don't try to hide behind a library of FAQ's and online forms that, more often than not, result in site visitors becoming frustrated by an organization's perceived unwillingness to speak to them. Whatever the method and whatever the user's impression of a company's Web site, it's sure to have an impact on the brand—and that should always be kept in mind.

FAQs

While certainly useful if constructed the right way, FAQs can also come across as both insensitive and irrelevant when they're not, as I discovered when reviewing the Formula 1 Web site for brandchannel in March 2006 (6). Although the site in general was a poor representation of the F1 brand, those behind its content blew it when writing the FAQs, and at the time I said:

> *Finally, and for those who may still doubt the extent to which formula1.com fails to get out of the pit lane, a trip to the FAQ section reveals a world-class abdication of responsibility that would send even the most junior of marketers diving for cover. Apparently, if the countdown clock on the homepage is showing the wrong time, it's likely your PC's fault for having the wrong settings; likewise with the site's quality of images. You should also read your local TV listings if you want to watch a race (you won't find this info on the site), while those who are looking for tickets should speak to the respective race tracks—regardless of the fact that you can buy tickets and travel packages through formula1.com on the homepage.*

Far from helping me with any questions that I may have had about Formula 1, the FAQ section of the Web site had the completely adverse effect and gave me the distinct impression that it was way out of touch with what was going on in the real world.

Key points to remember, therefore, when constructing FAQs are

- Cover all the bases and make sure that the resulting content is indeed representative of those questions that are frequently asked. Avoid being drawn into areas that may result in rambling ambiguity or are likely to cause conflict.
- Be careful of the tone and remember that the entire point of having a set of FAQs is to *help* visitors to a Web site get the best out of their experience. They should not be seen as a disingenuous barricade that will reduce the flow of an organization's inbound calls.

- Keep the language and terminology as basic and understandable as possible. Not everyone has a degree in IT, and it is important that any instructions or technical help be delivered in a clear and concise way so that inexperienced users can feel confident in dealing with a problem themselves.
- Always include some contact details so that users are welcome to write or call an organization directly should the FAQs not answer their query in full.

News and Investor Relations

Another area that's now commonplace on the Web sites of many organizations is that of news and investor or stakeholder relations. You could be forgiven for thinking that the latter is only relevant to businesses that are publicly listed, but it can also be used as a portal from which companies evangelize their work in the community, seek to attract new business partners, say how much they care about the environment, and generally bang on about a lot of cause-related stuff, most of which will be discussed in detail later in this book.

On the financial side, many companies also make use of an investor or stakeholder relations section to publish downloadable copies of their annual reports and chairman's statements against the backdrop of a real-time share price.

As far as reporting news is concerned, many people would argue that before any material is committed to the Web it should first be subjected to the basic criteria within an organization's communications strategy to make sure that it doesn't compromise the company or its brand portfolio—and I couldn't agree more.

As an example, I will share an experience with you that occurred when I was evaluating Tommy Hilfiger's Web site for an article I was writing for brandchannel (7).

While researching the Hilfiger Web site, I clicked on the link to the Rumor (8) section, expecting to pick up a load of innocuous stuff about fashion shows, new designs, and celebrity sponsorship deals. Imagine my surprise, therefore, when instead of being greeted by a load of upbeat messages about Tommy's new catalogue, I was confronted with a series of rantings that vehemently denied Mr. Hilfiger's involvement in a case of racial slurring that supposedly took place on an episode of *The Oprah Winfrey Show*. As if that were not enough, there was also a set of links to three types of statements (one from customers, one from corporate, and one from Tommy himself), either categorically denying that an incident ever took place or from customers stating that they didn't believe the rumors anyway.

Now, while I certainly don't purport to be an independent guru well versed in the art of PR, I still can't help wondering why such an amount of airtime was devoted to the subject on the Hilfiger site. My reason for making this point is that I am assuming that the rumors were only relevant in the U.S. Since I have spent most of the past few years in the UK and Australia, I certainly hadn't heard them. However, once Tommy decided to publish the content and context of the alleged impropriety on his Web site, I, along with the rest of the world, became acutely aware of an issue that we never would have known existed had it not been for the power of the World Wide Web.

In addition (and probably more disconcerting), we were granted open access to Mr. Hilfiger's reaction and, as we all now know, that can speak volumes for the culture of a company.

Having been brought up with traditional values, I can't really see what all the fuss is about. If it's true that Tommy Hilfiger has never even appeared on *Oprah Winfrey* (which is what it states on the site) and therefore couldn't possibly have made any remarks—racist or otherwise—why get so excited about it—and why draw so much attention to yourself in the process?

The rationale behind this point on news flow is that just like everything else that takes place on the Web, it's a form of communication and, as a direct consequence, any content or material that appears under its heading will have a subsequent impact on a brand. With that in mind, it's important to ensure that before any news is posted on the Internet, it should be vetted against the organization's current communications policy and, of course, that it's suitable for the eyes of a worldwide audience.

Search Engines and Site Maps

When I first started reviewing Web sites for brandchannel back in 2001, I used to have a real issue with companies that didn't afford their homepages the benefit of a site map, a search engine, or both.

More than five years in, my opinion hasn't changed but it still never ceases to amaze me how many organizations appear to take for granted that a visitor to their site will instantly find what he's looking for with a minimum of effort and stress.

Perhaps they spend so much time and energy on their online propositions that they become too intimately acquainted with them and automatically assume that everyone else will feel the same way. Or maybe it's a covert game that's played by techies to see how long they can keep people guessing as to where a certain type of content is hidden.

The fact is, as mentioned in chapter 2, more than half of the visitors to a Web site will stay there for less than sixty seconds because in this digital age of choice, they don't have to look very far before finding a competitor. With that in mind, a site map, a search engine, or any other type of tool that will speed up a visitor's search for relevant content and material should be considered a mandatory requirement by those involved in Web site design, because if users can't find what they're looking for quickly, they're off.

Site maps and search engines don't need to be complex beasts that devour Web space and bandwidth at a rate of knots either; they simply need to be visible, accessible, and, above all, usable, so that anyone looking for specific information can find it with ease.

· · ·

Key Points
The key points to remember from this chapter are as follows:

- An organization's history and background is an invaluable component of a brand's genetic makeup. Organizations can use this to their advantage by ensuring that their Web sites carry as much information as possible that is likely to result in a user developing a favorable impression of a company and its products.
- Messages should always be imparted with clarity and transparency, drawing attention to the elements that will invoke a series of positive emotions from visitors to a site.

- The best organizations treat feedback as a gift, are open with regard to their communication channels, and do not portray themselves as arrogant or aloof. The Web is not a substitute for direct customer contact and should never be treated as such.
- Care should be taken with news flow to ensure that it matches an organization's current communications policy and that its release will not have a negative impact on the brands to which it relates.
- Site maps and search engines should be mandatory components of all Web sites, as they expedite a user's search for relevant material. This way, they don't have to scroll through pages of content that they may well deem irrelevant.

ENDNOTES

1. *news.com.com/2009-12-962557.html*
2. Bedbury, Scott, and Stephen Fenichell. *A New Brand World: Eight Principles for Achieving Brand Leadership in the Twenty-First Century.* New York: Penguin, 2003.
3. *www.brandchannel.com/features_Webwatch.asp?ww_id=283*
4. *www.brandchannel.com/features_Webwatch.asp?ww_id=269*
5. *www.brandchannel.com/features_Webwatch.asp?ww_id=279*
6. *www.brandchannel.com/features_Webwatch.asp?ww_id=268*
7. *www.brandchannel.com/features_Webwatch.asp?ww_id=276*
8. *http://usa.tommy.com/opencms/opencms/companyinfo/ethicsvalues/ rumor.html*

4

It's a Small World After All

If you're trying to persuade people to do something, or buy something, it seems to me you should use their language, the language they use every day, the language in which they think.
—DAVID OGILVY

SO FAR IN THIS BOOK I HAVE TALKED A LOT ABOUT THE concept of brand association, a little about brand identity and brand awareness, and up until now, been careful not to go into too much detail about the traditional marketing base elements of positioning and segmentation.

That is because the concepts of positioning and segmentation are so fundamental to the success of any marketing plan and, of course, the formulation and execution of subsequent strategy, that referring to them as bit-part players simply won't do them justice. To that end, we are going to spend the next part of this book looking at both positioning and segmentation and how organizations attempt to replicate these associated concepts via the World Wide Web. In other words, this chapter will put the finishing touches to what we learned in chapters 1, 2, and 3 by exploring how organizations use the concepts of positioning and segmentation in cyberspace and effectively close the loop as to what the fundamentals of digital branding are, to ensure that when a brand goes online it's most definitely in line.

The common school of thought these days is that in tightly contested markets where competition is rife and a large choice of products and services exists, the point of differentiation between one company or another is the brands they represent and not the functionality of the products themselves. This assumption is based on the premise that the level of extrinsic features and benefits between the products and services is more or less in a state of equilibrium, yet there can be no denying the superior impact that some brands will have on our mindset when compared with those of the competition.

Picture yourself in an electronics store, for instance, looking at a range of portable color TVs. You're in front of a long aisle and stacked on either side are loads of miniature televisions, all bearing the names of such well-known companies as Sanyo, Samsung, Sony, Philips, Toshiba, Sharp, Sansui, JVC, Mitsubishi, and LG (Lucky Goldstar), to name but a few. By and large, they all have the same functionality. They have similar screens, the same number of channels, the same timer, the same memory functions, the same audio and visual inputs—the choice is endless, but which brand do you choose in the end and what was it that pushed your brain into gear?

More than likely, the brand you chose was the one that *you believed* would deliver the most for you based on all of those nice, positive emotions that we talked about in chapters 2 and 3. You were pushed into that decision, however, by the mental associations that you made between the brand and its subsequent attributes that have been burned into your brain by the parent company's positioning and segmentation strategies. Let's look at a slightly more detailed example.

The Hypothetical Pie Co.

Billy Bunter Inc. makes pies. In fact, it makes so many pies that just about everyone in the world who's ever wrapped their pearly whites around the crisp and golden outer crust and bitten into the succulent filling is almost instantly addicted to the Billy Bunter brand. As a result, Billy Bunter Inc. grows considerably and needs to engage some partners in order to facilitate its upswing in trade without compromising on the quality of its products.

One day, after a long and heavy meeting in the boardroom where many ideas were discussed and many pies were consumed, the CEO of

Billy Bunter Inc. told his management team that since the company excelled in the business of making pies, it should simply continue to concentrate on its core activities. Where possible, he wanted to out-source as many peripheral processes as he could in order to reduce the company's exposure to multiple suppliers, lower its cost base, and just get fully focused on making world-class pies. Without further ado, he then pointed to the company's finance director, Ivana Lotofanalisis, and instructed her to go and find an accounting firm that could look after as much of Billy Bunter Inc.'s financial workload as possible.

Ivana dutifully set about her task, and it wasn't long before she'd organized a series of meetings with a number of well-known firms in order to evaluate their capabilities and prices. Perhaps not surprisingly, the list of invitees included Mr. Deloitte, Mr. PWC, Mr. Ernst and Mr. Young, and, of course, Mr. KPMG.

Ivana had based her initial decisions as to whom she should con-sider to engage as a business partner on a set of criteria which included:

- Global reach—to help manage Billy Bunter Inc.'s foreign business affairs.
- Reputation—so as not to associate Billy Bunter Inc. with a perceived second-tier player that could have subsequent service failings and damage the company brand.
- Range of services—so that she could not only outsource as much of Billy Bunter Inc.'s financial management as the business was comfortable with, but so that she could call on the chosen partner to provide tax advice, auditing, and some general business consultancy if it were required.

In selecting the above criteria, Ivana had carried out some inde-pendent research on the Internet, discussed potential candidates with several industry contacts, and contacted her professional accounting association for advice. So what led Ivana to make her initial decision?

The answer to that one is, of course, quite simple—Ivana was both directly and indirectly influenced by the positioning and segmentation strategies of each of the companies in question and, as a consequence, was drawn to their respective brands like a magnet. In addition, the more questions she asked in line with her criteria, the more positive responses she received and the more her gut instinct told her that she was on the right course.

Whether she was or not may well never be known, since Ivana probably overlooked a number of businesses that could satisfy the needs of Billy Bunter Inc. but failed to gain recognition because they just don't have the same depth of visibility as the big four. That's because wherever you go in the financial world, you will see the names of KMPG, Ernst and Young, Deloitte, and PWC in perpetuity, as they're constantly supported by advertising campaigns, heavily involved in the sponsorship of professional bodies, and have built their reputations on extensive market share.

With this analogy in the back of our minds, let's now have a look at how brands attempt to position themselves online and how the market segments in which they choose to operate subsequently influence their Web offering. As usual and thanks to my experiences with brandchannel, we will be considering some real-world examples of brands that have done it well and some that have not—otherwise it wouldn't be any fun, now would it?

Brand Positioning

Theories on brand positioning are many and varied and, like everything else, have evolved over time. Rather than go for the textbooks, however, I thought it would be worthwhile exploring a couple of hypotheses that are available on the Internet—after all, this is a book about digital branding!

Jennifer Rice is founder of Mantra Brand Consulting, based in San Francisco (1). Mantra specializes in building brand identities and connecting them with the needs of potential customers by helping their clients build effective brand positioning strategies within their target markets.

Jennifer also has a hugely informative and entertaining Weblog (2), which over the past few years has developed into a very useful resource base for anyone who may be interested in exploring the latest schools of thought with regard to the concepts of brand identity and brand positioning.

In one of her online articles entitled "Brands as Ecosystem" (3), Jennifer argues that the relative strength of a brand is in direct proportion to the number and quality of connections that exist within a brand's own ecosystem, which is comprised of such things as the company it represents, its stakeholders, and, of course, its customers. Harking back to chapters 2 and 3 of this book, you will no doubt recall that I have gone to great lengths to stress how important the Internet is as a "point of engagement" and also how it can directly reflect the culture and ethics of the business it represents. I have also tried to stress the importance of making sure that whenever a brand goes online, it's in tune with the unique characteristics and personality of the offline brand and that a Web proposition should seek out opportunities to add value to a brand, not erode it.

This subliminal critiquing of a Web site's ability to emotionally connect a brand in cyberspace to that of its offline counterpart forms an inextricable link between a user and the perceived personality of an offline brand. In other words, a Web site reflects exactly how good, bad, or indifferent an organization is at articulating its brand positioning strategy within the realms of cyberspace—and that's what makes things like content, color schemes, context, and layout so fundamentally important to making a snap connection.

Suzanne Hogan is an identity and image consultant. She is also a senior partner at Lippincott Mercer—a U.S.-based business that specializes in "connecting brands to business with an unwavering focus on the customer" (4).

In an article written for the Lippincott Mercer Web site (5), Hogan argues that there are three essential factors involved in developing a brand's definition, the combined effect of which will subsequently drive the positioning of a brand in the marketplace. She lists these factors as:

- Vision—the ability to link a brand's positioning strategy to a company's overall vision.
- Meaning—the direct association of a brand's image and appearance to what it actually means in the marketplace.
- Parameters and relevance—the perceived limits of a brand's extension into alternative markets or segments that, when executed, will either enhance or compromise brand value.

Disney

When benchmarking some companies against her criteria, Suzanne Hogan cites Disney as a very good example of a well-defined brand and states:

> Few brands are better defined than Disney. The company's success is measured by no less than a 610 percent growth in the last decade, according to its most recent annual report. Nearly half of that growth came from new business areas, some that bear the Disney name and some that do not. Here is a company that not only understands its vision and meaning but clearly understands its parameters of relevance.

When I first started reviewing Web sites for brandchannel back in 2001, I found myself drawn to Disney due to the power and strength of its brand. Upon reviewing Disney online (6), I wrote:

> As Walt Disney once said, "You can create and build the most wonderful place in the world, but it takes people to make the dream a reality." Exactly the same principle can be applied when transferring a brand to the Web. For example, there is little point in constructing the world's greatest Web site, if the very cultural and conceptual values that established the brand in the first place become lost in a void of technological wizardry.
>
> In plain English, the site is a superb recreation of the Disney environment. There can be no mistaking the Disney-esque artistry and lampoon-like tones that accompany the homepage's navigational options.
>
> Disney.com is one of the better examples of brand association on the Internet today and represents a vibrant, safe, and educational environment for children to visit while retaining the philanthropic and emotional values that underpin the entire Disney concept.

As well as being impressed with the general characteristics and brand association of Disney's proposition on the World Wide Web, I referred to how the company made good use of the Internet's commercial possibilities by looking to enhance its revenue streams through other areas of the site, such as the shop, hotel, and entertainment sections.

See figure 4.1, a screenshot of the *Disney.com* homepage taken in July 2006.

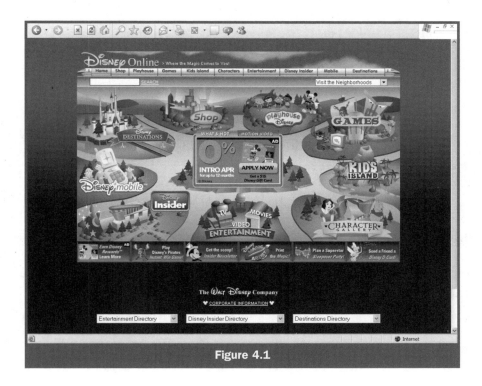

Figure 4.1

More than five years in and nothing much has changed as Disney continues to develop its brand through a very well-executed positioning campaign that now sees it extending and expanding its offering to include the likes of dedicated gift cards (a bespoke type of Disney credit card), more detailed vacation packages, and entertainment options, in addition to its other operational activities.

By following Suzanne Hogan's criteria of vision, meaning, parameters, and relevance and Jennifer Rice's philosophy of making the right connections, it is easy to make a number of observations with regard to how Disney has positioned itself online and how it has attempted to reflect and enhance the overall value of the brand.

Before looking at these, however, let's just step back and remind ourselves what Disney stands for. Within the "Disney Insider" section of the *Disney.com* Web site, the company introduces its business as follows:

> *Since its founding in 1923, the Walt Disney Company has remained faithful in its commitment to producing unparalleled entertainment experiences based on its rich legacy of quality, creative content and exceptional storytelling. Today, Disney is divided into four major business segments: Studio Entertainment, Parks and Resorts, Consumer Products, and Media Networks. Each segment consists of integrated, well-connected businesses that operate in concert to maximize exposure and growth worldwide.*

Because Disney is able to articulate its position with such clarity, the company can rely upon strong foundations to help evangelize its brand meaning and, as a direct result, extend its presence into other target markets. This structured and proactive approach has also increased the scope that Disney online has to connect with site visitors almost exponentially and has culminated in a Web site that has something for just about everyone. Indeed, whether you're visiting *Disney.com* to plan your trip, book some travel, buy some tickets, check out the latest movies, play some games, learn about the characters, or buy something from the shop, you will always be left with the same impression: Disney is a class act.

Now just Imagine what Disney online would look like if it followed the example of Nabisco!

Clearly, not everyone can have the luxury of working with a brand as instantly recognizable as Disney and so not everyone can start to construct his online offerings from such a position of strength. With that in mind and after having looked at what is a very good example of brand positioning on the Web, now let's take a look at something a little bit different—Aeroflot.

Aeroflot

Aeroflot is in the airline industry. As such, it has to compete with such blue-chip enterprises as British Airways, Cathay Pacific, Singapore, and Continental, while at the other end of the scale, contending with the budget-driven cattle class experts that specialize in heavily discounted fares, speedy on-stand turnarounds (the rapid disembarking and re-embarking of passengers in order to decrease the aircraft's time on the ground), and the subsequent arrival and departure at airports slightly off the beaten track.

At the turn of the millennium, Aeroflot had received some very poor publicity due to its safety record and level of service, so I thought that it would be a good idea to review its Web site for brandchannel to ascertain whether any of its problems were visible on the Web. After taking a look at its online proposition, I went on to write (7):

Vodka-guzzling pilots who encourage their sons to fly the planes, smoke-filled cabins reeking of cigars and an oppressive selection of trolley dollies who would stand a better chance of winning a medal in the Olympic shot-put than they would in a beauty parade—these are just some of the features of flying with that great Russian institution, Aeroflot (8).

Unfortunately, the homepage is about as welcoming as a wet weekend in a Siberian salt mine with basic graphics and weak technology making for a rubber-bands and string approach that do more than give the distinct impression that the whole thing's been done on the cheap. Delving deeper into the Web site doesn't get much better either and while most global airlines are offering real time bookings, the best that Aeroflot can do is offer an interactive flight schedule that's two years out of date!

In terms of site content, the About Aeroflot section is a must for poor PR and boasts such side-splitting claims as the company's pilot training centers being equipped with "flight simulators and other high-tech equipment." Can you believe that in this digital age international pilots would actually need such things before taking responsibility for the lives of 300 people? And here I was thinking that most commercial flyboys only needed to sit a driving test first.

Aeroflot's presence on the net is indeed a very poor attempt at restoring customer confidence and their Web site is unlikely to win any medals in terms of creativity and design. Perhaps then it is little surprise that over the past few years even seasoned world travelers have avoided the airline like the plague and that in backpacker circles the company even attracted a new name—Aeroflop.

As you can tell from the review, I was far from impressed with Aeroflot's Web offering back then—although at least it was in keeping with how the brand had positioned itself at the time!

These days, though, I am pleased to report that not only does Aeroflot have a much better Web site but also that the company seems to have taken a grip of many of the issues that were previously affecting the brand per se. As a result, Aeroflot is slowly but surely rebuilding its reputation and has greatly improved the level of clarity behind the brand's definition. Although by no means perfect, Aeroflot has shown that it is beginning to understand the importance of vision, meaning, relevance, and parameters of its brand within the global marketplace.

Figure 4.2 is a screenshot of the *Aeroflot.com* homepage, taken in July 2006.

From the image, you will note that not only does Aeroflot now have a real-time booking and reservations engine but that it also has a loyalty scheme, publishes discounted fares, and contact details on its homepage, and, in general, has the feel of an airline that genuinely cares about its customers and therefore wants to be taken seriously.

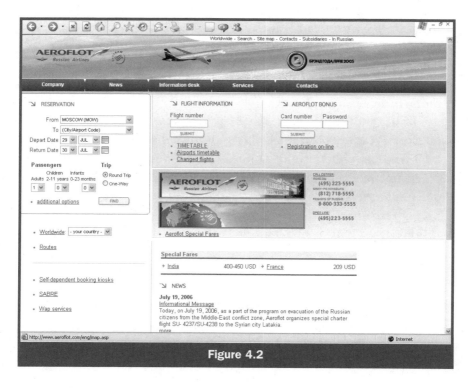

Figure 4.2

When subjecting the Web site to the Hogan and Rice test, we can also see that the introduction of some more functionality to the site along with the Aeroflot loyalty scheme has resulted in a much more engaging proposition from the customer's perspective and given the site more opportunities to connect with people. The extra effort and attention that the company has put into the development of its Web proposition has paid dividends further into the site, too, as a little bit of research reveals that Aeroflot is now much clearer about what type of strategy it is adopting to try and achieve its aims, the meaning of the Aeroflot brand, and the potential markets in which it can extend its presence.

These points are particularly evident within Aeroflot's comprehensive "Company" section, where it refers to its mission as "to provide most completely and safely one of the fundamental human freedoms—freedom of transportation" and also goes to the trouble of listing its strategic goals before specifically naming its intended market position.

It goes without saying, of course, that before Aeroflot could make the necessary improvements to its offering in cyberspace, it had to get its act together offline first. However, the point to bear in mind here is the impression that the Web site gave of the business back in 2001—and that which it reflects today.

In using the two examples of Disney and Aeroflot, I have really been looking to crystallize the importance of developing a reflective brand positioning strategy online. In doing so, I would hope that I have underpinned the importance of illustrating just how a Web site can affect the perception of a brand throughout the world. Remember, the World Wide Web is a global medium and, as such, its content can be viewed and interacted with from Taiwan to Tehran—regardless of whether a given organization deliberately sets out with that intention. To that end, a great deal of consideration should be given as to how a brand might appear online, so that it doesn't do its offline counterpart more harm than good.

A good analogy with regard to brand positioning on the Internet is to try and think of a Web site as a jigsaw puzzle, whereby viewing the component parts in isolation (although some of them might look very nice) only serves to present a disjointed and fragmented view of the business or organization that they are supposed to represent. When the parts are assembled in the right order, however, a viewer should be able to see the complete picture and instantly feel empowered to start building the associations and positive emotions with which the Web site's color scheme, layout, content, culture, and sheer brand presence are synonymous. Unfortunately, that's easier said than done!

Segmentation

In my view, market segmentation is a fascinating concept. Unfortunately, it's also one of the areas of marketing where there is absolutely no shortage of firms and individuals who would be delighted to take your money in exchange for a mythical silver bullet and on the proviso that you sit down and give them a damn good listening to.

Just consider for instance, one of Philip Kotler's descriptions of the concept (9):

> *Market segmentation is the sub-division of a market into homogenous subsets of customers, where any subset may conceivably be selected as a target market and reached with a distinct marketing mix.*

Now just stand back and think about that for a second or two—is it really possible to categorize a market to such an extent that a business can then target the specific, more lucrative sections or those that play to its strengths simply by tailoring its proposition to suit the constituents of each segment? Well, the answer is yes, it most definitely is possible, but the keys to success reside firmly behind a door that's quite clearly marked "classification," and this is where most organizations tend to come unstuck.

In the first instance, there are so many ways of segmenting a customer base these days that many software houses are making a lot of money based on data mining and CRM programs that are perpetually evangelized as being quicker, stronger, and better than the last, when the truth is that all of them are only as good as the information with which they are given to work. In addition, most of these systems tend to be purely transaction based, so they're not going to tell you about customers' behavior when it comes to paying their bills on time, how much of their existing budget may actually be spent on your products/services, or what their degree of loyalty might be.

The common term for segmenting a group of customers by behavioral type is known as "psychographics" (not to be confused with demographics, which is the classification of groups of people based on age, sex, ZIP code, etc.). Since the inception of psychographic analysis and the belief that it really is possible to segment customers by behavior, recent times have seen a great deal of emphasis put on concepts such as relationship marketing and other "softer" methods of attracting the "right" type of customer rather than just "more" customers. Psychographics is not always a straightforward process to implement, but the benefits of developing the right type of psychographic approach to segmentation are considerable, as businesses can then target the most lucrative customers with the most desirable profiles of any given market segment.

My personal belief is that, like anything else in life, it's a question of compromise and that there are so many benefits attached to developing and executing an effective segmentation strategy based on both transaction and behavior, that perseverance to find the right blend is more than worthwhile. After all, effective segmentation strategies dictate the ways in which businesses should be positioning their brands and subsequently form the platform upon which everything else is built. They channel the effective use of resources, the appropriate mode of advertising, and are instrumental in not just attracting but retaining customers too—so if you know a business that doesn't have a segmentation strategy, look at its level of performance and ask yourself whether it's managing to survive through luck or good judgment!

Coca-Cola

The most common method of segmenting customers on the Web is to do it by geography; after all, the Web is a global medium and a Web site is going to be visited by a lot more people than just those in the host nation. But what happens after that? How will the cultural influences of each country around the world shape the minds of visitors to a particular site? And from a company perspective, how important is it for a business to differentiate its messages based on the international markets in which it may or may not have a presence? For instance, potential customers in China are likely to have considerably different cultural beliefs than those from the Netherlands, so how should that conundrum be managed?

To answer some of these questions, let's look at how one of the world's biggest brands, the Atlanta-based Coca-Cola, goes about its business on the World Wide Web.

As with Disney, when I first started reviewing Web sites for brand-channel I immediately found myself drawn to the Coca-Cola brand because of its depth and presence. Excited by the prospect of reviewing the online offering of one of the world's most valuable brands, I had this to say about its inherent strength (10):

If there's still a one-eyed yellow idol to the north of Katmandu, you can be sure that right underneath it is a T-shirt-wearing native selling cans of Coca-Cola from a corporately liveried fridge—such is the exposure achieved by the world's most valuable brand. But, can Coca-Cola respond to the challenge of the World Wide Web and deliver us the real thing with their venture into cyberspace?

At the time and as I wrote in the review, Coca-Cola was concentrating on getting the basics of its Web proposition into gear and was really pushing hard on making sure that its positioning on the Web was reflective of what it stood for in the real world. It was also concentrating on providing an interactive and engaging Web site that was both informative and enjoyable for anyone who wanted to visit.

Since those early days and after having spent time cutting its teeth in order to define just exactly how it could use the concept of the World Wide Web to its best advantage, the monolithic brand known affectionately as "Big Red" has since grabbed the Net by the Ethernet cables and has one of the most lateral and holistic concepts around. Consider, for example, a homepage that provides access to up to 100 individual country-specific Web sites, where each one is written in the host nation's language, to the extent that even in the U.S., *coke.com* can be viewed in English or Spanish. Granted, some of the lesser known countries such as the Ivory Coast still have their Web sites under review, but this should in no way detract from Coca-Cola's intent—it wants to speak to as many people as it can in order to encourage them to buy its soft drinks—and it wants to use their language, the language in which they think.

Figures 4.3 and 4.4 are screenshots of the company's Swedish and Chinese homepages, taken in July 2006:

Figure 4.3

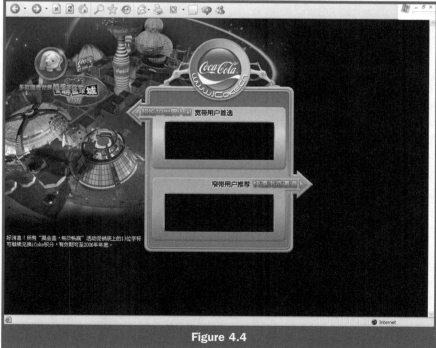

Figure 4.4

What's most impressive about the two examples above (and this is typical of almost all of Coca-Cola's country-driven sites) is that they are not simply straightforward translations of Coke's American Web site but rather individually tailored Web propositions geared to each nation's cultural and idiosyncratic tastes. The investment in time and effort that Coke has put into its Web proposition is absolutely indicative of a business that believes that the Internet is a marketing tool to be exploited, not neglected—and the results are plain to see. Little wonder, then, that Coca-Cola's willingness to embrace new concepts and strengthen its appeal have helped to ensure that it's still the world's most valuable brand.

Apart from using geography to segment a market online, many businesses attempt to structure their Web sites in such a way that they can specifically target users from one particular business or industry or, indeed, use their own product portfolios to try and guide visitors to the area of a Web site that best fits their needs.

You will recall the L'Oreal Web site that was reviewed in chapter 3—if not, then turn back a few pages and look at the screenshot in figure 3.3, which clearly shows L'Oreal's "Customize Your Experience" title down the left-hand side of the homepage. What's really clever about this proposition is that not only has L'Oreal recognized the importance of tailoring its Web site for a range of different audiences, it's also invited participants to segment themselves by giving them a number of different perspectives from which to view content, such as consumer, scientist, journalist, student, or jobseeker.

Puma

Puma, the German-based sportswear company, is a business that uses a technique similar to L'Oreal and also has its star in the ascendancy as far as its position on the Web is concerned. When reviewing its site for brandchannel I said of Puma online (11):

The homepage of Puma.com is both pragmatically engineered and sartorially complimentary. Designed with an empathetic eye for the customer, its architecture facilitates the navigation process with ease, while the dynamic use of Flash technology brings the entire proposition to life and adds a vibrant dimension to the experience.

Puma's driven urge to blend fashion with sport scores highly at "The Mongolian Shoe BBQ," where those craving exclusivity can design their own shoes, and at "True Love Never Dies," a trendy little partnership with those connoisseurs of denim, Evisu. The sophisticated and stylish Alexander McQueen and Puma collaboration evolves the concept even further, with the establishment of the "ManCat" icon and the introduction of a tailored range of footwear that will be as much at home in the cafe as at the gym.

Puma's running, cricket, baseball, and motorsport sites may smack of bread and butter, but each has plenty to offer in the way of product information, and they all stay in tune with Puma's Web strategy. The golf site is a particularly good example of the case in point, as with its subtle animation and focus on fashion, it acts as both a snapshot of the current catalogue and a poignant little cameo of a brand that's got its act together.

Figure 4.5 is a screenshot taken of Puma's homepage in August 2006:

Figure 4.5

From the screenshot in figure 4.5, it is a relatively straightforward exercise to define Puma's segmentation strategy since the layout and departmental listings clearly guide users toward the macro-categories of either sport or fashion, before breaking themselves down into further subsets of specific brands and activities. In addition, Puma has a "language chooser" in the top right-hand corner of the page that allows visitors to the site to select any one of ten languages in which to review the content. Unfortunately, at the time of writing the depth of language-specific content wasn't quite in the same league as that of Coca-Cola, but at least the intent is most definitely there.

New Zealand

Moving on from such commercial entities as Puma and Coca-Cola, it's important to understand that the process of market segmentation is not purely the bastion of large-scale corporations. As a concept on the Web, market segmentation can be used whenever the need arises to highlight specific areas of expertise, attraction, or, indeed, advantage. With that concept in mind, let's now look at some examples of organizations that have used segmentation to very good effect on the Web. We'll start with the country-based Web site of New Zealand.

New Zealand is a land of breathtaking beauty and very stark contrasts—facets which have led to its naturally endowed landscape being featured heavily in such Hollywood movies as *The Lord of the Rings*, *King Kong*, and *The Chronicles of Narnia*.

Economically, New Zealand is a country that's keen to learn and grow and is determined not to be hindered by its somewhat remote location. To this end, the New Zealand government has set about its strategy of developing and extending the country's reach and penetration within the trade and tourism sectors, in order to gain more exposure globally and exploit its natural advantages. As part of this process, the individuals concerned have been both proactive and enthusiastic in terms of evangelizing their country through the medium of the Internet. When reviewing the New Zealand Web site in January 2006, I wrote (12):

A ninth annual Webby Award winner, the homepage of NewZealand.com is a vibrant blend of heritage and enterprise, with both tourism and trade promoted in a decisive but considerate manner. Bedecked in images of raw, natural beauty and with multi-lingual functionality, the portal is easily navigable and appealing in its simplicity. Far from being superficial, however, the real allure of the Web site lies within its sub-culture, perhaps not too dissimilar to the country it represents.

One no longer has to merely wonder what it would be like to visit such exotic and conceptually idyllic locations as New Zealand. With the advent of the Internet, marketers the world over enjoy a perfect opportunity for seducing prospective clients with an array of digital imagery and sensory indulgence that C.S. Lewis himself would have envied. NewZealand.com exploits its medium to the full, with an innovative and world-class travel planner, complemented by compre-hensive transport and accommodation guides that together make it possible to plan an entire vacation while barely moving a muscle.

The business end of the site is a more regimented affair, with a process-driven undertone that unashamedly focuses on enterprise development. The attention to detail is outstanding, however, and as tight as an All Black scrum (13); links to MarketNewZealand.com and InvestmentNewZealand.com make the transition between external sites almost seamless. Indeed, the perceived cohesion between the different organizations is so impressive that it puts many a multinational corporation to shame.

A screenshot of the *NewZealand.com* homepage taken in August 2006 is shown in figure 4.6 on the following page.

As with the Puma example, one quick look at the homepage is more than enough to decipher the segmentation strategy of *NewZealand.com*, as the eye is instantly drawn to the headlines of both "Travel to New Zealand" and "Do Business with New Zealand," around which the rest of the site content revolves. It's not just surface gloss either, as clicking on either link reveals a wonderful depth of content where each site area is inextricably linked to the country's vision and brand positioning strategy.

Perhaps the best example of this approach exists within the trade and industry areas (although the tourist end of the site is brilliantly integrated too), which link external government, industry, and enter-prise Web sites together with *New Zealand.com* so that visitors to each section can do all the research and knowledge building they need, without probably even realizing that they've left the home domain.

Figure 4.6

Manchester United

Hot on the heels of corporations and countries is an online example of a soccer team that has used the Web to good effect in order to project a segmented approach to its global audience. Manchester United is an institution in English soccer and will always be a club that's close to the hearts of the current generation—for better or for worse (as I am a Newcastle United supporter, I most definitely fall into the latter category!).

Like many soccer teams, Manchester United recognized some time ago that it's part of the entertainment business, but it became different from most of its peers when it also recognized the extent of its overseas fan-base and deliberately targeted the associated opportunities that came with that discovery.

By harnessing the power of the Web and paying particular attention to China, where Manchester United has a very large following, the club has quickly been able to develop the process of unlocking the value it has built as a result of its domestic and European success on the pitch, by capitalizing on the superstar status of several members of the team and providing its new market with a host of exclusive content. When reviewing the Manchester United site for brandchannel some time ago, I said of the club's ambitions (14):

> It's clear from this Web site that Manchester United have got their act together in every aspect of the business. In recognizing the advantages of digital branding they've transferred the team's success on the pitch toward a global audience of millions, by embracing the power of the Web.

So how does a soccer team segment its customer base? First of all, there are two main categories of individual: those who can go to the games (provided they can get their sweaty palms on a ticket) and those who can't—and because of their location, the good folks who live in China tend to be in the latter category.

While the first area of classification (people who go to the games) is easily broken down into subsets such as season ticket holders, corporate hospitality buyers, family members, and fan club members, the second category obviously needs a bit more thought—and that's where clubs such as Manchester United have been very cute in terms of leveraging the power of the World Wide Web.

For example, far from being fazed at the prospect of not being able to cater to people who couldn't attend any matches, sports teams like Manchester United have been quick to unleash the power of the Internet on anyone who may feel geographically disenfranchised and as a result have taken not just the games, but the personalities, the trivia, and, of course the merchandise to the end of the very phone lines of anyone who's willing to pay the subscription fee.

To illustrate the case in point, a screenshot of Manchester United's Chinese homepage taken in August 2006 is shown in figure 4.7 on the following page.

Figure 4.7

Even for those who don't speak Mandarin, it is still easy to see exactly what Manchester United is seeking to achieve by evangelizing such facilities as the "One United" membership scheme and the "SMS service."

Because of the World Wide Web, no one who has his heart set on identifying with the Red Devils of Manchester or indeed any other sports team with a marketing department that's remotely switched on, need ever fret again about feeling isolated or concerned about being detached from the brand he knows and loves—provided, of course, that he is willing to pay for the privilege.

Other Methods of Segmentation

Having covered most of the main types of segmentation on the Web, which by and large tend to come in the forms of geography, product, industry, or consumer group, I couldn't possibly close this chapter without taking a look at some of the other, perhaps less popular methods that are employed by organizations—and be warned, some of these are colorful!

First, let's consider luxury brands and how they go about segmenting their business on the net. A few years ago, I wrote an article for brandchannel entitled "Luxury Brands Snub the Web" (15). The article was geared toward looking at why most luxury brands refuse to sell their goods online, and in it I wrote:

> *Rolex doesn't, Clarins doesn't and even American legend Harley Davidson doesn't, but Louis Vitton, Dior, and Givenchy on the other hand do. Why do some brands go where others fear to trade and proactively sell their products in cyberspace, while others take a more intransigent stance towards the concept of E-Commerce?*
>
> *For most companies, the advent of the Internet as a global distribution channel provided an unparalleled medium by which to enhance brand awareness and improve market share. So why then are so many luxury brands refusing to ply their trade online? The answer, as usual, is as financially driven as it is historically. High-value brands have meant high-value margins for well-heeled companies who have prided themselves on exclusivity.*
>
> *So when it comes to maintaining their position of price supremacy, luxury brands all over the world have tended to treat the use of generic distribution channels with the same distaste that royalty display for the tabloid press. They prefer to imagine that by refusing to sell their wares online, they are endorsing their prime positioning within their preferred routes to market and ensuring that they can continue to control their carefully chosen distributors, who remain quite firmly stuck in the middle.*

It's now more than five years since I wrote that article, and very little has changed insofar as the number of luxury brands that still turn their noses up at the thought of trading online. Although one or two may have softened their stance a bit, the majority still tends to avoid the prospect of selling online like a trip to the dentist. Instead, they make their customers pay through the teeth by pointing them toward an array of distributors whom the brand owners believe will evangelize the positive qualities of their products and extract fair value for doing it.

To that end, it is quite common for luxury brands to segment their propositions online by introducing distribution channels as a subset of either geographical or portfolio-based scenarios, in order to encourage users to get off their backsides and trot down to a store before physically making a purchase. For the best examples, simply close your eyes and think of a brand that you know is very unlikely to trade online and then look up its Web site and *voilà*, the absence of an online store will be quickly glossed over by the introduction of some high-brow dealerships that more often than not come complete with a ZIP code finder so that you can determine your nearest outlet before actually going there in person.

If, on the other hand, you currently find closing your eyes too difficult right now, take a quick look at *TagHeur.com*, which at the time of writing provided a classic illustration of the very case in point.

Finally, and in closing this section, there is an area of the Web that regularly segments its customer base not just by product or geography or indeed by industry but more by personal taste—and that, of course, is the adults-only segment that is dominated by pornography.

In May 2006, Brandchannel's Abram Sauer wrote a profile article on Bang Bros, the hard-core Web site that, in its own words, "reached out and rocked the Internet like never before." In the article (16), Abram said that Bang Bros was "On the cutting edge of the online porn profit model," and that it had been so successful in terms of standardizing its offering across a whole host of its Web sites that it had even been able to trim back on its free content and trailers.

The point that Abram was making was that Bang Bros doesn't just own one Web site, it owns a whole series of them and the titles that it has chosen for each one directly reflect their content and, as a consequence, are set up to attract users with a particular taste or fetish.

For a full list of the Bang Bros sites and, of course, to fully appreciate the academic argument, your curiosity can be fulfilled at *BangBros.com*. For those without an Internet connection, however (and

I would advise those of a nervous disposition to look away now), some of the more self-explanatory segments include the likes of Bang Bus, Boob Squad, Big Mouthfuls, MILF Lessons, and Mr. Camel toe—to name but a few!

• • •

Key Points
The key points to remember from this chapter are as follows:

- A brand's positioning strategy should be seen as the fundamental driver of a Web site's design and content.
- Web sites should communicate a brand's vision, define its meaning, establish its parameters and relevance, and also attempt to connect with people in as many ways as possible.
- A Web site should complement the offline brand by perfectly matching its positioning in the real world. It should also enhance brand value, not erode it.
- The concept of market segmentation is every bit as viable on the Internet as it is in the real world.
- When identifying the correct method of segmentation for a Web site, consider all target markets and attempt to tailor the content accordingly.
- Where possible, attempt to strike a balance between transactional and behavioral segmentation criteria in order to appeal to the same audiences and cater to the same tastes as the offline brand.

ENDNOTES
1. www.mantrabrand.com/
2. http://brand.blogs.com/mantra/
3. http://brand.blogs.com/mantra/2004/11/brand_as_ecosys.html
4. www.lippincottmercer.com/aboutus/index.shtml
5. www.lippincottmercer.com/publications/a_hogan01.shtml#top
6. www.brandchannel.com/features_Webwatch.asp?ww_id=1
7. www.brandchannel.com/features_Webwatch.asp?ww_id=19

8. *http://travel.guardian.co.uk/article/2004/jul/22/travelnews1)*

9. Kotler, Philip. *Principles of Marketing.* Englewood Cliffs, NJ: Prentice Hall, 1997.

10. *www.brandchannel.com/features_Webwatch.asp?ww_id=13*

11. *www.brandchannel.com/features_Webwatch.asp?ww_id=274*

12. *www.brandchannel.com/features_Webwatch.asp?ww_id=260*

13. A rugby scrum is when 16 men, 8 from either side, pack down against each other with a channel between the two sets of players. The ball is then put into that channel and each set of players try to drive the opposition away from the ball. The New Zealand All Blacks (so called because they play in an all black strip) are arguably the best in the world at it.

14. *www.brandchannel.com/features_Webwatch.asp?ww_id=36*

15. *www.brandchannel.com/features_effect.asp?pf_id=33*

16. *www.brandchannel.com/features_profile.asp?pr_id=282*

5

Okay, You Built It; That Doesn't Mean They're Coming

Customers buy for their reasons, not yours.
—ORVEL RAY WILSON

IF YOU'RE ANYTHING LIKE ME, YOU WILL SHARE MY DISTASTE for telemarketers who always seem to call when you're right in the middle of tea. You will also take a real exception to being approached in the street or the airport by some credit card evangelizing youth and throw 99.9 percent of all the junk mail you receive straight in the circular file. Although I haven't yet discovered a permanent cure for avoiding the exponents of that last technique, going ex-directory and pretending to be on your mobile are very sound methods of managing the first two!

I recognize the need for certain types of direct marketing, but I fail to see why it needs to be intrusive and I generally do not like having my personal space invaded. Yes, I am becoming a grumpy old man and quite frankly who cares—because I, like most of the planet's population, prefer to be engaged on the basis of curiosity and need rather than being force-fed something that I just don't want.

Unfortunately (and this is probably a sign of impending middle age), it would seem that when it comes to appraising promotional activity that I've turned into something of a prude. Gone are the days when I was attracted to the bright flashing lights that pulled me like a tractor beam into the amusement arcades of the UK's coastal resorts. Gone also are the times that I had to walk home because I'd blown my last two-bob coin on a video game. These days, I much prefer the rifle to the machine gun, so I tend to gravitate to the more clinical campaigns rather than the "shoot 'em up" mass marketing efforts. While I may reticently agree that there is still a place for the more "in your face" promotions, I'm afraid I have little respect for them and when I am confronted by the brands they represent, I feel a great deal of empathy with a certain Naomi Klein, the author of *No Logo* (1).

Despite my avid dislike for being badgered, hectored, and, I am sure, deliberately targeted by ivory-toothed salespeople, it would appear that there are still enough supporters of this type of promotional activity to perpetuate its existence. Imagine my disgust, therefore, when the concept rapidly made the ascent into cyberspace, courtesy of the much-maligned Spam and those abominable pop-up windows. Now banner ads I can understand, but pop-up windows—I ask you, what is the point? Surely with today's standard of education, the establishment of professional marketing bodies, and, of course, the communications media that we have at our disposal, we can do a bit better than that.

My belief is that despite the many conversations that take place in the corporate halls of power, the general public is just not as dumb as many people think, and these days, most people prefer to be invited rather than "pushed," and seduced rather than "pulled." In addition, don't these so-called corporate gurus understand the impact that certain types of promotional activity can have upon a brand?

With that question in mind, this chapter will focus on the tools and techniques that organizations and businesses apply on the Web in order to improve traffic flow and get that hit counter spinning at an exponential rate. Because search engines and their associated manipulation was discussed in chapter 1, it is not my intention to cover them again here. Instead, we will look at some of the more imaginative and innovative ways in which companies attempt to attract and retain customers on the Web and, of course, the subsequent impact of such schemes on the brand.

Online Clubs and Memberships

Toward the end of the last chapter, we took a quick look at how Manchester United had introduced an online, subscription-based membership scheme in order to give its fanatical followers exclusive access to content such as player interviews, video clips, and SMS messaging. Other examples of teams that do exactly the same thing are the majority of England's premier soccer clubs, such National Football League teams as the New York Jets, and, of course, those that take part in the world of motorsport, such as Ferrari and McLaren, to name but two.

Some online clubs and membership schemes are fee-paying and others are not, but all of them share the common denominators of being purely designed to satisfy the needs of those who wish to get as close to a brand as possible while simultaneously providing the businesses concerned with valuable information about their subscribers. They are not just confined to the world of sport either, as during the past few years there appears to have been an explosion in the amount of companies who believe that by dangling a series of content-driven carrots that are clearly marked "exclusive," they will improve their level of brand loyalty by strengthening the bonds and connections that may or may not already exist within a customer's mind. In return for providing such content, of course, companies can improve their level of market intelligence by storing the details that each user supplies on submission of his profile and data mining it later, where it is invariably used in the formulation of various marketing strategies and the targeting of particular segments.

Although there can be no denying that online subscription-based clubs and memberships are a good way of ensuring those who feel that they have a certain affinity with a brand can be given the opportunity to identify more closely with it, some are obviously better than others and not all of them require a subscription. Consider Fender, for example.

Fender

As far as rock music is concerned, Fender is a classic brand with a rich and vivid heritage that's predicated on both its associations with many contemporary musicians and, of course, the quality of its guitars. Indeed, as a result of being either strummed, plucked, or even downright thrashed by such axe-wielding giants as Jimi Hendrix, Eric Clapton, Mark Knopfler, and Kurt Cobain, Fender has maintained its status as an iconic brand with almost mythical qualities for the best part of seventy years. When reviewing the Fender Web site for brandchannel some time ago (2), I said:

> *Visitors to Fender's Web proposition certainly have plenty to look at, as once through the company's global gateway there are so many options to occupy your time that your brain would be less busy bashing out a pentatonic scale.*
>
> *You can chill with the stars in the Players Club and receive a lesson from the likes of Eric Clapton or select from video clips that could have you playing in the style of Hendrix in no time.*

What's really interesting about Fender's Web proposition is that once users log onto the "Players Club" page, they get free access to exactly the same types of premium content that many businesses charge for. Although there is the option to sign up and join the club as a member in order to receive free newsletters and updates from the world of Fender guitars, visitors to the site are under no obligation to do so and instead are free to download lessons, music, and interviews with artists until their achy-breaky hearts are content.

Because Fender believes that it has a duty to both "inspire and entertain" and to evangelize "a passion for playing the guitar," it has quite obviously decided to keep the content in the Players Club free and openly available and only request contact details from those who wish to subscribe to the newsletter. Because this approach speaks volumes for a company that prides itself on a sense of free spirit and the right to musical self-expression, it drives a strong affinity with Fender's brand values and enhances the company's credibility.

Figure 5.1 is a screenshot of Fender's "Players Club" page, taken in August 2006:

Figure 5.1

Hard Rock

As we are currently in rock music mode, let's take a look at another example of an online club (fee-paying this time) that resides at *HardRock.com*—the online version of the heavily themed cafe, hotel, and casino chain. Having been a patron at many of Hard Rock's establishments throughout my traveling days, I decided quite some time ago to review the Hard Rock Web site on behalf of brandchannel (3). In doing so, I said:

Nations may well be divided by cultural differences, but one certainty remains in that no matter where you are, you can usually find a Hard Rock café or at least a pirated T-shirt bearing the ubiquitous logo.

The Hard Rock brand has grown over the years to include much more than just the cafés and its intent to promote a cause-related cocktail of commercialism and style has helped transform the business into something of a supergroup.

By implementing a somewhat more mercantile approach than those laid-back people at Fender, Hard Rock uses its online club to promote a range of benefits associated with its cafes and to try and keep users loyal:

Figure 5.2 is screenshot of Hard Rock's "All-Access Membership" page, taken in August 2006:

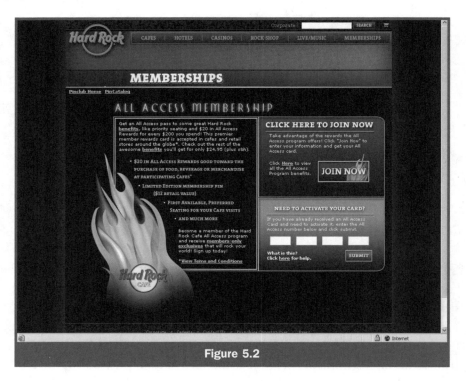

Figure 5.2

From the screenshot in figure 5.2, it is possible to identify the promotional techniques employed by Hard Rock in all of their online glory, as visitors are enticed to join its "All-Access Membership" scheme with a smorgasbord of benefits that include priority seating, an introductory discount toward the purchase of food and beverages, and of course, "A limited edition membership pin," which I'm sure has got the train spotters among you just "shivering with antici . . . pation"—if I may quote the great Tim Curry!

Galvanized by the company's mercantile nature and enthused by the medium of the Internet, the team at Hard Rock have quite clearly put their house in order in terms of seeking to generate more business by using the organization's Web site to promote its cafes. To that end, and in turn for a fee-paying subscription, Hard Rock customers can look forward to getting closer to the brand and making good use of several exclusive benefits that should see them treated as a priority during future visits to the company's eateries.

Perhaps what is somewhat strange about this approach, however, is that historically Hard Rock has been a business that has predicated itself on philanthropy and has always gone to market with a cause-related edge. Who could forget, for instance, the role that its New York restaurant played in the aftermath of 9/11 when it fed streams of workers who were toiling around the clock and the subsequent benefit gigs that have been held at several Hard Rock premises? Would it not have been better therefore to reward loyal visitors to its restaurants with free membership to its scheme and to publicize that on its Web site rather than to simply charge a fee for all?

Adidas

By way of variation, not all businesses class their membership schemes and the subsequent provision of preferred content to people who subscribe as actually carrying the status of a club. Adidas, for example, simply asks users to provide their contact details and complete a personal profile in return for receiving information regarding the release of new products, the latest events, and special promotional information.

When reviewing the Adidas Web site some time ago for brand-channel (4), I had this to say about the sports market in general—and in my view it still sums up Adidas's approach:

These days, there can be few international business arenas that attract the same amount of publicity as the ruthless world of professional sport. And while the real contest has historically been between athletes, it's now been transferred to the big label brands, who are all too aware that when it comes to enhancing the value of their sporting apparel, it's the win and not the way you play that matters.

A screenshot of the benefits that subscribers to *Adidas.com* can expect to receive is shown in figure 5.3 and is accurate as of August 2006:

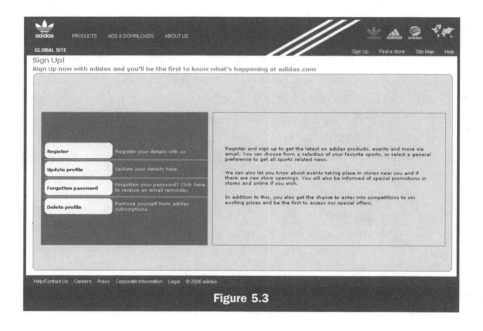

Figure 5.3

On the surface of it, this may look like a very good deal given that there is no cash to part with and that the title of the scheme, "Adidas Subscriptions" tends to come across as a lot less formal than a membership program or an online club—so have I been a bit too harsh in terms of my summation of the Adidas brand culture?

Not in my opinion, because in the world of professional sport no one can expect to receive anything for nothing, and if you take a good look at Adidas's online subscription form, illustrated in figure 5.4, you can evaluate the content yourself before making up your mind as to the extent of the company's data-mining activities:

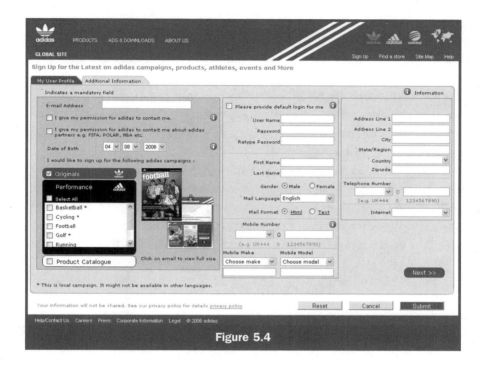

Figure 5.4

As one can see from the screenshot in figure 5.4, Adidas is looking for some rather chunky detail from its subscribers in return for providing them with a perceived range of benefits. Indeed, not simply content with soliciting the usual criteria of name, address, ZIP code and e-mail, Adidas is also looking for your date of birth, your mobile number, and the make and model of the phone it relates to.

So how does all of this unashamed gathering of research material affect the Adidas brand? Well, as I mentioned in my brandchannel review of the Web site, the world of sports apparel is an intensely competitive market these days and companies are now virtually tripping over each other (as well as tripping each other up) to try and gain an edge. Given that Adidas is one of the biggest kids in the playground, it's right up there with the very best of them and so it's very little wonder that it is actively looking to maximize its potential for market penetration by enhancing the functionality of its Web site.

Of course, there are many other examples of online clubs and sub-scription-based schemes on the Internet these days and it would be impossible to list them all here, so in discussing the examples of Adidas, Hard Rock, and Fender, I hope that you now have a feel for both what they are about and what they are used for. In underpinning that point, it is important to understand that from a digital branding perspective, both the context and the content of the online club or scheme in question must fit within the overall parameters of the brand that it represents and not simply look as though it is a cheap shot at gaining more revenue or an unnecessary extension of the brand's range and scope.

It is also important to bear in mind that whatever data is sub-mitted to an online club or membership scheme will subsequently be used by the business in relation to its future marketing strategies and as such, visitors to a site should only impart as much information about themselves as they naturally feel comfortable with.

The Online Community

Many online communities have evolved from companies' mailing lists and subscription-based clubs, although they differ because they are often used to create an environment where like-minded souls can meet and exchange information as a result of their mutual interests instead of simply acting as a conduit to facilitate the flow of information between a host company and a user. In other words, the communica-tion process is very much a two-way street and everyone is empow-ered to make an equal contribution. In many instances, the exchange of information is engineered by chat rooms, forums, bulletin boards, and blogs, all of which provide a capable platform for those who feel they have something to say and are only too keen to share it with anyone willing to read it.

The power of online communities and the ways in which they can identify with brands and subsequently impact their value was high-lighted by a Nielsen study (5), the results of which disclosed that somewhere in the region of 1.8 billion Web pages are viewed each month by members of an Internet group. So with this sort of volume, we probably shouldn't be surprised at the breathtaking speed at which such illicit subject matter as Pamela Anderson's sexual olympics,

Britney Spears' drunken misdemeanours, and George Bush's gaffes and bloopers are catapulted into our homes courtesy of sites such as *YouTube.com*.

As with any sort of community, the online versions don't take long before establishing their own culture and generating their own set of rules along with a subliminal pecking order—indicative in many ways (as any academic will tell you) of the good old Hawthorne Experiments that were inflicted on the workers of the Western Electric Co. in Cicero, Illinois, back in 1924 (6). Because of this, most organizations that host online communities like to control the types of content and feedback that is discussed within their environment and, as a result, ensure that their forums, chat rooms, blogs, and bulletin boards are all appropriately moderated for fear of some disenfranchised malcontent either terrorizing the conforming members or partaking of the odd piece of rabble-rousing.

There are many examples of indigenously hosted online communities on the Web, and one never seems to have to look very far to find them. Organizations at the forefront of the concept would probably include eBay, Google, Yahoo, Friends Reunited, and of course, Microsoft. In addition, financial services groups, such as the UK's Hemmington Scott, have for years provided their members with a free information exchange, where users can openly discuss the relative success and failure of UK stocks and equities, and also what to buy and sell.

In addition to the indigenously hosted communities, some purport to being either completely independent or detached from the influence of the corporate world. As such, they quite often carry a significant weight of opinion within certain industry sectors and as a consequence, have been targeted by many multinationals for the processes of manipulation and advertising. A very good example of this type of scenario is the community-based travel site, *IgoUgo.com*—a winner of several Internet awards and the owner of a membership base that numbers around 350,000.

Figure 5.5 on the following page is a screenshot of the IgoUgo. homepage as of August 2006.

Although there is no doubting the sincerity of the contributors to Web sites such as *IgoUgo.com* and, of course, the quality of their feedback and advice, it is still interesting to note the types of brands that

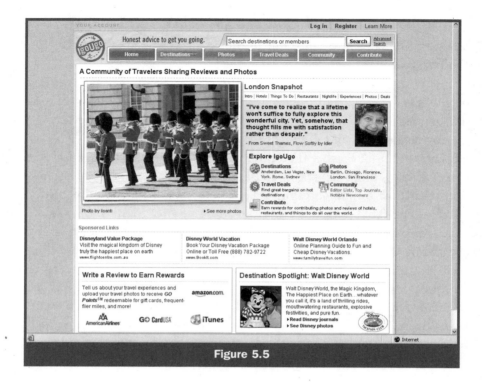

Figure 5.5

get to feature as "Sponsors." Take a look, for instance, at IgoUgo's "Destination Spotlight" section and the participants of the "Go Points" scheme.

Clearly, the mutual benefits associated with building and sustaining an online community and then encouraging the right type of sponsorship can pay dividends for all concerned. For instance, if you were at the helm of a sharp-minded business and suddenly became aware of a large and viable demographic that could be targeted directly over the Internet, wouldn't you be interested? Likewise, if you just happened to be the philanthropic soul who set the community up in the first place, wouldn't you be swayed by a large corporate carrot?

Perhaps not surprisingly, the growth in popularity of online communities has not gone without notice to a number of businesses that possess an eye for the entrepreneurial, and just as Verisign created a niche for itself within the digital brand management market, organizations such as Communispace have developed propositions by which to facilitate the growth of what they describe as the concept of "Customer Engagement" (7).

What companies such as Communispace do is actively develop and promote an online community in order to focus on a particular market or industry sector before subsequently collating the resulting data, courtesy of a software program that's built into the Web. Clients are then given access to the data either openly or anonymously, depending upon their relationship with the host organization, before using it to define their marketing strategies.

A large part of the attraction of dealing with companies such as Communispace is that because clients know that they are dealing with "real" people who share an active interest in the markets in which they operate, they should be guaranteed a number of benefits. These could include objective feedback should they wish to use the community to test-market new products, a willingness from members to participate in additional research, or indeed an informed opinion on the credibility of the competition. The fact that research is facilitated on the Internet should also mean that companies get to receive their feedback in a fraction of the time that it would normally take through traditional research methods and I would imagine, at a significantly lower cost.

Given the surge in popularity of online communities and the associated appearances of businesses such as Communispace, it should be safe to assume that the concept will be around for some time—particularly if the rapid success enjoyed by "Second Life" (8) is anything to go by.

For those who haven't come across the Second Life phenomenon yet, the concept revolves around people in the real world developing a "second life" within a virtual world that only exists in cyberspace. Once registered, residents of the Second Life community can choose how they appear to other residents in the form of characters called Avatars, before starting their own businesses, buying real estate, and enjoying many different types of activities that just aren't possible during their normal lives on Earth. They can also make money by withdrawing and converting their Second Life currency (linden dollars) into U.S. dollars whenever they wish to do so.

Now before your eyes start glazing over and you start muttering under your breath that people should get out more or take up a healthy pursuit, just consider for a moment that as of August 2006, the Second

Life community had almost a million residents and was grossing more than $300,000 within each twenty-four hour period. In addition to and at the same time as I researched these figures, I came across an announcement on the BBC (9) that British Pop supergroup Duran Duran was planning to build a virtual island within Second Life and use it to play live concerts—obviously the band's ambitions have outgrown "Planet Earth."

Like everything else, it will be interesting to see what the next stage of evolution brings in terms of online communities as more and more of the bigger names and brands cotton to the power and influence that such brotherhoods can bring—but I would certainly think that we haven't seen the last of initiatives such as Second Life.

Playing Games

Another way of attracting increased traffic to a Web site is by ramping up the entertainment on offer by loading it with flash-enhanced or java-based games—Nabisco being an extremely prominent example of the current case in point.

From a branding perspective, games can be designed in a number of ways, the execution of which is usually dependent upon the host company's marketing strategy. Some games ensure that they feature the brand directly in order to gain maximum exposure, while others allude to the brand through the use of associated characters or contain references to the brand through either highly visible or discreet forms of advertising. Although there are obviously many games available on the Internet, we will simply attempt to focus on the major types of scenarios that drive the digital branding concept.

AdverGaming

This relatively new term is used to describe the blatant use of branding that a Web site's host has incorporated into either its online game or games portfolio. Although AdverGaming is most prevalently directed at children, it is quite common throughout the Web and can often turn up when you least expect it—Wikipedia highlighting two wonderful examples from Dyson and Nurofen (10).

Critics of AdverGaming believe that it is a cynical attempt by businesses and corporations to entice young or impressionable individuals to a Web site before continuously exposing them to a brand, in the hope that they will visit the site more frequently and, in addition, tell their friends about it so that they can get involved too.

This process has become known as "Viral Marketing," as its success is based on the circulation of content through word of mouth, e-mail, blogs, or any other type of communications channel that exists within a social network. To perpetuate the "Viral" effect, the majority of Web sites that use AdverGames tend to carry a link titled "send your score to a friend," or something very similar, so that on every occasion a game is played, its prospects of improving traffic flow increase.

Because AdverGaming appeals to an individual's basic desire to improve his high score and be competitive within his peer group, it can often be quite addictive and as such it has proven to be a very successful way of increasing Web traffic and building brand awareness at the same time.

By way of an example, figure 5.6 is a screenshot of an AdverGame from *Pepsi.com*, taken in August 2006.

Figure 5.6

To take part in the game in figure 5.6, users play the central character of the "Pepsi Man" (although they can choose other characters) who is frantically challenged to complete an ever increasing cycle of orders to earn tips. At the end of the game, the amount of tips earned are totaled and ranked in a series of leagues so that users can determine how successful they've been. Pepsi then publishes a list of the highest scorers so that they can gain some recognition for their erstwhile endeavors.

Needless to say, as the AdverGame concept has developed and grown on the Internet, so have the associated content providers, and, should you ever be interested in developing a game for a Web site, there are a number of businesses that will gladly accommodate you. Perhaps the most obvious provider (as it is the holder of the *AdverGame.com* (11) domain) is Skyworks Technologies, which has a ready-built library of more than 100 games to choose from. Other providers of unashamed viral-based interplay include Arkadium (12), Blockdot (13), and the appropriately named Skive Creative (14).

Character-Based Association

Not all businesses use such a barefaced method of promoting their brands when designing their games for the Internet, and some prefer to use their associated characters to play the lead roles, rather than the brands themselves. This technique tends to play more on the subliminal connections that a brand already has with an individual without being quite so blatant. Although character association is usually not as transparent an advertising method as directly driving the brand itself, it's still an extremely powerful tool and can have exactly the same consequences in terms of its "viral" spread.

The most obvious exponent of character-based association in the development of Web-based games is more than likely Disney, which for years has built its online entertainment package around such iconic personalities as Winnie the Pooh, Goofy, and, of course, Mickey Mouse. As its Web proposition has developed, however, so has its online games portfolio and Disney now has an extensive range of character-based games in its portfolio, some of which are illustrated in figure 5.7 on the next page:

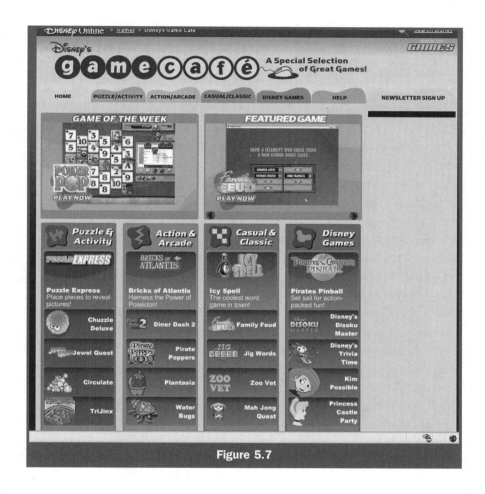

Figure 5.7

Although Disney is probably at the forefront of character-associated game play, it's certainly not alone as a visit to Web sites like Kellogg's (15) and M&M's (16) will regularly reveal characters such as Snap, Crackle, and Pop, and those diminutive but colorful spokescandies habitually put through their paces in both a bid to entertain and, of course, to retain some affinity with the brands they represent.

Brand-Sponsored Games

Because the Internet can be used to connect people, it's frequently used to host multiplayer games that either have their software installed on a PC or, instead, are linked via one of the mainstream consoles such as Sony's PlayStation, Nintendo's Gamecube, or Microsoft's X-Box. As a result of the surge in popularity of online game play, many of the games now played on the Web also attract a significant amount of interest from many multinationals who see the games market as a prime point of promotion.

If you think that the placement of brands in mass-produced games for the console market is a relatively new concept, its time to think again, as in 2005 around $80 million was spent by advertisers on both "in-game" branding and the sponsoring of popular gaming events (17). The technology that facilitates the placement of a brand inside the video game is also becoming increasingly sophisticated too, as a visit to the Web site of Massive Incorporated (18) will prove to the extent that it just might blow your mind.

Billing itself as an "audience aggregator," Massive Incorporated's gaming network brings together millions of users from around the world who share a passion for gaming. The company's sophisticated technology lets users play each other via the Web across a range of best-selling games with titles such as "Splinter Cell" and "SWAT" while simultaneously loading the game with advertising. Because Massive's software is "dynamic" and runs by downloading material from a centrally held Web server on a real-time basis, it can also dictate the specific period of time that an advert is seen before switching it for another as well as the places in which it appears. The shape and form of the advertising can be anything from the livery on a vehicle, a backdrop on a billboard, the side of a soda can, the top of a pizza box, or the image on a TV screen.

In Massive's words: "The player always sees the latest ad campaigns in the context of the game environment and in this way, games are transformed from static, permanent billboards for only a handful of advertisers into a dynamic, evolving advertising channel."

Given that Massive has hosted in excess of 35 million game sessions since its inception and that (according to Nielsen Research figures that it proudly displays on its Web site) the average young male spends up to 25 percent more time gaming than he does watching TV, you don't have to be a rocket scientist to see the attraction of advertising with the company.

That's not all, either; far from resting on their laurels, the team at Massive Incorporated have pushed the envelope even further and in

July 2006 launched additional functionality that makes advertisements "interactive" and actually encourages gamers to engage with them. The first company to use the software was Toyota.

By way of illustrating just how far the level of capability attached to the console market can go on the Web, I couldn't possibly close this section without mentioning the Nintendo Wii and the Sony PlayStation 3, or PS3 for short.

Sony's new machine is so sophisticated, for example, that whenever one of them goes online it will automatically link to every other PS3 that is currently attached to the Internet and then surrender any spare processing capacity it has to a team of American scientists for the purposes of research. The scientists (attached to the distributed computing project called "folding at home" or FAH) will then run a series of calculations on the PS3 network in order to examine such things as how the shape of proteins, critical to most biological functions, affect diseases such as Alzheimer's. Now if all that isn't sexy enough, here's the real stinger—the scientists at FAH believe that if they can get a crack at a network consisting of 10,000 PS3s or greater, they will have a processing power at their disposal that's almost four times as fast as the world's most powerful supercomputer, IBM's BlueGene/L, and be able to perform up to one thousand trillion calculations per second (19).

While your still digesting that thought, let's consider how Nintendo has revolutionized the console sector by releasing its new machine, Wii: Equipped with new motion-sensitive controllers, Wii brings a level of reality to the gaming sector that's never been seen before, by allowing players to swing a virtual golf club, tennis racquet, baseball bat, or even a pair of boxing gloves and become physically immersed in game-play.

No doubt by the time you are reading this book things will have moved on even more and the next time you encounter a gaming experience you will probably be confronted by the ability to order a pizza that is subsequently delivered by a look-alike of Scarlet Johansson or Jessica Alba—or is that just wishful thinking on my part?

Offline/Online Vouchers

Having more than likely terrified the life out of some readers with that brief insight into the speed and depth of brand development, and

exposure in the online gaming sector, I'd like to offer the possibly com-
forting news that there is still a place on the Web for the more traditional promotional approaches—and they don't come much more
traditional than the humble coupon or voucher.

Although there are many different ways in which businesses and
organizations use coupons, vouchers, or promotional "codes" on the
Internet, their intention is always the same—to increase sales or traffic
flow by attracting more visitors to their Web site.

One particular exponent of the offline/online approach is that
employed by the Canadian confectionery distributor Ferrero, which for
a number of years has included a "magic code" inside its Kinder
Surprise chocolate eggs. The people who buy the eggs (invariably kids,
of course) are then encouraged to visit the Web site of *Magic-Kinder.com*
(20), where they input the code as requested and in return, are
granted access to a game or character-based scenario that can either
be downloaded or played online. Naturally, Ferrero is not alone in
employing this type of promotional technique, and if you keep your
eyes open, you can find similar types of codes on the packaging of
breakfast cereals, soft drinks, and other types of confectionery.

Moving up the price points to larger ticket items, promotional
codes and vouchers can also be used by e-tailers (supermarkets, hotel
groups, etc.) to apply a discount to certain purchases, while other
organizations actively seek to attract a certain demographic by piggy-
backing on other companies' loyalty programs. The rental car company
Hertz, for example, has a considerable discount scheme and often
seeks to evangelize it by offering members of certain professional
bodies and loyalty programs a reduced rate when booking online.

By way of role reversal, many businesses also allow visitors to their
Web sites to print a coupon or voucher that can then be used in their
outlets in exchange for a discount or additional products or services. I
have to admit, for instance, to being no stranger to Pizza Hut's
Australian site, which allows all of its registered users to view and print
the active discount coupons that relate to their local restaurants before
exchanging them for discounted pizza!

Competitions

As with coupons and vouchers, there is seemingly no end to the
opportunities that exist to improve a Web site's traffic flow by giving

something away for nothing—as long as users are prepared to put in the hard yards, of course. Indeed, whether it's solving puzzles, entering draws, playing games, or answering quizzes, the Web has a home for all of them and gone are the days when it was only possible to enter by putting your answers on the back of a post card or enclosing a self-addressed envelope.

Although there is always plenty of availability in terms of competitions online, the quality and content can vary greatly depending upon such things as the commitment of the sponsor and its anticipated level of return. As a result, many online offerings can be perceived as dull and the majority of them will achieve very little. Now and again, however, it is possible to come across a particular technique that stands head and shoulders above everything else, which was absolutely the case when Google teamed up with Sony Pictures to produce the Da Vinci Code Quest in the second quarter of 2006.

Unashamedly viral and mutually designed to give both Google and Sony Pictures maximum exposure, the quest involved users being asked to solve a series of Da Vinci-themed brainteasers within a timeline that coincided with the release date of the film. In total, the Da Vinci Code Quest ran for twenty-four days and could only be completed by people who both registered with Google first and, of course, showed the necessary mental resolve to complete all of the puzzles. As a direct consequence, and because the majority of the conundrums were set around Google's search facilities, the users who demonstrated the necessary staying power and subsequently completed the quest either became well versed in Google's technological attributes (which was obviously the intention) or no strangers to blogging sites such as Mike Salisbury's (21), which brazenly posted the solutions each day. Ahh, the power of the Internet—where there's a will, there's most definitely a way!

Other Stuff

As I've said many times within this book so far, one of the great things about the Internet is its fluidity as an interactive medium. Because of this and, of course, the speed of its development, there has been seemingly no end to the new and innovative gizmos, gadgets, and associated paraphernalia that can get you online—anytime, anyplace, or anywhere. Indeed, the days when visitors to the Web were confined to a 14K modem and telephone socket are now nothing but a distant memory to some of us, having been long since replaced by a generation of 3G-brandishing teenagers whose thumbs can key-text messages faster than most of us can type.

For organizations that have adopted a bleeding-edge approach to the technological revolution that has invaded our homes and lifestyles faster than anyone could have predicted, the challenges have come thick and fast—and so have the opportunities.

In the early days of the Internet, visitors to a corporate Web site (if you were lucky enough to find one) were deemed privileged if they so much as got a breakdown of the company's core activities, let alone were captivated by the offered content. These days, however, it's a much different story and whereas it might once have been innovative to allow selected users to download the odd bit of corporate wallpaper, such an approach today would be seen by some as archaic.

Take Budweiser, for example. This globally recognized brand has always been seen as adventurous when it comes to developing its ad campaigns and certainly not shy in splashing the cash when it comes to securing a prime-time viewing spot.

When I reviewed the Budweiser Web site for brandchannel a few years ago (22), the company had recently started its "Whassup" campaign and I remember being impressed by its attempts at innovation on the Web. At the time, I wrote:

> *Fans of the whassup adverts will not be disappointed, as the site contains a catalogue of downloadable goodies that are sure to turn your desktop into a hive of interaction. Files on offer include Frank and Louie screensavers, movies, audio clips, electronic postcards and a free "deskplayer" from which you can whassup your friends.*

Even back in 2001, Budweiser had its act together in terms of producing engaging types of content and now more than five years on, the company has done it again with a whole new twist on the e-card scenario, a screenshot of which is shown in figure 5.8.

At the time of writing, Bud's e-card campaign is titled "Giving Lip" and gives users the opportunity to create their own talking e-card by either selecting an image from the library or uploading one of their own. The really fun part, however, comes when the user is asked to type a message to a recipient which is then decoded and played back in a choice of different accents, thereby converting the user's text into a full-fledged audiostream, as the image simultaneously lip syncs—clever or what?

A screenshot of Budweiser's "Giving Lip" homepage is shown in figure 5.8:

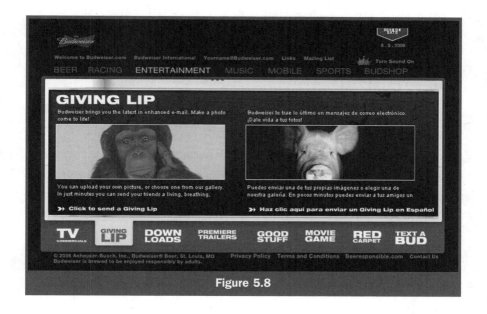

Figure 5.8

Innovative augmentations such as "Giving Lip" have helped to firmly establish Budweiser as something of a pioneer as far as Internet-based promotions are concerned. As a result, the company has continued to see visitors to its Web site flowing like Guinness at an Irish wake.

Granted, not everyone can be as adventurous as Budweiser because not everyone has the same marketing budget or, indeed, the investment in Internet technology. With that in mind, let's now have a look at some of the more common and lower cost gimmicks that businesses load their Web sites with in order to try and drive up traffic flow and make their propositions more palatable.

Wallpaper

This stuff never fails to appear and can contain anything from the typical high-resolution brand marks and logos to images that depict the modeling of product material by celebrities. Once the sole domain of the humble desktop PC, the inception of 3G mobile has made the use of wallpaper even more ubiquitous and it's now possible to personalize almost every Net-ready device that you would want to get your hands on with a variety of images and themes. Indeed, as far as wallpaper is concerned it seems that there is quite literally no end to the variety of stuff available that can be downloaded from the Web, with almost everything getting an airing—from the official badges and crests of sports teams to the latest bikini-clad babes on the beach, courtesy of publications like *Sports Illustrated* and of course, the global "lads mag" FHM.

Screensavers

Only one step ahead of wallpaper in terms of their technology, screensavers usually consist of a montage of images and audio files, animated or still-framed, that seek to occupy screen-space just prior to a device entering "low-power" mode. Just like with wallpaper, it is possible to download almost every conceivable type of content directly from the Internet for use on a device, although many organizations now fit their own versions (along with the prerequisite wallpaper) to employees' machines in order to discourage them from picking up undesirable material from the Web. Most corporately branded Web sites offer downloadable screensavers of one description or another, with perhaps the most visible and entertaining residing in the beverage and entertainment sectors.

Downloadable Audio Files

Although not as prevalent as they once were due mainly to the improvements in bandwidth and the "real-time" availability of sound-related content, some branded audio files can still be found on the Net if you look hard enough; however, their context can range from the sublime to the ridiculous. Indeed, sometimes one can be forgiven for wondering just who was smoking what when a decision was made to stick a sound on a Web site on the pretense that it would either engage potential users or add value to a brand. Downloadable files can also vary in length, and while some last just a split second, others can go on for several minutes, depending on what purpose they have been designed to serve. Just a couple of examples of downloadable audio files (and make up your own mind about their quality and what they actually bring to the party) are the DB9 engine sound at *Aston Martin.com* (23) and the sound of a beer being poured at *Grolsch.com* (24).

Should you decide to save either of these sound files to your PC's hard drive, I am sure that you will have hours of fun and entertainment swapping your system's default sound files for those which you have just downloaded—alternatively, you could get out more often.

Podcasts

As downloadable audio files move slowly toward obsolescence due to the ever increasing improvements in technology, so the next generation of audio content relentlessly picks up pace. By and large these days, most of the audio content you will come across on the Web is either embedded into a site in order to augment the visual content and enrich your Web experience (at least that's what it's supposed to do) or it is streamed onto the Web site via another source—that is, live radio.

In 2003, the introduction of Podcasts provided yet another angle to this concept, as it opened up the Web to millions of wannabe broadcasters who were desperate to make themselves heard (difficult to believe on the Internet I know, but it was only a matter of time!).

The word *Podcast* is a hybrid of *I-Pod* and *broadcast*, and it involves the posting of audio content on a Web site, which can then be downloaded by a user before being either replayed on a PC or uploaded to a mobile MP3 player or other like-minded device. In the early days of Podcasting, the majority of content was dominated by music but now it is possible to listen to radio shows, watch videos, and generally do anything that the technology permits. Most corporate entities use Podcasts to add value to their Web propositions by filling them with content that is designed to have a positive impact on the brand or brands in question, while others pay for advertising space in existing Podcasts in much the same way that they would for airtime on a radio show.

Examples of some major brands that have already identified Podcasts as a viable way to increase visibility are American Express with its Travelcast initiative (25) and BMW with its audiobooks (26).

Videos

For many Web sites, the next logical step from audio has always been video, and its evolution has developed in much the same way that John Logie Baird, the inventor of television, followed Guglielmo Marconi, the inventor of radio. As technology has progressed, what started with the occasional download that could only be viewed in the time it took for your latte to go cold has since developed into highly impressive embedded screens that nonchalantly play their content as if it's the most natural thing in the world.

Because the use of video on the Internet has grown significantly during the last few years, the medium now has many of the traditional qualities associated with advertising at the movies and on TV. As such, the influence of video-related material within a heavily branded Web site can be seen as substantial, which is why the concept will be discussed in more detail in the next chapter—so for now we will just take an overview.

One of the real advantages of using video on the Web is that it broadens the opportunities for people to connect with a brand by instantly appealing to their senses of sight and sound. As a result, it can be used to drive a number of both preconceived and desired brand associations by seeking to evoke a series of predetermined emotions. Companies often look to achieve this by displaying sequences of videos that are shot within the context of the brand in question or by linking the Web-based audio and visual content with that which people would normally see on TV. To that end, many corporate Web sites now allow copies of their current TV campaigns to be viewed from the Web—and let's face it, who hasn't read an e-mail carrying an attachment of a particularly funny advertisement that's been aired on TV in a country that's different from one's own?

Mastercard is a good example of a brand that has really grasped the nettle as far as posting its TV content on the Web is concerned. It now has its current library of ads residing at the domain name of *priceless.com* (27). Likewise, other large multinationals such as

Budweiser and Coke have also had many dalliances with transferring their TV ads to cyberspace.

Despite the presence of such large corporations on the Net, however, and the undoubted quality of their ads, my personal favorite has to be the video for the Australian company Inghams and its chicken Kievs (28). If you are interested in seeing it, there are links at the end of this chapter that contain two versions of the video—one that appears on TV and one that definitely doesn't.

Software Downloads

Another method of promoting a brand on the Internet and ensuring that users retain their sense of association with it is to encourage them to fill up their hard drives and portable electronic devices with as much corporate content as possible. More often than not, Web sites achieve this by heavily promoting the availability of free downloadable content by making it as engaging and entertaining as possible (i.e., Budweiser). While some of the more mundane items such as screensavers do fall into this category, I am principally talking about stuff that's more imaginative—like the buddy icons at Warner Brothers (29), the clock at Veuve Cliquot (30), and the vast selection of ringtones and other associated material that's far too vast to reference. As there is absolutely no shortage of this type of downloadable content on the Web, I am sure you have already had several experiences with it and perhaps even spent many a frustrating hour or two trying to remove the stuff that your kids have so generously and lovingly installed on your machine.

Section Summary

Finally, in closing this discussion on the types of promotional content that many corporate brands employ to increase traffic flow, I hope I have given at least some indication of the sheer size and scope of the opportunities that exist and underlined once more the power of the Web as a communications medium. For those who are willing and are happy to put in the effort, there is absolutely no shortage of tools and techniques that can help attract more users to a site—and there is really little excuse when many of the more recognized brands fail to measure up to the expectations they have built within the minds of their consumers. With that in mind, perhaps the next time you log onto a Web site you will have a look at the types of promotional material and the associated techniques that an organization has employed in order to ensure your return—or not, as the case may be.

• • •

Key Points
The key points to remember from this chapter are as follows:

- Promotional techniques should fit within the context of the brand and not be seen as an attempt to climb aboard the latest theoretical bandwagon.
- Online communities are a growing concept and are capable of providing businesses with a lot of valuable feedback with regard to how a brand is perceived.
- Beware of AdverGames, as they are now being heavily criticized for the viral nature of their spread.
- There is still plenty of mileage in the more traditional methods of promotion, such as codes and vouchers, provided they are used appropriately.
- Where possible, stay innovative and keep the content fresh—the Internet community is attracted to creative and imaginative material that has a clear point of differentiation.

ENDNOTES

1. Klein, Naomi. *No Logo*. New York: Picador, 2000.
2. *www.brandchannel.com/features_Webwatch.asp?ww_id=77*
3. *www.brandchannel.com/features_Webwatch.asp?ww_id=57*
4. *www.brandchannel.com/features_Webwatch.asp?ww_id=6*
5. *http://communities-dominate.blogs.com/brands/2006/02/ nielsen_study_h.html*
6. *www.referenceforbusiness.com/encyclopedia/Oli-Per/Organizational-Behavior.html#THE_HAWTHORNE_EXPERIMENTS*
7. *www.communispace.com/*

8. *http://secondlife.com/*
9. *http://news.bbc.co.uk/1/hi/technology/5253782.stm*
10. *http://en.wikipedia.org/wiki/Advergaming*
11. *www.advergame.com/*
12. *www.arkadium.com/advergames.html*
13. *www.blockdot.com/*
14. *www.skivecreative.com/*
15. *www.kelloggs.com*
16. *www.mms.com/*
17. *www.usatoday.com/tech/gaming/2006-07-10-ad-games_x.htm? POE=TECISVA*
18. *www.massiveincorporated.com/*
19. *http://news.bbc.co.uk/2/hi/technology/5287254.stm*
20. *www.magic-kinder.com*
21. *http://mikesalsbury.com/mambo/content/view/447*
22. *www.brandchannel.com/features_Webwatch.asp?ww_id=9*
23. *www.astonmartin.com/eng/thegallery/soundgallery*
24. *www.grolsch.com/defaultcom.htm*
25. *http://home3.americanexpress.com/corp/uk/2006/travelcast.asp*
26. *http://podcast.bmw.com/en*
27. *www.priceless.com/film/film.html*
28. *www.inghams.com.au/consumer/media/media_release/ Kiev_Swearing_Wanker.wmv www.inghams.com.au/consumer/media/ media_release/Kiev_Swearing_%20Bloody_Idiot.wmv*
29. *http://looneytunes.warnerbros.com/Web/loot/loot.jsp*
30. *www.veuve-clicquot.com/en/the_clicquot_touch/lighten_up/ index.asp?page=lighten_up*

6

Functionality Now and for the Future

The best thing about the future is that it only comes one day at a time.
—ABRAHAM LINCOLN

WHEN I FIRST STARTED SURFING THE WEB BACK IN 1995, all I had to play with was an old PC that had a hard drive no bigger than a memory stick, a 14K modem that took an eternity to connect and a "Mosaic" browser—which, believe it or not, was considered an absolute revelation at the time, as it was the first commercial "Net-ready" browser that was capable of running on Windows and not Unix.

In those early days, the content on the Web was about as enriching an experience as a long-haul flight in economy class, and the process of surfing from home was every bit as bumpy, too. Indeed, what with the tenuous nature of dial-up connections, the slow speed of data exchange, and the associated landline costs, the concept of the Internet was difficult to justify to a loved one who would much rather watch the latest installment of *Coronation Street* with you. As if that were not enough, any attempts to placate said spouse would invariably be met with a suspicious scowl, as the precise moment she decided to hover over your shoulder to see what the Web was all about always seemed to coincide with an inadvertent stumbling across some of the more unsavory and un-policed material that pervaded the Net at the time. Despite those early drawbacks, however, I, and many like me, had become hooked by the Internet's potential and, collectively, we marveled at the speed of technological progress as adoption rates grew and one corporate entity after another slowly got online.

Today, of course, it's a completely different World Wide Web. Within just a decade, bandwidths, memory size, processing rates, and hard drive capacities have multiplied exponentially and galvanized a living, breathing, interactive medium, the likes of which we've never seen before. Content and material have also become completely dynamic and now appeal to the senses in an increasingly absorbing way, thereby stimulating the brain cells and providing a much more rewarding and engaging experience than anyone could have envisaged in the past.

By way of illustrating just how much technology has moved forward, the BBC recently ran an article on its Web site entitled "Happy Birthday—How the PC has changed" (1) and used it to depict the twenty-fifth anniversary of IBM's first home PC.

Launched in 1981, the cheapest IBM model would have set you back around $1,600 and for that, all you got was the PC and the keyboard—there was no monitor, and disk drives were an optional extra. In terms of technology, it came fully equipped with a state-of-the-art 4.7Mhz processor, a whopping 16K of memory, and was capable of displaying up to four different colors for graphics and twenty-four different colors of text.

For about the same price today, anyone willing to part with his cash should be able to pick up a computer with a processor that's 750 times more powerful, memory that's 65,000 times bigger, and a hard drive with the equivalent storage space of more than 1 million of those good old floppy disks—now that should create some space at the bottom of the wardrobe!

By way of showing some appreciation for the progress that's been achieved, and to try and get some sort of fix on what may lie ahead, we are going to spend this chapter looking at some of the technology that has been instrumental in the Web's evolution and how it has contributed to the digital branding concept by enriching functionality. We will also attempt to identify just what is meant by the term *dynamic Web experience*, evaluate its impact on brands on the Net, and consider the types of functionality that many organizations use to drive up brand value.

Java, Flash, and Techie Stuff

Before we dive headlong into the field of functionality and start "ooo-ing" and "ahh-ing" at some of the things that organizations now do on the World Wide Web, let's take some time to appraise the process behind the improvements in Internet-related software and gain some appreciation of the events that have helped shape today's experiences in cyberspace. Although some of the content is of a technical nature, try and stick with it as it's important to understand just how far the Web has come in such a short space of time and, of course, the subsequent impact that new technology can have on digital branding.

Java

Many businesses claim to have invented the "first big thing" on the Internet or to have produced content that's both groundbreaking and innovative. In spite of the rhetoric, however, few companies have actually come up with the goods and as far as most people in the know are concerned, the introduction of Java technology back in the 1990s remains one of the truly global landmarks.

Now while the Web-heads and the techies among you are probably yawning with inherent boredom as a result of already feeling well acquainted with Java, please bear with me while I try to explain the concept to those who aren't blessed with the same level of technical competence—such as my good self.

In short, Java is a dynamic programming language that facilitates the transmission of small executable programs known as either applets (if they run on your PC) or servlets (if they run on a server), which automatically run on demand. Because of its self-executable nature and multi-platform capability, Java technology was instrumental in transforming the Web from a one-dimensional information provider into a living, breathing, dynamic environment that can be completely interactive in terms of material and content. To quote the Java Web site:

> Java technology opens up a wealth of exciting possibilities for consumers. It enables just about any application—including games, tools, and information programs and services—to run on just about

any computer or device. From desktop PCs to mobile handheld devices and cell phones, Java technology today is just about everywhere.

The story of how Java developed is both colorful and interesting. It's also living proof of that old adage "if at first you don't succeed." Contrary to popular belief, Java was never originally conceived for the Internet but instead came about because of the perception of a need to create a universal language that could be used to link together a series of commonly used electronic devices.

The story starts back in January 1991, when Bill Joy, James Gosling, Mike Sheradin, and Patrick Naughton, among others, got together in Colorado to discuss a plan initiated by Sun Microsystems to develop a system that would allow millions of electronic handheld consumer devices (phones, organizers, etc.) to communicate with each other via a central point. Originally called the "Stealth Project," the team at Sun subsequently changed the name to the "Green Project," as they set about writing a programming language that was capable of functioning independently of the platform that hosted it.

The initial language that was produced is largely accredited to James Gosling, who christened it "Oak" after looking at an Oak tree that sat outside his office window. Gosling was forced to change name, however, after discovering that another programming language already had a patent for it. There then began a protracted process of deliberation that coincided with the team's development work, during which time names such as "Java" and "Silk" were discussed. Eventually, the team settled on "Java" as their preferred option (some believe the name was chosen after a trip to a coffee shop, which may explain the current Java logo) and in 1995 gave birth to a brand that Scott McNealy, the chairman of Sun Microsystems, has since described as "probably a bigger brand than Sun itself." (2)

In 1992, following the introduction of the new language and a hardware platform in the form of a PDA (personal digital assistant) known as *7, the "Green Project" became housed under Sun's "FirstPerson" initiative and the process of finding a viable target market began in earnest.

Unfortunately, progress was slow, and while the technology received a few plaudits, several potential partners failed to see a fit between it and their businesses until Sun got a bite from Time-Warner as a result of the latter's 1993 foray into the digital TV market.

Spurred on by the prospect of having their technology installed in set-top boxes for digital TV, the FirstPerson team began re-focusing their attention on that market only to lose out on the Time-Warner deal to SGI (Silicon Graphics Inc.). The team then failed again when attempts at attracting other digital players such as 3DO also came to nothing. Eventually, and as a consequence of becoming frustrated by the perceived lack of progress, FirstPerson was scrapped by Sun in early 1994.

Notwithstanding Sun's decision, several members of the FirstPerson team including Bill Joy and Patrick Naughton persevered with the technology. It was in the summer of 1994 when the "Eureka" moment arrived, as Naughton had the idea of trying to get the language to run on the Internet while spending one of his weekends writing a Web browser.

To his absolute delight, Naughton discovered that the World Wide Web was the perfect place for Java's independent language technology. By the end of the year, he had co-written a browser called WebRunner along with Jonathan Payne. WebRunner was unique at the time of its launch because it was the first browser that could support moving objects and host dynamic, executable content. Its development and introduction was a monumental breakthrough and one that hadn't gone unnoticed by many of the large corporations.

As 1994 turned into 1995, WebRunner became known as HotJava and the programming language itself was officially christened as Java, before subsequently being released to the world and incorporated by Netscape and Microsoft in both of their respective Web browsers— Java had arrived on the global stage in no uncertain terms.

Just one year after the launch of Java in 1996, Microsoft announced its ActiveX technology and proudly proclaimed that just like Java, it was capable of running video, animation, and active scripts across multiple platforms. With Microsoft now running its technology right alongside Sun and Java, the new age of digital media was upon us and the Web had become dynamic in every sense of the word. In many ways, it would never be the same again.

Flash

Flash technology is owned by Adobe. It is probably the best-known vector graphics technology on the Internet and is used extensively in the creation of animation. Now before you start panicking and go leaping for the glossary, let's simply define what vector graphics technology is.

Your computer usually displays images by recognizing the colors of pixels within a data file and displaying them on your monitor. Clear, high-definition images have a lot of pixels and therefore necessitate bigger files, whereas low-definition images have fewer pixels and quite often lose their quality when the image is enlarged. This type of digital imaging is most commonly associated with bitmap files or concepts such as raster graphics.

In the case of vector graphics, the image isn't actually made up of pixels but instead is depicted mathematically. This means that when recognizing a code that relates to vector graphics, your computer actually "draws" the picture based on what it has deciphered and doesn't simply reproduce pixels in a file (3). The advantages of using vector graphics over raster graphics are smaller file sizes, low bandwidth capability, and of course, the facilitation of image manipulation without any loss of quality to the original. The biggest disadvantage of using vector graphics, however, is that because they can't be used for direct replications of the real world (i.e., photographs), they are really only suitable for animation work—but, boy, has their development made a difference in that area!

The history of flash technology starts with Jonathan Gay, whose childhood fascination for building things from colored LEGO slowly evolved into a dream of becoming an architect before he revolutionized the way in which animation was produced on the Web.

Moving on from playing with LEGO, Gay got his hands on an Apple computer when he was still in high school and messed around creating games such as a clone of "Space Invaders" before creating his first graphics editor, which he entered in the school's science fair. Shortly afterwards, he acquired an Apple Macintosh and was subsequently taken by his father to a Macintosh users group where he met up with the group's organizer, a man named Charlie Jackson.

Jackson took a shine to the young Jonathan Gay. As he wanted to start a software business but didn't have the cash to pay expensive programmers, he gladly gave the student the use of a very expensive computer in return for letting him write some games. A short time later, the pair released "Airborn!" and then "Dark Castle," which proved to be such a popular seller that it both paid for Gay's college education and stuck Jackson's company, Silicon Beach Software, right on the developer's map.

It was principally while writing the games that Gay got experience in linking animation to digitized sound, although he was to return to developing graphics editing programs such as Superpaint II and Intellidraw before starting his own company (with the help of some funding from Charlie Jackson) in 1993.

Gay's business was known as FutureWave Software and in its early days focused on the concept of Pen Computing (using a pen to write on a screen instead of a keyboard), developing a product known as SmartSketch. Unfortunately, due to several reasons beyond FutureWave's control, SmartSketch wasn't the hit that was intended and Gay was forced back to the drawing board before discovering his "Eureka" moment—which, strangely enough, turned out to be not too far away from the time when Java was launched.

It was while attending the annual SIGGRAPH computer graphics conference in 1995 that Gay got the idea to turn SmartSketch into an animation product, as apparently this thing called the Internet was looking as if it might be quite popular and could possibly be used for people to send and receive graphics and animation. Gay explains (4):

> At the time, the only way to extend a Web browser to play back animation was through Java. So we wrote a simple animation player that used Java and was horribly slow. We stubbornly kept at it though, and in the fall, Netscape came out with their plug-in API. Finally, we had a way to extend the Web browser with decent performance (this was the ancestor of Macromedia Flash Player). As it grew close to shipping time, we changed the name of our software to FutureSplash Animator to focus more on its animation capabilities.

Just one year after deciding to produce an animation product for the Web, Gay and FutureWave got two pivotal breakthroughs when MSN adopted the software for its Web site and Macromedia almost simultaneously approached Gay to discuss the prospect of working together, having been impressed with the FutureSplash Animator software that Disney was using online. The rest, as they say, is history, as FutureWave was sold to Macromedia in December 1996 and FutureSplash Animator became Macromedia Flash 1.0.

Move forward a decade and Flash is now celebrating its tenth anniversary, with "Flash Professional 8" being branded by Adobe as "the industry's most advanced authoring environment for creating interactive Web sites, digital experiences, and mobile content." The company also believes that its "Flash Player" software is installed on about 600 million Internet-connected PCs, laptops, and mobile devices all across the world.

Although Java and Flash were the real pioneers in terms of producing dynamic, animated content for the Internet, they weren't completely capable of linking up businesses' ERP platforms to the Web. For that process, organizations were primarily turning to XML.

XML

XML stands for extensible markup language; however, it should not be confused with HTML—the Internet authoring standard known to the world as hypertext markup language. The fundamental difference between the two languages is as follows:

HTML is the Internet standard for writing and creating Web pages. It is predominantly used to display data and dictates such things as the size, typeface, and color of text as well as the positioning of links and images.

XML is used to structure, store, and send data readily over the Internet. It is also somewhat "platform independent" and can be used across a considerable range of applications.

Needless to say, given XML's ability to structure and store information and then use it almost ubiquitously, it rapidly became the preferred choice of programming for businesses that were early adopters of a good old-fashioned buzzword of the eighties—"EDI" or electronic data interchange. The principle reason for doing so was that through its introduction, XML quite literally introduced a common standard for sending and receiving files of data that almost instantly dispensed with the need for teams of tired techies to camp out in company meeting rooms in order to get two competing IT platforms to "talk" and "correspond" with each other.

Not surprisingly, when XML was first invented and released by the editorial board of the World Wide Web Consortium back in the late 1990s, it was very quickly seized upon by many large corporate enterprises to facilitate such things as the exchange of purchase orders and invoices so as to expedite the trading process and negate the need for paper. From there, it became a relatively minor step for businesses to exploit XML's potential even further and develop their online "real-time" shopping experiences by linking their respective back-office systems to a front-end on the Web and start pushing the boundaries associated with e-commerce. Never again, for instance, would customers need to be asked to peruse a range of online catalogues before filling in an ugly looking form that simply resulted in the generation of an e-mail, which was subsequently picked up by a desk jockey and keyed into a company's operating system. (So the next time you log onto a Web site that still operates this way, you may want to ask yourself why!)

Section Summary

Although other businesses and associated individuals will undoubtedly press home their points with regard to their involvement in the Web's evolution, in my opinion, there have been few more significant developments than the introductions of Java, Flash, and XML. Sure, it could be argued that all of these things are predicated on bandwidth and the perennial improvements in hardware; however, I see the whole thing as a cycle, where advancements in one area drive those in another and vice versa. To steal Jennifer Rice's analogy, the Web is part of an ecosystem that has numerous touch-points with its stakeholders. It is both a dependent of and a contributor to the evolutionary process that surrounds those stakeholders and is therefore inextricably linked to them.

Before Java, Flash, and XML, the Web was simply a vast library of data that was somewhat one-dimensional in terms of its experience. Now, it is a dynamic, interactive, vibrant, and highly commercialized medium that has given birth to some of the world's most valuable brands. Long may its development continue.

Functionality

So with all the sexy dynamic content in place at the front end of a company's Web proposition and its ERP platform nicely linked to the Net courtesy of XML, what is functionality and what does it mean?

Well, no doubt you will be pleased to hear that my definition of the concept is relatively straightforward and that it simply provides the engineering behind the *purpose* or *purposes* of a Web site. As such, it is not limited to a single dimension and it can quite often be multifaceted. For instance, let's consider three different businesses, Tesco, FedEx, and something very close to my heart, Newcastle United Football Club.

Tesco is a retailer based in the UK. It uses its Web sites (*Tesco.com*, *Tesco.co.uk*) to enhance the value of its brand by providing its users with detailed information about its store portfolio, associated products, and services and comes complete with an online shopping function that can subsequently be used for the home delivery of orders.

FedEx is one of the world's biggest providers of supply-chain services. It uses its Web sites (global derivatives of *Fedex.com*) to enhance the value of its brand by providing users of its services with the opportunity to dynamically interact with its ERP platform by enabling them to manage their accounts online, choose delivery options, track and trace consignments, and discover more about the company's service portfolio.

Newcastle United is an English Premiership Soccer Club. It uses its Web site (*nufc.co.uk*) to enhance the value of its brand by providing its users with the ability to view exclusive videos, listen to live match commentary, and partake of the club's promotional activity.

As you can see, Tesco, FedEx, and Newcastle United are very different businesses but they all have one thing in common—they have attempted to harness the Internet and its associated functionality in order to increase brand value and profitability by providing visitors to their Web sites with an engaging and interactive Web experience.

Thanks to technologies such as Java, Flash, and XML, there is now quite literally no end to the possibilities of using functional components on a Web site to boost a brand's value within the hearts and minds of its target audience. Nor is there an excuse for a Web site failing to live up to expectations. Indeed, no longer should visitors be prepared to put up with second-rate content and material and no longer should they be treated as second-class citizens. By their very nature, consumers on the Web are inquisitive, concept-savvy, and smart—aren't you?

You'll now be glad to hear that most of the technical and theoretical stuff is more or less taken care of, so without any more rhetoric from me, let's start looking at how some organizations attempt to use the concept of functionality to improve the value of their respective brands and build a dynamic Web experience.

Video

Yes, this has been discussed in previous chapters but only at a superficial level and only from the perspective of either using it as premium content or to complement a current advertising campaign. So let's get into a bit more detail.

Most of the videos that you see on the Web are known as "streaming videos" which are sent to a browser on a continuous basis, where they are subsequently decoded and played. Because they are sent continuously, the browser can both play and download the content simultaneously after undertaking a short "buffering" period.

In chapter 2, we looked at the Bratz Web site and how the homepage played a video of an advert in order to complement the rest of the visible content. In chapters 4 and 5, we talked about videos being sold as premium content to those who were willing to pay and briefly discussed the sports and pornography markets as obvious beneficiaries of the technology.

In this chapter, we will look at something slightly different whereby streaming videos are used to build brand value by either educating a potential market or providing potential consumers with more information on a particular product or service.

Let's look at the example of Budgy Smugglers (usually spelled Budgie Smugglers). If you've never heard of them, don't worry, as neither had I until I moved to Australia. By way of explaining the brand when covering the Budgy Smugglers Web site for brandchannel, I articulated the concept as follows (5):

For years, Australia's Bondi Beach has been synonymous with richly painted images of sun, sand, surf, and droves of well-honed bodies bronzing dutifully under cobalt skies. Now a small Sydney company wants to make sure that it's famous for its swimwear too—especially those skin-tight trunks, known affectionately to the locals as "budgie smugglers."

The very mention of the Budgy Smugglers name is guaranteed a giggle in Australia. The brand takes its name directly from an age-old Aussie colloquialism, used to describe a certain type of male, figure-hugging beach attire, which, when viewed from the front, looks as though the wearer may well be attempting to conceal a domestic budgerigar (a small parrot). Although prominent on Australia's beaches for decades, budgie smugglers have seldom been seen outside of the Antipodes since the 1970s and the days of Mark Spitz— a trend that Lachlan Harris and Tom Malone, partners at Budgysmuggler.com, would like to change.

At first glance then, one need not be a rocket scientist to evaluate the challenge facing the team at Budgy Smugglers (which is a 100-percent Web-based business). So as a small Australian company with an image that's completely founded within its island continent, just how is the Budgy Smugglers team going to ensure that the brand gains more exposure and that its subsequent target market is educated as to the culture that's associated with the brand and business in general?

Of course, the answer is simple—either spend millions of dollars in the sponsorship of Australian swimming icons such as Ian Thorpe and Grant Hackett or make sure that your Web site does the best job it can of evangelizing the brand that you're trying hard to build (OK—obviously, if you did have millions to spend you would do both, but just indulge me for the moment).

With the latter point in mind, let's take a look at figure 6.1 (facing page), which is a screenshot of the *Budgysmuggler.com* homepage taken in August 2006.

As mentioned earlier, Budgy Smugglers is solely a Web-based business and has a skin-tight advertising budget when compared with the likes of Speedo, so in attempting to kick sand in the face of its competitors, it has paid a lot of attention to its Web proposition and made very good use of incorporating streaming videos to get its message across. By doing so, it can ensure that the light-hearted nature of the brand and its fiercely patriotic roots are clearly communicated to an

Figure 6.1

audience of millions and, as a consequence, open up the possibility for increased sales. As I said earlier, none of this is rocket science!

Another example of a brand that uses video to try and educate its audience is Gore-Tex. When reviewing the Gore-Tex site for brand-channel in August 2006 (6), I described the brand as follows:

> *Gore-Tex is arguably the best known family brand of W.L. Gore & Associates, the US-based business that made its fortune from polytetrafluoroethylene—or PTFE to you and me. Used extensively in the manufacture of outdoor clothing and footwear for such well-known names as Berghaus, Sprayway, and North Face, Gore-Tex material has dominated the great outdoors for years, and as anyone who's been up a mountain will testify, is second to none when the weather kicks in.*

Given the qualities of Gore-Tex and its reputation for doing what it says on the tin, you won't be surprised to hear that it's just a tad sore on the pocket when investing in a set of tweeds that are made of the material. Naturally, this gives Gore-Tex a problem—how can a brand in its position encourage people to see the value in its product range without compromising its proposition? The answer again is simple—either invest a lot of cash in ensuring that the typical nose-ring wearing, hair-cut avoiding, tree-hugging part-timer who sells the gear through its range of distributorships on extremely busy weekends is well-versed in the manufacturing process, or educate the public through the inclusion of value-added material on a Web site.

In the case of Gore-Tex, the company has included several videos of product testing on its Web portal, which when viewed, really do give a valuable perspective on the amount of time and effort that go into making its material the preferred choice in the marketplace. The "Raintower" and "Walking" videos are particularly interesting, and a screenshot of the link to the former is attached below in figure 6.2:

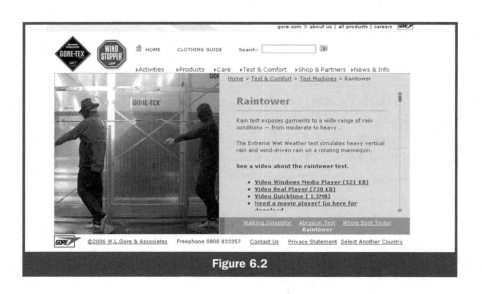

Figure 6.2

Unfortunately, at the time of writing, neither of the Gore-Tex videos were streamed and instead had to be downloaded before being viewed (and asking potential customers to have to go and do something in order for a business to get its point across is never a good idea). Imagine what an enhancement they would have been, therefore, if they were automatically streamed to the homepage's primary viewing area and dynamically used to complement the material being offered.

By coincidence, the team at Gore-Tex had already recognized some of the limitations associated with their original Web proposition when I started writing this book and not long after my article appeared on brandchannel, they contacted me to let me know that they were enhancing their online offering with the introduction of two new and branded sites—namely *Gore-Tex.com* and *Windstopper.com*.

The generation of these two new sites was the output of some twelve months work for the Gore-Tex branding and Web development teams, and the key focus areas of the new propositions were emotional connectivity, education, and usability. Having taken a tour of both *Gore-Tex.com* and *Windstopper.com* and had some subsequent conversations with Michael Petillo and Katie McGrail of Gore-Tex, both of whom were instrumental in developing the new portals, I can honestly say that their efforts have paid off. Indeed, not only are both sites now much more representative of the Gore-Tex brand in general, but they are also much more dynamic, fluid, interactive, and educational, and are a credit to everyone involved.

As you can see from the two examples of Gore-Tex and Budgy Smugglers, there is a lot more to video than just using it as premium content or enabling it to play the latest round of adverts. Indeed, like TV, radio, and of course, the movies, it is a medium in itself and its capabilities in terms of enhancing the value of a brand and creating a more rewarding and enriching Web experience should never be underestimated.

Online Bookings

These days, most people take it for granted that businesses such as ticketing agencies, theatres, sports and entertainment venues, hotels, rail companies, and airlines are able to facilitate bookings online and offer prospective punters (customers) the opportunity to choose their seats based on a set of preferences that range from price to comfort level. After all, the technology exists and the companies want your business, so why wouldn't they pursue their mercantile ideals by tempting you to commit to a Web-enabled sale? Just imagine how you would feel, for example, if you were booking a vacation in the Far East and one of the most popular airlines in the region didn't allow you to book online—what would your immediate reaction be, and what would you think about the brand?

Well, before you start accusing me of losing my marbles, let's have a look at Dragonair.

A relatively new airline with an up-to-date fleet and a very strong presence in Hong Kong, Dragonair has its ownership split between China National Aviation Company (44 percent), CITIC Pacific (30 percent), Swire Pacific (8 percent), and Cathay Pacific (18 percent). When reviewing the Dragonair site for brandchannel late in 2005 (7), I said:

> *Throughout Chinese history, the dragon has been revered as an ancient symbol of mystical power and strength. By locking it into a logo and embellishing it as a brand, Dragonair hopes to weave the spirit of the legendary beast into the very fabric of its business. However, in transferring the concept to the Web, has the company risked interpreting the symbol of national pride as simply hot air?*
>
> *At first glance the multi-lingual portal portrays a subtle blend of East and West, which nicely reflects the origins of the company. The rich red and white hues mingle with an easily navigable Web design and help convey a functionality that one would expect to be underpinned by China's premier point of competitive advantage—value for money.*
>
> *Unfortunately, the company's brand message of "The Beauty of Flying" cannot be aligned to "the beauty of buying," as the Web site fails to recognize the importance of online booking, a significant exclusion given the gaggle of airlines currently offering the facility of self-service. Although Dragonair does cater for its frequent flyers by providing online check-in, customers can only use it if they are departing major cities. Either there is still some work to be done in aligning available Web technology with the company's logistical capabilities, or the marketing team needs a wake-up call.*

As you can see, I was fairy critical of Dragonair's omission of an online booking system with the rationale behind my statements being driven by a perception of a "we know what's best" or a "not invented here" attitude within the company's ownership.

Just a few days after the article appeared on *brandchannel.com*, it was also run by *Business Week Asia*'s online publication, which very generously solicits open feedback on the articles that it publishes. Needless to say, my Dragonair article struck a chord with a reader who went by the pseudonym "BeenToChina" (how very cosmopolitan of you!). He or she replied to it as follows (8):

> *Nickname: BeenToChina*
>   *Review: I think it would have been a good idea to ask Dragonair for comment regarding its Web site. My experience in China is that there is still a large amount of trust in buying things online, and the society is still very much cash based. I suspect the lack of online booking and transparency of its fares has little to do with technology and more to do with cultural norms.*
>   *Date reviewed: Dec 17, 2005 5:20 PM"*

Well, listen here, Mr. or Ms. "BeenToChina." Transparency only has one "A" in it, and clearly your Phileas-Fogg-like dalliances have yet to lead you to Web sites such as China Airlines (9) or China Southern (10), both of which offer online booking. And another thing: I have flown with Dragonair and found their service excellent!

Furthermore, I also contacted Dragonair during the writing of this book for a statement with regard to its omission of an online booking facility and on August 29, 2006, this was their reply:

> *Since 2004 we have been offering online booking for promotional campaigns. We are currently working on introducing an Internet booking service for all our flights and hope to have this up and running in the near future.*

So there you have it—it was coming all along, they just hadn't quite got around to it! In putting the matter to bed, therefore, I have attached a screenshot of Dragonair's homepage in figure 6.3 (following page), which clearly shows that as of August 2006, the company had not yet offered its customers the facility of booking a flight on its Web site.

Now without the tongue-in-cheek rhetoric and by way of setting the record straight, the review facility on *Asia Business Week* is a very

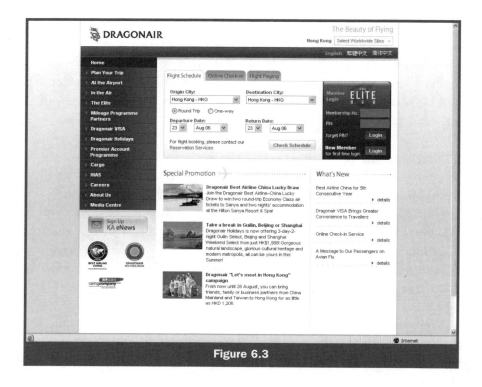

Figure 6.3

good way of soliciting feedback and, of course, like any other level-headed writer, I treat it as a gift. Indeed, in Asia there are some very distinctive reasons why online trading has yet to catch on to the extent that it should (education, Internet access, and the lack of plastic money being just a few of them) but these are gradually being eroded each day, thereby reducing the number of available excuses for not getting jiggy online.

The use of an online booking system to improve the functionality of an online proposition has tremendously augmented the Web sites of many of the types of businesses listed at the start of this section. In their most basic forms, online booking systems will quite often just let you buy a ticket depending on how much you want to spend and where you want to sit. The more sophisticated models, however, have all sorts of bells and whistles on board and come complete with the facility to demonstrate "virtual views" at entertainment and sporting venues; sometimes they even allow users to select extras such as pre-booking food and drinks at intervals, which can either be collected or brought to your seat.

Likewise, many members of airline loyalty schemes now use online booking systems to check in for their flights and choose the exact seat in which they wish to sit. They can also make adjustments to their ticket types, change arrival and departure dates, and generally interact with the host company's mainframe in a controlled and risk-free way, just by adhering to the parameters that have been laid down during the system's design.

Because online booking systems are extensively used within the travel and entertainment industries, it really isn't surprising that some of the biggest beneficiaries of the technology have been tour operators, many of whom are now enjoying access to much bigger audiences courtesy of the World Wide Web. Perhaps a very good example of a Net-based brand that was specifically developed to take advantage of this concept is Expedia.

Originally founded within Microsoft as far back as 1995, Expedia Inc. was divested from the business in 1996 before going public in 1999. Today, Expedia Inc. is the largest global online travel business and the fourth-largest travel company in the world. Aside from owning the brand of *Expedia.com*, it also owns the brands of *Hotels.com*, TripAdvisor, and Classic Vacations. According to its corporate Web site (11), Expedia Inc. is now on a mission "to become the largest and most profitable seller of travel in the world, by helping everyone, everywhere plan and purchase everything in travel."

The strength of Expedia Inc.'s proposition is that through Web sites such as *Expedia.com*, it is able to offer a completely holistic package for anyone who is planning a trip or vacation, regardless of whether he's just after a single flight or looking to book additional hotels and car rental. Holidays, cruises, and activities too are all covered in detail, thanks to Expedia Inc.'s network within the travel industry. With a number of country-based sites now added to its already extensive portfolio, Expedia looks set to give many indigenous travel operators a good run for their money. To illustrate the depth of Expedia's proposition, a screenshot of the *Expedia.com* homepage taken in August 2006 is illustrated in figure 6.4, on the following page.

I hope this example of Expedia and the associated discussion of online bookings has backed up my belief that if you happen to own a brand in the travel or entertainment industries and you're intent on sticking it on the World Wide Web, you really should be looking to

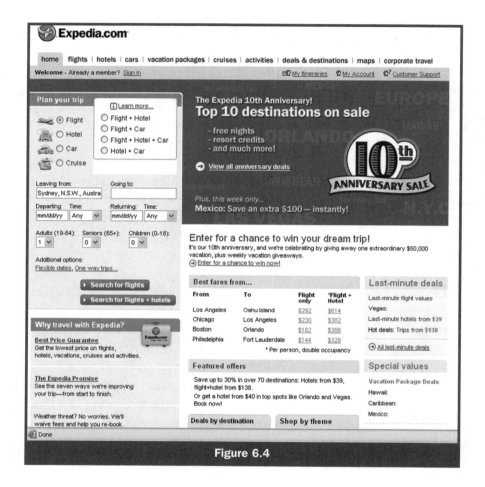

Figure 6.4

complement it by developing a real-time online booking facility. Not only will that let your business develop an additional revenue stream, but it will also enhance the value of your brand by showing visitors to your Web site that your company can cater to the cyber-community by taking its Net presence seriously. It will also broaden the brand's exposure by making it readily available to the many people around the globe who might just want to experience it—stranger things have happened!

Online Shopping

If that last series of comments on online bookings has stimulated your gray matter somewhat, strap yourself in for this one, because the subject of online shopping has always been a minefield for anyone with an interest in e-commerce—not to mention being top of the "sweary words list" for luxury brands the world over.

To underline that point, let me share with you a recent conversation I had with a chap named Todd Moore, general manager for Lowrance's Asia Pacific business.

Headquartered in Tulsa, Oklahoma, Lowrance specializes in the manufacturing and distribution of GPS mapping and sonar equipment for the recreational fishing market. When I asked Todd to state the biggest threat to his business, he said without hesitation, "The Internet, because it has opened up boundaries for purchases that were previously locked by geography."

In other words, Todd was really concerned that his business in Australia could be damaged if prospective customers who were looking to buy Lowrance products did so in markets where prices and margins are lower (due to lower production overheads and increased competition) and then imported them to Australia themselves. Now take that analogy and multiply it by the number of businesses that you think may exist in the world and simultaneously trade either directly on the Web themselves or indirectly through licensed distributors, before standing back, lighting your pipe, and admiring the extent of the problem— "Yes," said the actress to the bishop, "it's positively enormous!"

Personally I love this issue, because coming from a working-class background in the UK (which is a geography that's always had the rough end of the stick when it comes to paying a premium compared with markets such as the U.S. and mainland Europe), I think it's great that many brands have experienced an overdue and radical reality check regarding their geographically biased pricing strategies. Before everyone gets excited and instantly starts associating me with the Socialist Workers Party, however, let's just park the debate of premium brands and the Internet for the moment and come back to it in the following chapter where we can dig into it in more detail than is necessary here.

So back to Internet shopping then and all that it entails. One of the fundamental points to bear in mind when rushing to open the cash registers in cyberspace is that unlike a lot of the Web's commercial functionality, Internet shopping relies extensively on a company's fulfilment capability and its channel management strategy in order to make it fly. It is simply not the same as hosting an online booking system that is predicated on selling capacity, as it is absolutely dependent upon a solid logistics and supply-chain platform that can cater to all forms of service and delivery—including product returns and refunds. In addition, the more SKUs (stock keeping units) that are placed online, the more complex the supply chain gets, and the more critical it is that each customer order is habitually completed in full.

Furthermore, because of the speed of trade on the Web and the immediate availability of price-comparing software, organizations that do trade online need to be pretty darn clear where their competitive advantages lie or they'll find themselves in trouble soon enough.

By now, I am sure you've realized that the concept of Internet shopping is so lateral and holistic that I couldn't possibly do it justice in just one section, so I'm afraid you're going to have to wait until the next chapter to see where we are going with that one, along with the inextricable linkages that it has to premium-branded goods. For now, then, let's just be clear that as far as the average retailer is concerned (luxury brands excluded), the ability of its customers to trade online is every bit as important as it is for them to visit a store, so it's vital that they not feel short-changed when visiting the Web site in question.

Software and Product Downloads

Having covered the concepts of both online bookings and online shopping to one extent or another, let's now have a look at a relatively new market that has only been allowed to develop thanks to the functionality of the Web.

Software and product downloads can come in a variety of forms, shapes, and sizes. They can be represented by things like music, programs, and movies, and they can either be designed as saleable units in their own right or given away as a type of free sample. Software and product downloads can also be used to enhance a USB-compatible device to upgrade its capability or to update aging programs on an existing PC. All things considered, they are a marvel of the modern Web and a fantastic addition to a branded Web site.

One of the best examples of a brand that uses software and product downloads to augment the sales of its hardware is Apple and its iTunes program. However, if you know your history, you will be acutely aware that Apple has owned a golden ticket once or twice before (particularly when it dominated the PC market in the 1980s) and consequently lost its way. Indeed, before Apple launched its iPod around five years ago, it was a business in trouble with a plunging market share and very little light at the end of the tunnel.

Enter 2001 and Apple, from somewhere right out of the blue, completely revolutionized the domestic and portable music markets with the launch of both iTunes and the first 5GB iPods that together gave users the capability to carry their music anywhere. Today, and as a result of the perpetual advances in technology, Apple's iPods are smaller, thinner, and capable of carrying up to twelve times as much data as they did when they first came out. Aside from just carrying music, they now carry pictures and video too. In short, the inception of the iPod has transformed Apple's business from an aging, flagging monolith into a streamlined, sexy proposition that now includes a growing retail chain to boot.

Although Apple is probably the easiest example to recall when considering the use of software downloads to augment a company's brand, it's by no means the only one. Take Garmin, which is a competitor of Lowrance and a global leader in the field of electronic cartography.

I reviewed the Garmin Web site for brandchannel in early 2006 (12) and in doing so I said of the brand in general:

> *Garmin is the undisputed king of GPS-driven cartography. For the past 20 years or so, its tried and tested teams of techies have quite literally moved heaven and earth to ensure that whether one is traveling by land, sea, or air, Garmin is the technology used to avoid getting lost.*
>
> *The brand prides itself on functionality, which is probably just as well because there's very little room for intuition when it comes to landing an aircraft in fog. Garmin.com has obviously been designed with the same ethos in mind—and while that's great for ease of navigation, it's probably not for the thrillseekers.*

To help you visualize exactly what I was talking about, a screenshot of the homepage of *Garmin.com* taken in August 2006 is illustrated in figure 6.5.

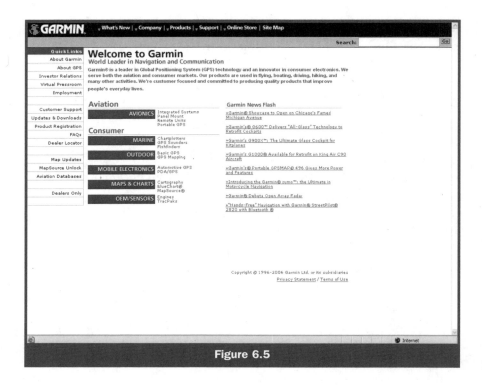

Figure 6.5

As you can see from the screenshot in figure 6.5, *Garmin.com* is a clinical piece of machinery that operates as a fully functional component of the company's brand proposition and loses very little through its lack of dynamic content. Indeed, just one look at the links that are located on the left-hand side of the page should give you a fair idea of what *Garmin.com* is about, and if you own a Garmin device, I'm sure that you're no stranger to that section of the site. Allow me to explain.

Having bought a Garmin Street Pilot (a portable vehicle-based GPS system) when I first moved to Australia in 2005, I have found it to be invaluable in terms of helping me find my way around Sydney without burning gallons of fuel or running into the back of an unsuspecting local while leafing through an A–Z street directory. Moreover, when I registered it on *Garmin.com* via a USB link direct to my PC, I was given the option of updating the mapping software or buying extra geographical chips should I ever have the need to take the unit overseas. As a real added bonus, I was then directed to a "places of interest" site that specializes in updating Garmin software and was instantly able to load my Street Pilot with the location of every listed speed and red light camera in the state of New South Wales—now who was it that said that the Internet would never catch on?

Clearly, Garmin has done a lot with its Web site in terms of using it to enhance the value of its brand by providing users of its equipment with an invaluable set of options that can help them stay in touch with the world as it changes beneath their feet. They are not alone, however, as many organizations are now using similar types of functionality to upgrade and augment devices such as PDAs and cameras and encourage brand loyalty by offering users of their sites a service that's second to none.

Track and Trace

One of the great things about the Web is that it's capable of supporting all sorts of businesses, regardless of whether they're B2B or the traditional B2C. As mentioned earlier in this chapter, FedEx is a business that can easily straddle both sectors and is well known for its global logistics capabilities. FedEx is also a very forward-thinking outfit, as it was one of the first organizations of its kind to use the Internet's functionality to provide its customers with an interactive experience that's based on its core services in order to add value to its brand.

For example, if you're an account holder with FedEx, there's a number of things you can do on the Web to save yourself time and money. Not only can you do the easy stuff like organize a shipment, print the labels, and subsequently book a collection, for instance, but you can also track and trace the consignment through every point on its journey at which it is scanned by a FedEx agent and at the very end of its travels, obtain a POD (proof of delivery).

FedEx doesn't stop on the Web with just its freight business either, as in addition to booking haulage and thanks to FedEx Kinko's, you can use the Web site to buy everything from stationery supplies to office furniture and have it shipped directly. If that's not enough, you can then feel free to organize some online print runs of your own personal files or create a set of greeting cards that can subsequently be collected at your nearest Kinko's outlet—now that's holistic functionality!

Obviously, FedEx is not alone in terms of using track-and-trace technology to enable its consumers to keep an eye on their packages wherever they may be in the world, as the likes of TNT, DHL, and obviously UPS do exactly the same thing. What is unique about FedEx in this arena, however, is the ways in which the company has consolidated its portfolio of businesses and integrated them via a single site to enhance its online offering and add more value to the brand.

Managing Transactions

As we discovered during the discussion on XML, one of the first uses of the Internet for the purposes of e-commerce was the exchange of orders and invoices in order to speed up the trading process and negate the use of paper. Little wonder, then, that it's now possible to manage all of your finances online without ever visiting a bank—unless, of course, you only trade in cold hard cash (and even then you could get it from an ATM).

Although some organizations have stuttered in terms of their approach over the years and the subject of security quite often rears its head, it is now quite likely that if you are reading this book, you manage at least part of your financial affairs either directly through the Web site of the hosting organization or through a third-party site. And why not? After all, the benefits of doing so are more or less obvious—there's no need to leave the house, no need to join an endless queue, and no need to worry about opening hours when you've got a PC close at hand. The benefits to the institutions are substantial, too, which is why many of them now operate dedicated Internet-only businesses (such as the UK's EGG and First Direct) that offer much lower charges and better rates of interest as a result of having very little need for infrastructure.

In addition to the major banks, many credit card businesses have wasted little time in getting in on the Internet act with the likes of American Express shamelessly promoting its class-oriented, color-coded cards and encouraging its customers to manage their accounts on the Web. It doesn't end there, either, as these days many utilities and service providers have built considerable exposure in cyberspace so that regardless of whether you're buying water, energy, or even just paying a phone bill, it's now more than possible to choose your preferred provider based on your individual preferences and then manage your account on the World Wide Web.

As if all of this isn't enough, there are also the insurance companies and health care providers. Who hasn't yet searched for an online quote for car, home, life, or marine insurance either directly through a company Web site or by using a Web-based broker?

All things considered, it would seem there is no end to the mercantile pursuits that can be facilitated by the Web's functionality and that the opportunities to use what's available in terms of technology to jack up the value of a brand or brands are really too good to be put on the back burner.

Before we get carried away, however, we need to be aware that even though we have covered a number of the more popular uses of the Internet in terms of its engagement with many people's lives, we have really only caught the very tip of the iceberg and there are many other ways in which the Web can be used from an interactive perspective—with many more being developed each day. With that in mind, I am really looking forward to seeing more innovative and exciting methods of customer engagement as the Internet develops—and, of course, saving both time and money in the process.

• • •

Key Points

The key points to remember from this chapter are as follows:

- Technology on the Internet is constantly improving and perpetually brings new opportunities for the Web-conscious brand.
- Because of the improvements in Internet software, it is no longer necessary to spend millions of dollars to create a dynamic and enriching Web experience for customers.
- Web site functionality is an absolutely critical point of engagement between a brand and its customers.
- The type of functionality that's used on a Web site should afford company stakeholders the perfect opportunity to interact with a mainframe to the mutual benefit of all.
- Organizations should ensure that the types of functionality they place on a Web site is reflective of their core processes and is of a "value-added" nature to the customer.

ENDNOTES

1. *http://news.bbc.co.uk/1/shared/spl/hi/pop_ups/06/technology_ibm_ pc_anniversary/html/1.stm*
2. *www.javaworld.com/jw-10-1996/jw-10-javaname.html*
3. *www.imagearts.ryerson.ca/abal/lectures/flash/flash_concept.html*
4. *www.adobe.com/macromedia/events/john_gay/page04.html*
5. *www.brandchannel.com/features_profile.asp?pr_id=280*
6. *www.brandchannel.com/features_Webwatch.asp?ww_id=291*
7. *www.brandchannel.com/features_Webwatch.asp?ww_id=257*
8. *www.businessweek.com/innovate/content/dec2005/id20051215_ 440605.htm?chan=search*
9. *www.china-airlines.com/en/index.htm*
10. *www.cs-air.com/en/*
11. *www.expediainc.com/phoenix.zhtml?c=190013&p=home*
12. *www.brandchannel.com/features_Webwatch.asp?ww_id=286*

7
The Luxury Brand Debate

He who rejects change is the architect of decay. The only human institution which rejects progress is the cemetery.

—HAROLD WILSON

FOR SOME ORGANIZATIONS, THE ADVENT OF THE WORLD Wide Web provided an unparalleled global platform from which to evangelize the points of competitive advantage associated with their premium-brand portfolios and, as such, was welcomed with open arms. Other businesses, however, considered the Internet a barefaced menace, and instead of recognizing its positive communicative qualities, treated it as an implement of humiliating exposure of which the Gestapo would have been proud.

The void between these polarized perceptions of how the Web should be seen as a marketing tool by prestige providers of goods and services has consequently become a battleground—a no-man's land populated by the brave, the foolhardy, and, of course, the barbarian hoards of rampant consultants!

On one side of the barbed-wire fence sit the bulls. Early adopters of Internet technology and survivors of the dot-com holocaust, they are resilient, innovative, and apparently impervious to either the removal of geographical boundaries or the threat of margin erosion. On the other side of the fence are the bears. Nervous and indecisive, they see the growth of the Internet as a major strategic threat and are dug in so deep behind their logos and brands that they run the real risk of being awarded a snowy white feather in exchange for their cowardice and procrastination.

At first glance, the differences between the two camps appear to be both complex and multifaceted. The bulls, for example, are happy to ply their trade online, have geared up their Web propositions accordingly, and taken an aggressive and innovative investment approach toward the new technology. Conversely, the bears have refused to acknowledge the upsurge in online sales, seem unclear as to the positioning of their brands online, and continually harp on about the "boutique-shopping experience."

Having spent many an hour attempting to cut through the rhetoric associated with the constituents of all parties involved, it is now my humble opinion that those against online branding and trading have spent a long time hiding behind a wall of semantics, which have often been used to mask a distinct lack of clarity around a brand's direction. On the other hand, businesses that have actively preached lucidity and demonstrated a clear brand strategy, have generally found no reason at all for a hugely successful offline brand that predicates itself on the concept of exclusivity not to be successful on the Web.

That is not to say, of course, that all luxury brands are automatically guaranteed to be triumphant online but instead reinforces the mantra in this book that says that if a business can truly reflect the intrinsic and extrinsic values of its brand in cyberspace at every point of engagement, there is no reason at all why it should not continue to be successful. Why? Because the Internet is simply another distribution channel that needs to be managed accordingly—and it really is as straightforward as that.

For those who disagree, I would readily recommend a reality check in the form of the 1837 fable, "The Emperors New Suit" (1), by Hans Christian Andersen, and I have included a link at the end of this chapter for those who haven't read it! Alternatively, they can either keep telling themselves something often enough until they believe it is true or reflect upon an article by Flavio Quaranta and David Sadigh (2), founding partners at IC Agency and experts in the field of online marketing, which beautifully highlights the lengths to which some people will go in order to disguise their ignorance of the influential medium known as the World Wide Web.

In the article, Quaranta and Sadigh claim that in 2003, they asked the CEO of a watch brand if he should reconsider the use of the company's Web site as a means of defining its online strategy. In replying, the CEO came out with two absolutely priceless quotes that are probably worth a lot more than his watches.

Indeed, after initially stating that his clients were looking for "individual service that we can offer them primarily through our exclusive boutiques," the individual in question went on to say that "the Internet is not appropriate for a brand such as ours," and then managed to go one better with the mealy-mouthed comment that the "watches were not luxury products but rather prestige timepieces, and that these two categories were, in fact, radically different."

Taxi for the geezer who has absolutely no idea what his brand stands for or how he wants to develop it!

Thankfully, the growth in Internet adoption rates and the associated explosion in online shopping have managed to change the mindset of many organizations that proudly ply their trades at the premium end of the market and, as a consequence, more and more businesses are becoming increasingly articulate with regard to their Web-based strategies. Let's face it, though, with markets like the United Kingdom experiencing year-on-year growth in online shopping by more than 30 percent to July 2006 (3) compared with Main Street growth of 2–3 percent and UK consumers expected to spend more than £30 billion on the Web during the course of the year, the arguments against selling one's products online are diminishing by the day. Despite these somewhat spectacular statistics, however, plenty of companies still seem to think that if they bury their heads in the sand in perpetuity, this ghastly electronic toy of generations X and Y will at long last run its course and eventually be confined to the same part of the cupboard as the hula hoop and the Rubik's Cube.

How they wish! With the dot-com crash now confined to the history books and *Boo.com* (4) just another story over a beer, the reality is destined to be somewhat different, and if you're anything like me, you'll be having a whale of a time watching some of the world's most affluent brand portfolios scrambling around like Bambi on ice for a position within an environment that they could have and should have identified with several years ago.

In this chapter, we will attempt to explore the grounds of argument for and against the marketing of luxury and high-value brands on the Web and seek to identify several of the perceived barriers to entry. We will also pay particular attention to the concept of online shopping and try to identify a number of the tools and techniques that such brands use in their endeavors to control this "new" distribution channel and replicate their offline success.

Online Shopping

Of all the hot topics associated with the marketing of luxury brands on the Internet, this one is without doubt the hottest of them all. It's so hot in fact that it couldn't possibly be any hotter if Beelzebub himself were using it to cook up a barbecue in Hades using nothing but habanero peppers and a bottle of "Blair's Death Sauce" (5)!

The Internet is brim full of articles quoting many different reasons as to why luxury brands get agitated at the thought of trading on the Web. Many of the arguments are quite often esoteric and involve every conceivable theory that's ever done the rounds in a lecture theater. I had a go at uncovering some of them in 2001 when writing an article for brandchannel called "Luxury Brands Snub the Web" (6); however, by no means did I get them all, and, if anything, the ensuing period of time has only allowed many of the long-term opponents of online trading to further entrench their positions and intensify the debate—although at long last, the cracks are starting to appear within their ranks.

To help illustrate this point, and as we have already touched on the online marketing of "prestige timepieces," let's take a good look at Rolex, one of the world's most instantly recognizable manufacturers of chronometers and a brand that's synonymous with both opulence and affluence. When covering Rolex for brandchannel in 2001 (7), I said of the brand and its prospects on the Internet:

Since its birth at the turn of the century, this powerful brand has become an icon of sophistication and a possession revered by the world's high achievers (a point nicely illustrated by Sir Edmund Hillary, who took his to the summit of Mount Everest). But today's desire for digital consumerism and the mass market medium of the

World Wide Web has meant a host of new challenges for luxury goods and many brands are struggling to retain their exclusivity when transferring their products to the Net.

I then went on to make the following comments about the Rolex Web site:

The Rolex environment oozes with class; several key areas are enhanced by some excellent Flash technology and a range of musical audio files. For all of its good points though, you're still left looking for that "used Rolex Locator," which doesn't exist, or the facility to book an appointment at your local Rolex Dealer after completing an online form to supply them with some purchase information. However, despite these minor criticisms the site does succeed in convincing the customer of one vital point—if you're going to buy one of these sartorial watches, it's going to cost you a lot of hard-earned cash.

Five years down the track and little has changed at *Rolex.com*, as the screenshot in figure 7.1, taken in September 2006, clearly illustrates:

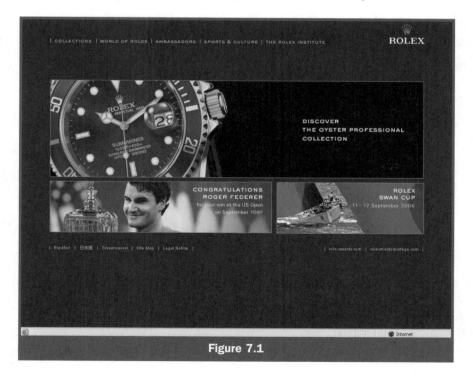

Figure 7.1

Just like it did half a decade ago, *Rolex.com* continues to focus its attentions on educating visitors as to the cultural values and history that pervade the brand in general and has little or nothing by way of encouragement for anyone wishing to get his hands on a watch. To underpin this point, Rolex proudly states by way of a link to a legal notice that's clearly visible on its homepage that "Genuine Rolex products are sold through official Rolex Jewelers and are not available on the Internet."

Obviously the team at Rolex hasn't spent much time on Google then, whereby the entering of a simple set of search terms will instantly reward anyone who would like to get his hands on an "Oyster," "Daytona," or "Yachtmaster" with an array of online establishments that are only too keen to take your cash in exchange for a new or used timepiece! So what's happening here, and what does Rolex make of it all?

For me, the disposition of Rolex absolutely epitomizes the luxury brand debate and should give you a feel for the arguments being offered with regard to online trading. On the one hand, Rolex is flatly refusing to have anything to do with selling its products on the Internet and instead is continually trying to educate its audience about the brand's premium points of value by associating it with opulence at every opportunity. On the other hand, the exclusivity created by Rolex and the subsequent demand for its products, have motivated several entrepreneurial businesses to try and take advantage of the company's demeanor on the Web by getting in underneath the Rolex distributor network to capitalize on the company's blind spot.

In attempting to define the arguments more clearly, let's now take a look at some of the more detailed aspects of trading online and focus in particular on the barriers that luxury brands perceive as inhibiting the concept. In doing so, you can make up your own mind as to their degrees of credibility!

Lack of Purchase Experience

Ah yes, the old "buying my products is an experience" line, which nearly cost Levi's its shirt when it had a big fall-out with Tesco in a battle over pricing that straddled the millennium (8).

In essence, the "purchase experience" argument revolves around the fact that certain manufacturers of luxury goods believe that in order to

fully appreciate the brand they are buying, customers need to be subjected to the culture, ambience, and knowledge that only a specialist
retailer can provide. This method of selling is quite often referred to as
the "boutique-shopping experience," and retailers use it to differentiate
themselves from the competition by seeking to reward each and every
customer with a level of attention and satisfaction that's fully commen-
surate with the price they are paying for a particular product or service.

The argument is founded on the fact that many luxury and high-
value products can often be described as "sensory" because of their
dependence on the extrinsic qualities of sight, touch, and, in the case
of fragrances and some cosmetics, smell. As such, they are believed to
depend highly upon personal contact that just cannot be replicated on
the World Wide Web.

Although most of this reasoning may well be true for first-time
users of a product, once the identity and loyalty factors kick in thanks
to a company's branding strategy, the primary drivers for purchase
often switch from extrinsic to intrinsic, and are most often motivated
by many of the emotional associations that we have regularly discussed
within this book. So, if a brand can replicate these emotional aspects of
association in cyberspace, it surely must be attractive to the online
consumer who is already loyal to the brand per se.

In my humble opinion, there is now very little to stop the manufacturers of luxury brands re-creating much of the purchase experience
process in cyberspace (perhaps with the exception of the seriously big-
ticket items) thanks to the advancements in Internet technology, bandwidth, and hardware. In addition, the argument for the "boutique-
shopping experience" does not cater to the many individuals who have
neither the time nor the inclination to go wandering around in order
to buy a brand with which they already have a strong affinity.

Put these points together with the growth in online shopping and
the presence of several successful Web sites that do nothing else but
specialize in the sale of luxury and high-value goods (some of which
are covered later in this chapter) and as far as I'm concerned, the perceived lack of a purchase experience as a barrier to trading online represents nothing more than a thinly veiled attempt to disguise the fact
that the owners of a premium brand have failed to correctly manage
either their distribution channels or their pricing strategies. Or perhaps
even worse, they may still be on the fence with regard to the Web in

general and have little in the way of a management plan to deal with the medium's growth.

By way of an illustration, let's consider the row between Levi's and Tesco that I vaguely alluded to at the beginning of this section.

This little catfight can be traced as far back as 1998, when Levi's got upset at Tesco taking advantage of price disparities in several foreign markets (the U.S., Canada, and Mexico) and exporting its products to the UK without authorization. Tesco then went on to galvanize its substantial store network, selling the imported goods at a significant discount to the market and undercutting Levi's British distributors to the point that they were bleeding.

Not surprisingly, Levi's threw its toys right out of the proverbial playpen in a fairly major way, and the ensuing legal battle raged on through the courts for a number of years before finally coming to rest long after the millennium—in favor, believe it or not, of Levi's.

What's interesting about this story is that all that Tesco did was commit a very entrepreneurial, if not obvious, act of arbitrage, the likes of which goes on at consumer level millions of times each year when people go on vacation—albeit on an infinitely smaller scale. So has Levi's, in managing to curtail Tesco, actually missed the bigger picture?

Since the advent of the Internet, it has become increasingly unnecessary for people to travel abroad just to find a good deal, and instead, they can shop from the comfort of their very own homes provided that they can find themselves an e-tailer that ships internationally—and more such companies are springing up all the time. With that in mind, any business or organization that has a set of price disparities across a number of geographies is going to get caught with its trousers down if its products are sold on the Web by either unmanaged or unauthorized distributors.

The brands that are most vulnerable to being completely blown out of the water when being traded on the Net internationally are those which have a range of standardized products and are not geographically dependent. Examples could be a specific type of fragrance, a fashion accessory, or an electronic product that is eminently usable regardless of its point of origin. Indeed, brands that possess these qualities are an absolute sitting duck for the fleet-footed entrepreneur or the value-conscious consumer who is actively seeking to save or make a fast buck on the back of an international price disparity.

On the other hand, it is very possible for products of a brand that require a large degree of customization that's predicated on personal contact to put forward a very strong case for the purchase experience argument. For example, buying a car from Aston Martin or a made-to-measure wedding dress from a particularly high-brow fashion house is likely to involve a substantial amount of discussion and subsequent consideration before the actual purchase is made, so it is highly unlikely that they would initially be bought online. That said, these types of purchases are usually few and far between, and time is now running out for the opponents of online trading who continually cite the purchase experience as a realistic barrier to selling on the Web.

Target Market not Available

This argument most often revolves around the owners of a luxury or high-value brand refusing to accept or acknowledge that their preferred demography either has access to the Internet or even if they did, would not be interested in shopping online. As such, it is quite often used as a supporting act by those who would cite the "boutique-shopping experience" as a good enough reason to refuse to trade on the Web.

Let's have a think about this one for a minute, then. How many people do you know who own a PC with Internet access, and what sort of demographic would you put them in?

In the introduction to this book, we discovered that 16 percent of the world's population now has access to a Web-enabled PC. In terms of getting a handle on the rate of adoption, a study back in 2004 (9) stated that by 2010, the world should have around 1 billion PC users on its books—however, in May 2006, it was found that the world already had 900 million users (10), which subsequently meant that the 2004 forecasts looked hugely conservative.

On the financial side, between 2000 and 2005 the world's GDP has consistently grown between 2 percent and 4.5 percent, with China, the world's most heavily populated country, growing at an unprecedented rate and averaging around 10 percent for the same period (11).

In addition to these numbers, we learned during the early part of this chapter that in the UK (which is fairly typical of the Westernized world), consumers are expected to spend around £30 billion on the

Web during the course of 2006, with more growth expected in 2007 (some global figures for online sales are discussed later in this chapter).

Put all of these statistics together and it's not particularly difficult to start drawing some conclusions—Internet sales are rising, adoption rates are increasing, and, globally, people have more money to spend. To avoid conjecture, however, and by way of giving the demographic doubters a final poke in the eye, let's look at an example that proves beyond all reasonable doubt that there actually is an online market for e-tailers of luxury goods and premium products—and that it's growing.

In April 2004, Amazon officially launched its online jewelry proposition after having taken more than 100,000 orders during a test period that lasted several weeks. Since then, Amazon has found that sales of products through its jewelry store have rocketed almost exponentially and have regularly achieved triple-digit growth when measured quarter on quarter (12). In terms of price points, Amazon jewelry starts at the extremely affordable $24.99 and escalates to upwards of $10,000.

Now do the mathematics: if Amazon Jewelry took 100,000 orders for products at only $24.99 within a trial period that lasted around six weeks during 2004, it would have had minimum sales of around $5 million for the quarter, which have since risen substantially. The truth is, however, that given Amazon's range of price points, $5 million could be a very conservative starting point and the actual number is probably much higher.

Now before you go off the deep end and accuse me of contriving an argument, I am aware that selling a few thousand bracelets at $24.99 is hardly going to turn the heads of manufacturers of luxury and premium goods. After all, these people are connoisseurs of sophistication and style and are extremely well educated when it comes to articulating their market positioning and their preferred range of demographics. So instead I will say only this:

In 2005, the most valuable product that Amazon sold through its online jewelry store was a pair of diamond earrings—and they went for $94,000 (13). Now, will someone please stand up and tell me that the high-value consumer just doesn't exist online?

Loss of Exclusivity

This debate tends to revolve around an organization's fear of its brand or brands becoming overexposed as a result of trading on the Internet and subsequently becoming devalued. This can certainly happen if a premium brand finds itself being sold on the Web through a variety of e-tailers that either don't fit the parent company's distribution profile or have managed to procure some wholesale product through a subtle act of arbitrage (*a la* Tesco and Levi's). It can also happen if a luxury brand fails to design and implement its Web proposition correctly and falls short of consumers' expectations with regard to content and presentation.

These arguments aside, however, trading on the Internet is not the only way in which a brand can lose its kudos—as Burberry will testify.

The history of Burberry can be traced back as far as 1856 when Thomas Burberry, a twenty-one-year-old draper's apprentice, started producing gabardine (strong woven twill) and opened a small outfitter's shop in Basingstoke, England. It was almost a lifetime later, however, in the 1920s, when the famous checked pattern that is synonymous with Burberry today (and is registered as a trademark) was first introduced by way of a lining to a trench coat. Slowly but surely, the company continued to build its reputation and in 1955 was awarded the royal seal of approval when it received a Royal Warrant from Queen Elizabeth II. In 1989, Burberry received another Royal Warrant from His Royal Highness, the Prince of Wales.

Despite its regal plaudits, Burberry was never really a brand that appealed to the premium end of the mass-produced market, and as such, looked destined to lurch from one crisis to another until Rose Marie Bravo took over as CEO in 1997. Bravo's appointment proved to be a real turning point for the business, as under her stewardship and within only a few short years, she transformed the image of Burberry from a crusty middle-class riding crop of a brand into a stylish and sexy lifestyle offering that carried instant recognition and appeal. As a result, Bravo became known as a dynamic and driven entrepreneur and in 2004, *Time* magazine christened her "The Most Powerful Woman in Fashion."

Unfortunately for Burberry, an unexpected side effect of the company's success was the adoption of the brand as the preferred mode of dress by Britain's professional underclass, commonly known as "chavs" and the nick-naming of the plaid as "Essex Tartan." The problem has since become so much of an issue for Burberry that it has been forced to re-think a significant part of its overall brand strategy and take an iron grip of both its channel management and its distribution policies.

For anyone who is unfamiliar with the concept of a "chav," a brief look around on Google should be sufficient to provide a concise definition. However, for the purposes of this text I would describe them as a tribe of loutish peasants who have an acute aversion to work, refuse to pay full price for anything, are usually dripping with cheap gold jewelry and possess a stunted, swaggering gait that, although it is believed to be cool, can only be described as laughable.

The online encyclopedia, "Wikipedia," perhaps gives a more articulate version:

> *The term "chav" refers to a subcultural stereotype of people fixated on fashions such as flashy "bling" jewelry (generally gold), and designer clothing with the beige Burberry pattern (most famously the baseball cap which has since been discontinued by the company).*

If the above descriptions still leave you a little vague with regard to "chavs" and their associated culture, worry not, as there is plenty of information on the Web with regard to the phenomenon. That said, I thought I should include a link to a couple of my favorites (14) at the end of this chapter, as well as a screenshot in figure 7.2, as I believe that together, they encapsulate the concept rather nicely!

Figure 7.2

As you can imagine, Burberry was horrified at the unfortunate publicity that its brand had attracted when its products first became known as the consummate apparel for chavs throughout the United Kingdom, but worse was to follow when toward the end of 2005 one of its prime clothes horses, the sultry Kate Moss, admitted her dalliances with drugs and subsequently undertook a very public period of rehabilitation (Burberry subsequently renewed Moss's contract in 2006).

Needless to say, all of this negative PR put Burberry's senior management into overdrive to try and think of a game plan that would keep the company's brand on the proverbial straight and narrow, and it wasn't long before the outputs subsequently manifested themselves in several fleet-footed maneuvers around product availability and a range of public statements on positioning. After the dust had settled, the company seemed to gain just a little bit of relief and is now a lot more comfortable about playing down its overexposure to the UK's *l'enfants terrible* and is instead focusing its energies on cultivating itself within the North American market.

Of course, there can be no way of telling whether the Internet actually contributed to Burberry's depth of appeal to such an unfortunate market segment in any way at all, and in truth it probably didn't. That said, Burberry's experiences with overexposure carry a lesson for us all—and the importance of managing one's distribution channels could not be more glaringly obvious.

Price Comparison Software

By way of extending the argument as to the importance of managing a set of distribution channels (and seeing the Web as one of them), this is as good a time as any to have a look at the Internet shopper's weapon of mass destruction and the retailer's worst nightmare, the price comparison Web site.

Developed purely for the purpose of providing its user with the best possible price for a specific type of product, the price comparison Web site has become the scourge of the Internet for any type of business with lucrative margins and is as handy as a cluster bomb for the click-happy consumer. It can also act as a galvanizing tool for owners of premium brands who are—shall we say—a bit loose in terms of managing their routes to market and in danger of being caught with their hands inside the cookie jar.

Examples of price comparison Web sites include Kelkoo (which is cited in the example below) and the U.S.-based *activeshopper.com*, although there are plenty of others on the Internet that can easily be found via one of the major search engines. Regardless of which one you choose to play around with, they all have exactly the same purpose and function of scanning their active databases in order to find you the best possible deal.

By way of working through an example of just what a price comparison Web site can achieve for a consumer, let's take a look at a typical price evaluation that I ran on the Yahoo-owned Web site Kelkoo (15) for a JVC GZ-MG77 camcorder in September 2006, having first checked out said item via the online shopping facility on the Web site of the high-brow UK retailer John Lewis (16).

For the princely sum of £749 including tax, John Lewis will deliver the camcorder to your door and give you a two-year guarantee on the product, which on the surface is not a bad deal.

Figure 7.3 is an illustration of the camera's product details as displayed on the John Lewis site.

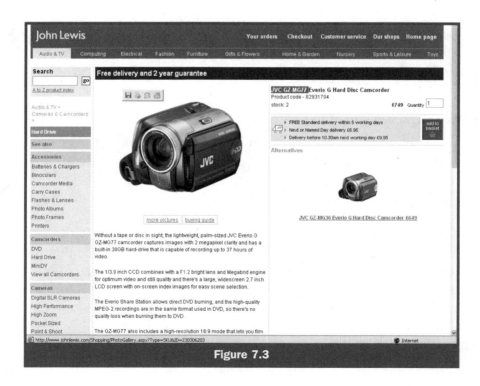

Figure 7.3

Kelkoo, on the other hand, can do much better, as when the make and model number of the camcorder are entered into the Web site's search engine, the user is confronted with a number of different e-tailers whose price points start at £489 including tax (albeit with only a twelve-month manufacturer's guarantee). Figure 7.4 is a screenshot of the Kelkoo results:

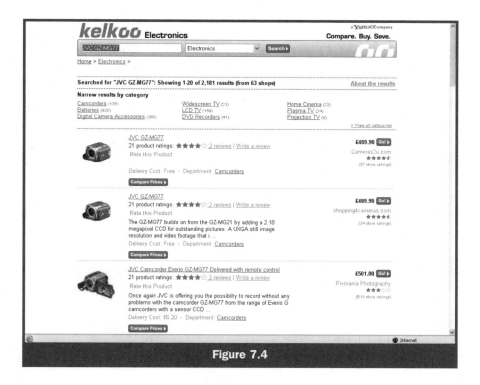

Figure 7.4

Clearly this isn't quite an apples-with-apples comparison, as there is a one-year difference in terms of the guarantees offered, and sometimes (but not always) there can also be disparity over the cost of delivery. In this case, however, the consumer simply has to ask himself whether or not he would like the security of an additional twelve months guarantee from John Lewis in exchange for a price differential of £260—hhhmmmm, I think I know the answer to that one!

Of course, there will still be cries of "foul" from those of you who are skeptical about the use of price comparison Web sites, and I am sure that you will already have several questions, such as the reputation of the e-tailer and the origin of the product. On doing your homework, however, you will doubtless discover that your concerns are ill-founded and that e-tailers such as those that are featured on Kelkoo are more than credible businesses that are very easily monitored and have either taken advantage of a simple act of arbitrage or are willing to accept a much lower margin than many of their Main Street counterparts—which is yet again testimony to the importance of managing a set of distribution channels.

For me, the absolute irony of price comparison Web sites is that they more or less fly right in the face of most arguments that luxury brand owners use for not directly selling their products on the Web—in particular, those surrounding "the purchase experience" and the perception that a brand's "target market" does not exist online. Indeed, it could easily be argued that what the advent and growth of price comparison Web sites actually says in unequivocal terms is that people have undoubtedly been sold on the brand and that they just want to get their hands on it at the best possible price—and, of course, that's a matter for the brand's owners to resolve.

As we move into the future, we should all be aware that as organizations become more efficient at managing their channels on the Web, the likelihood of uncovering such large price disparities on products that are so readily identifiable will not last indefinitely and, at some point in time, the owners of the brands in question are sure to tighten up their policies.

That argument aside, I hope that this very simple example of what can be achieved via a price comparison Web site has whetted your collective appetites for shopping on the Web and has really focused your mind on how easy it is to achieve a good price for a mass-produced item that is not bound by geography and is easily identified by its brand, make, and model number. As discussed previously, though, items that require a lot of customization require a high degree of personal contact, and I'm afraid that in the short term the Web has not yet found a way around that one. Likewise, you may prefer to visit a couple of stores to try out a specific product and actually hold it in your hands before returning to the Net with a vengeance to try and track down the best possible deal.

Cannibalization

In completing the discussion on channel management and by way of examining yet another excuse that luxury brands often use for not trading on the Web, let's have a look at cannibalization. No, this doesn't involve a scarlet-faced great white hunter squatting in a simmering pot while the surrounding, chanting natives eagerly carve up capsicums in the hope that they may be used as garnish but instead concerns the perception of having to sacrifice offline revenue in return for growing online sales.

This type of reluctance to engage in an emerging channel isn't really anything new and can quite often signify anything and everything from a cautiousness to invest to a large degree of ignorance as to the Internet's capability. Indeed, the rationale of staying away from Net-based trading for fear of losing traditional sales does tend to make one a tad suspicious about the overall strategy of the organization in question and perhaps more importantly can quite often leave the door that's marked "competitor threat" wide open to those who are quick to spot a weakness. A good example of one such scenario is Kodak's now well-documented reaction to the introduction of digital cameras.

For more than a century, Kodak was a major force in traditional photography, and its brand was an icon all over the world. It was also one of the first ever Web sites that I reviewed for brandchannel back in 2001, when I described the brand as follows:

> In 1888, George Eastman introduced his innovative KODAK Camera with the slogan, "You push the button—we do the rest" and began to develop a brand that would dominate the global photographic market for over a hundred-years. How times have changed since then, with intense competition from the Far East and Asia providing an ever present-threat to Kodak's brand security and the explosion in digital imaging ensuring that Kodak's R&D is constantly pushing the boundaries of advanced photographic technology.

Unfortunately, Kodak quite obviously didn't push its R&D buttons fast enough, as the company was somewhat slow out of the blocks when the world went technology daft. The company totally misinterpreted the surge in popularity of those newfangled digital cameras. The end result was more or less a bloodbath, with Kodak being humiliated by an incredible drop in sales of around $1.8 billion over a two-year period and its shares dropping to their lowest level in twenty years during 2003. At the time, the company's CEO, Daniel Carp, said (17):

*We are acting with the knowledge that demand for traditional prod-
ucts is declining, especially in developed markets. Given this reality,
we are moving fast—as digital markets demand—to transform our
business portfolio, with an emphasis on digital commercial markets.*

As everyone knows, hindsight is a wonderful thing, but in Kodak's
case quite a lot of grief could have easily been avoided with a little bit
of foresight, had it actually heeded the warning signs that were per-
vading the market like wildfire. Then again, maybe Kodak genuinely
recognized the threat but decided to stay away from taking an early
position in digital imaging for fear of cannibalizing its sales of traditional film!

With the benefit of the many arguments on channel management
that we have covered in this chapter still very fresh in your mind, I
would trust that you will now feel that the notion of losing sales
within a traditional set of channels as a *fait accompli* of trading on the
Web is at best a cheap way of disguising the lack of an effective online
strategy and, at worst, arrant nonsense.

These days, the Internet is hardly a new experience and one would
have thought that by now, people would realize that the design and
specification of a complementary online offering is an absolute prerequisite for growing offline sales. Conversely and just as importantly, the
degree of success that a brand enjoys offline will more often than not
determine the volume of traffic that it can subsequently attract to its
Web site, and thereby lies the opportunity.

As discussed in chapter 4 when we looked at Jennifer Rice's theory
of brands being virtual ecosystems with many interdependencies, the
relationship between the online and offline representations of a brand
can present a number of opportunities to improve its perception
within the hearts and minds of its target market. As such, the possibility of trading online should be seen as a real chance to steal a march
on the competition and drive up brand value. Indeed, with Internet
adoption rates doing nothing but growing and with sales on the Web
continuing to soar, it shouldn't take a member of MENSA to work out
the consequences for a brand that perpetually sits on the fence.

As we have discovered throughout this chapter, the real argument
revolves around the management of a company's distribution channels
and its ability to capitalize on new market opportunities as its environ-

ment evolves. The winners will be those who have a clear strategy, have thought through the implications, and have prepared for the changing times ahead. And the losers will have missed out because they have failed to take advantage of one of the most seismic changes ever to affect their industry.

Fulfillment Capability and Customer Satisfaction

Of course, not all of the reasons a business might put forward as barriers to trading online are purely conceptual. For instance, an organization may be inhibited from selling its brands on the Web as a result of not having a viable supply chain, available infrastructure, or simply because it does not possess the physical resources (such as the ready cash to invest).

As discussed in chapter 6, the capability of a business to trade its brands online is predicated upon both its channel management strategy and its fulfillment policies—even if they are managed by a third party. For instance, just consider where a clothing retailer would find itself if it decided to launch an online shop with little idea as to how it intended to manage exchanges and returns. Likewise, its lead times and cost structures for delivering product to remote locations and the subsequent effects of picking and packing small volumes of product within its warehouse or stocking locations.

Fulfilment capability is a big deal. Not just because of the physical logistical requirements that need to be evaluated before taking the plunge online but because of the consequences that the ensuing service levels will have on customer satisfaction and, of course, the brand or brands concerned. In addition, the growth curve needs to be carefully thought through, as there is no point in releasing a model today that might well fall over tomorrow at the first sign of an uplift in volume.

Take Tesco, for example, which launched its home shopping facility in 1996 and by 1999, had built up sales to around £125 million (18), which represented about 0.6 percent of total turnover. During this period, Tesco's fulfillment was managed by its retail stores which picked, packed, and delivered grocery orders to customers, as the company believed that it would not be able to achieve the economies of scale needed for a fulfillment center model until it reached volumes of around 5,000 orders per week, each with a value of at least £100. The very next year at the turn of the millennium, Tesco quadrupled its online sales and delivered 30 million items directly to the homes of its customers across the length and breadth of the UK.

Today, Tesco still picks and packs its customer orders directly from its stores and does so 150,000 times each year (19), which arguably makes it the owner of the world's biggest home delivery service. In terms of the financials, Tesco's online sales for 2005 reached £719,000,000, which, although up by 24 percent over the previous year, was still only representative of 2 percent of the company's total turnover—meaning that there should still be plenty of upside for growth in the future.

Of course, there are many other examples of the explosive growth in online shopping and indeed the challenges that organizations face as a result of trying to manage a perpetually rising trend. Amazon and eBay, for instance, are seen by many as the industry's leading lights, but that doesn't make them immune to criticism as both organizations discovered to their dismay in 2005 when each was marked down between 4 and 5 percent in the American Customer Satisfaction Index (ACSI) (20) as a result of their service performances the previous year. In their defense, retail consumers spent around $117 billion online, which was an increase of some 26 percent over 2003. Amazon, in particular, had widened its product portfolio considerably, which resulted in a significant amount of extra volume permeating through its supply chain.

In a subsequent interview for *TechWeb.com*, Claes Fornell, a University of Michigan business professor and founder of the ACSI, made his views clear in terms of where the problem with the lower customer satisfaction scores manifested itself:

> The online folks have suffered from the influx of more business, which they haven't been totally prepared to handle. It's going to become more and more challenging, to say the least. They're going to have to find the balance between adding more and more products, and maintaining the level of service that customers are used to.

Perhaps as a sign of the adaptability of both Amazon and eBay and, of course, the seriousness with which they treat the ACSI, the results for 2005 revealed that both businesses had gotten their brands back in line and had more or less recovered the ground they'd lost the previous year. Of more interest, however, was the fact that during the same period online sales grew another 23 percent to $143 billion and that, according to the ACSI, the levels of customer satisfaction achieved by e-tailers remained substantially higher than that of the national aggregate (21). Remind me again—just who it was that said that trading on the Internet would never take off?

The Winds of Change

With adoption rates increasing and connectivity on the rise, the argument for luxury brands commencing trade on the Internet has become more and more compelling. By way of adding some substance to this reasoning, let's consider an extract from a brandchannel paper that was written by Uche Okonkwo in April 2005 (22):

> *The demand for global luxury online sales is on the increase. Recent reports indicate that the wealthy are almost all online and are pleased with making online purchases. In most developed economies Internet penetration is as high as 95% and the ratio of wealthy people who have bought products worth above $250 online versus the rest of the population is 3:1.*

These numbers were endorsed in September 2006 when Christel Whelan, founder and managing partner of Catch Interactive, said in an interview with AME Info (23):

> *Internet penetration is on the rise at a high pace in most countries. In 2005, the United States' online penetration reached a whopping 69%. On a European scale, Sweden is considered the highest in Internet usage with 75% of its population online, the UK & Germany also have high online usage with 62% and 59% respectively. The demand for online luxury is on the increase. Recent reports indicate that the wealthy are almost all online. We are all quite familiar with Saks Fifth Avenue, Chanel & Louis Vuitton, but have we heard of e-luxury.com, ice.com or mondera.com? Marketers of luxury in the States & Europe have embraced these sites as part of their communication platform.*

The Cyber Boutique

As awareness of the amount of high-income consumers who actually use the Internet increases, so too has the amount of luxury brands that recognize the medium as a viable distribution channel, and, as a consequence, a number of major players have started to look for partners who can help them with life on the Web. Two such businesses that are only too pleased to be of service are *eLUXURY.com* and *Net-a-porter.com* (24), both of which were launched in June 2000 and have since claimed to be the Web's premier portals for the upper-class consumer. Despite those similarities and, of course, the superficial gloss, the underlying companies couldn't be more different.

eLUXURY, for example, is owned by LVMH (Moet Hennessy Louis Vuitton SA), which in turn is 51-percent owned by the charismatic French businessman Bernard Arnoult. According to *Forbes Magazine* (25), Arnoult was the seventh richest person in the world in March 2006, with a net worth of around $21.5 billion. Upon launching eLUXURY, Arnoult threw upwards of $150 million at the concept and gradually nurtured the business through the dot-com crash to self-sustainability. In terms of its portfolio and breadth of availability, eLUXURY predominantly sells brands that are owned by LVMH, such as Dior, Louis Vuitton, and Roberto Cavalli (although others, such as Dolce and Gabbana are sold on the site) and will only ship goods to the United States. Figure 7.5 (facing page) is a screenshot of the eLUXURY homepage as of September 2006.

Net-a-porter, on the other hand, was started in the UK by former fashion editor Natalie Massenet with only $1.3 million (26). Under her guidance and leadership, Net-a-porter also survived the dot-com crash and has since grown into a business with an annual turnover of around $50 million.

Stabling brands such as Jimmy Choo, Viktor & Rolf, and Cacharel, Net-a-porter has more than given eLUXURY an entertaining run for its money and unlike its competitor, is willing to ship its products anywhere in the world. In leveraging the power of the World Wide Web, Net-a-porter proudly proclaims on its site (27):

> *NET-A-PORTER is the first and only luxury fashion Web site to target a global market, understanding that the same brands are in demand internationally. To meet this demand, we offer you a seam-*

Figure 7.5

less, international shipping formula that allows deliveries to be made with taxes and duties pre-paid, expediting your valuable packages through international customs. So no matter where you live in the world, NET-A-PORTER is your local fashion shop With the combination of NET-A-PORTER's unique traits—the authoritative fashion editorial; a highly aesthetic and easy to use Web site; access to the world's hardest to find international labels; customer care that exceeds expectations; and a sophisticated international shipping system, NET-A-PORTER leads the online fashion pack as the world's most successful luxury global boutique and e-commerce destination.

Figure 7.6, as shown on the following page, is a screenshot of the Net-a-porter homepage, as of September 2006.

Obviously, the most striking differences between the two businesses today are that Net-a-porter has quite categorically set out its stall to appeal to a global market, whereas eLUXURY is focusing on just the U.S., and that while eLUXURY has the comfort blanket of its

Figure 7.6

own brand portfolio, Net-a-porter sees itself more as a cyber-distributor. Perhaps more of note, however, is that during the last five years both businesses have shown that it is most definitely possible to trade luxury brands on the Web and they are both now seen as role models for how it should be done.

Grasping the Nettle

Naturally, if a brand is confident enough of marketing itself on the Web, it need not feel obligated to use a third party and, instead, can retain any margin that would normally be forfeited to a distributor by hosting its own online shopping facility.

Just a few years ago, examples of such behavior from premium brands were as rare as hen's teeth, but with the increasing realization that the Web is here to stay and that luxury consumers are very much to the fore, a number of businesses have subsequently made some very noticeable changes in the way they appear on the Web.

One such example is Gucci. When I reviewed the Gucci site a few years ago for brandchannel, I was distinctly unimpressed with the company's online proposition and I wrote (28):

First impressions of Gucci's Internet offering are that it's more of a wallflower than an active participant and that the company is suffering from an attack of inertia when dealing with the potential of the World Wide Web. Quite the opposite of the clothing that's made the fashion house iconic, the homepage is drab and exudes mediocrity when it should come to the party with a strut and a swagger. The content is basic, the photographs bland and the lackluster sections seem to pervade in monotony as navigation around this limp-wristed effort becomes a whole lot more of a chore than a pleasure.

Since then, Gucci has really taken a grip of the way it portrays itself on the Net and has made good use of technology to add some depth to its site. It has also taken the bull by the horns as far as online shopping is concerned and now proudly proclaims to service the likes of the U.S., Germany, France, and the United Kingdom directly from its home in cyberspace.

Ditto Giorgio Armani, which as a very similar type of brand to Gucci has also been happy to sit on the fence in the past with regard to Internet shopping. These days, however, the company has decided to go ahead and bite the bullet, and if you happen to live in the U.S. and possess the necessary means and motivation, you can quite happily look forward to a number of Armani's products arriving on a doormat near you!

Conclusions

As you are now acutely aware, the online branding of luxury and high-value goods on the Internet has been a big issue for a number of years, and the subsequent online shopping debate has regularly raged in the background. In recent times, however, there have been some real signs that the fires are starting to recede and that has been helped in no small way by the growing recognition of the speed of Internet adoption rates and the quality of the online consumer.

Despite these facts, there are still a few brands (Rolex, Cartier, and Tag Heur) that seem determined to hold out for the longer term and continue to demonstrate an avid intransigence toward the concept of trading online. Let's hope they realize soon that no brand is an island and that if they are intent on staying away from the Web as far as online shopping is concerned, they must ensure that their traditional distribution channels are bulletproof, bombproof, and fireproof in order to avoid being left without a chair should the music suddenly stop.

I will leave the last word on Web-based shopping to the late George Eastman of Kodak, whose slogan of "Just push the button and we'll do the rest" could easily be applied to trading online—here's hoping that there aren't too many big brands who fail to heed the fate suffered by his company, when it so badly misjudged the impact of a new and emerging technology.

• • •

Key Points

The key points to remember from this chapter are as follows:

- The Internet represents a genuine distribution channel and should be managed as such.
- Online sales through Internet shops are rising at a pace that far outstrips those in the traditional Main Street.
- The luxury consumer is definitely online and possesses both the means and motivation to actively shop on the Web.
- Although more and more luxury brands now recognize the need to trade online, there are still many others who refuse to do so.

ENDNOTES

1. *http://hca.gilead.org.il/emperor.html*
2. *www.europastar.com/europastar/magazine/article_display.jsp? vnu_content_id=1002157482*
3. *http://business.scotsman.com/ebusiness.cfm?id=1277142006*
4. *http://extremefood.com/category.php?id=ds_hotsauces*
5. *www.brandchannel.com/features_effect.asp?pf_id=33*
6. *www.brandchannel.com/features_Webwatch.asp?ww_id=4*
7. *http://news.bbc.co.uk/1/hi/business/2163561.stm*

8. *http://news.com.com/A+billion+PC+users+on+the+way/2100-1003_3-5290988.html*

9. *www.c-i-a.com/pr0506.htm*

10. *http://devdata.worldbank.org/external/CPProfile.asp?PTYPE=CP&CCODE=CHN*

11. *www.platinum.matthey.com/media_room/1146661213.html*

12. *www.findarticles.com/p/articles/mi_m0EIN/is_2005_Dec_23/ai_n15968391*

13. *www.ugoplayer.com/music/inmeburberrry.html*

14. *www.kelkoo.co.uk/*

15. *www.johnlewis.com/*

16. *www.buzzle.com/editorials/9-26-2003-45888.asp*

17. *www.foresight.gov.uk/Previous_Rounds/Foresight_1999__2002/Retail_and_Consumer_Services/Reports/@Your%20Home/trends.htm*

18. *http://money.guardian.co.uk/ethicalliving/story/0,,1698649,00.html*

19. *www.techWeb.com/wire/ebiz/60401092*

20. *www.findarticles.com/p/articles/mi_m0EIN/is_2006_Feb_21/ai_n16072532*

21. *http://72.14.253.104/search?q=cache:Q4E6zAnZ6CsJ:www.brandchannel.com/images/papers/269_Lux_Goods_Online.pdf+luxury+brands+on+the+Internet&hl=en&gl=au&ct=clnk&cd=1*

22. *www.ameinfo.com/95192.html*

23. *www.eluxury.com/*

24. *www.net-a-porter.com*

25. *www.forbes.com/lists/2006/10/QD7M.html*

26. *http://domainsmagazine.com/Domains_6/Domain_1039.shtml*

27. *www.net-a-porter.com/About-Us/Our-Company*

28. *www.brandchannel.com/features_Webwatch.asp?ww_id=15*

8

It's All in the Best Possible Taste

The charity that hastens to proclaim its good deeds,
ceases to be charity, and is only pride and ostentation.
—WILLIAM HUTTON

A NUMBER OF YEARS AGO, I WROTE AN ARTICLE FOR
brandchannel that was designed to highlight the impact of poor publicity on a brand. It was also designed to highlight the associated
increase in the concept of cause-related marketing, as many organizations attempted to identify suitable countermeasures by which to
offset any unfortunate dalliances with impoverished communities, various regulating bodies, or, indeed, the global environment (1). The
article was entitled "Brands Get the Blame" and in it, I discussed such
things as the poisonous gas leak involving Union Carbide that killed
8,000 people in Bhopal, India, in 1984 and the grounding of the *Exxon
Valdez*, which in 1989 leaked more than 11 million gallons of crude oil
right along the shoreline of the Kenai peninsula.

Aside from the very public nature of these incidents and their dramatic effect on both people and the planet, I said in the article that
such cataclysmic events were rare and that recent research had sug-
gested that the true measure of an organization was how it responded
to the challenge of upholding its corporate code of ethics. To this end,
I highlighted a number of accusations of corporate malpractice relating

to such things as a company's reliance on cut-price labor, its attitude toward the global community, and its treatment of foreign employees. In citing some genuine examples, I said:

> *CBS reported in 1996 that Nike was mistreating its workers in Vietnam. The report claimed that contracted staff were subjected to a regime of both mental and physical brutality and made to work in appalling conditions in order to fulfill their daily quotas. Although the company tried to play down the story, their attempts were thwarted when the* New York Times *ran a front-page narrative concerning a leaked internal inspection document by the global accountancy firm, Ernst and Young, which found that some workers in Vietnam were working in "unsafe conditions." The document declared that tests at a factory near Ho Chi Minh City showed employees were "exposed to carcinogens that exceeded local legal standards by 177 times in parts of the plant and that 77 percent of the employees suffered from respiratory problems" (New York* Times, *November 1997).*
>
> *Another sporting brand to have suffered from accusations of poor corporate ethics is Adidas. In November 2000, the UK's* Observer *claimed that Indonesian factories supplying the company were using child labor and that workers as young as 15 were expected to work a minimum of 70 hours a week. The paper also claimed that the picture was very similar in Thailand, where one woman reported that she had to work 12-hour shifts, 7 days a week in order to get paid the equivalent of US$1.50 per day.*

In concluding the article, I made the observation (thanks to my degree in the glaringly obvious) that there was an inextricable link between a brand and its code of ethics and, of course, the ways in which it was subsequently perceived by the general public. I also noted that in their responses to the criticisms and allegations of surreptitious behavior, a number of the world's most valuable brands had gone on the offensive and that through the birth of organizations such as CERES (Coalition for Environmentally Responsible Economies), there appeared to have been a rapid change in attitude on issues such as poverty and the environment. As a result, I concluded that the concept of cause-related marketing looked set for a lengthy run.

Almost six years after writing that article, my beliefs look well founded, as the cause-related bandwagon has rolled on and on, to the extent that it is now creaking under the strain of the many organizations who would wish to evangelize their caring, sharing natures and their commitment to philanthropy. It has also evolved and developed something of a class structure, with many of the world's blue-chip multinationals moving away from the cause-related tag and evolving the concept further by embracing such ideologies as "corporate citizenship."

By now, it shouldn't surprise you to hear that the cause-related phenomenon is alive and well on the Internet with an ever increasing number of businesses and brands carrying dedicated site sections espousing such things as their social and environmental responsibilities, corporate sponsorship programs, and care for the community. Add to this the endless stream of other sites that have sprouted up to try and collect on behalf of charities and good causes and the dedicated charity-driven shopping malls such as *igive.com* and *givingmall.org*, and perhaps the general public could be forgiven for asking whether it's all become too much or whether the original charitable theme has been lost within a frantic stampede for positive PR.

By way of addressing the argument, *Promomagazine.com* ran an article in 2003 by Carrie MacMillan entitled "Cause and Effect" (2), which highlighted the concerns of an increasingly skeptical public with regard to the motives of several organizations that were actively running cause-related marketing campaigns. One of the points that MacMillan argued in her article was that instead of acting in the best interests of the causes and charities that they had aligned themselves with, many business were simply seeking to ramp up some positive publicity as a result of their associations with a worthwhile cause. In citing just one example of the decline in consumer support, MacMillan said:

While most sponsorship and cause-related tie-ins do reflect positively on the corporate partner, the boom in cause marketing has created a backlash with some consumers. Studies show that public confidence in major charities faltered over the disbursement of more than US$2 billion collected after September 11.

In developing her argument and in moving away from the corporate perspective by researching the thoughts of a number of charities regarding cause-related marketing, MacMillan made some interesting observations. Barbara Brenner, for instance, executive director of the San Francisco-based Breast Cancer Action (BCA), alleged that a number of companies had actually spent more money on advertising the fact that they were involved with a charity than they had physically given in donations. Brenner is quoted as saying:

> *There is increasing concern about cause-related marketing. We say just make a gift, write out a check and take out an ad saying you did it. Don't tie it to a product and exploit purchase decisions.*

In making her views even more public, Brenner decided to highlight her concerns to the great American public and subsequently took out a full-page advertisement within the *New York Times* in order to draw attention to businesses that she felt were questionable in terms of their motives. One such organization was American Express, which at the time was running a campaign called "Charge for the Cure," in support of the Susan G. Komen Foundation (a charity that's dedicated to the research and education of breast cancer).

Brenner's principal criticism of the American Express campaign was:

> *The [AmEx] ads say in big, bold letters that every dollar counts, but if you read the fine print you realize that you'd have to use your card 100 times to generate a dollar. We're asking people to think about these issues and to ask questions.*

So with charities such as Brenner's openly asking questions about the credence and depth of commitment displayed by some businesses and the growth in awareness of an increasingly savvy public, is the cause-related concept about to run its course? And if most of the world's consumers are indeed becoming more skeptical about the roles of charities and the ways in which funds are raised, how is this disposition being transferred to the World Wide Web?

In considering these questions and the thoughts of Barbara Brenner, we will spend this chapter looking at how the Internet is used to augment and enhance an organization's cause-related marketing strategies and how the concept has evolved. We will also try to examine the role of the "giving mall" and how businesses use such outlets in order to evangelize their support of good causes, along with some of the other methods used for raising funds.

Corporate Philanthropy and the Web

According to the most recent Interbrand survey, the world's five most valuable brands (3) are Coca-Cola, Microsoft, IBM, GE, and Intel. Let's take a look at them and evaluate what they do on their Web sites to ensure that they convey the right blend of philanthropy and philosophy to their digital customer base.

Coca-Cola

Coca-Cola is ranked number one by Interbrand and is believed to be the world's most valuable brand. Its code of ethics can be accessed via the homepage of *Coca-cola.com* and by clicking on "Select Corporate Links."

Once inside this section, visitors can access such evangelical goodness as Coca-Cola's "Commitment to Wellness" policy, which contains details on everything from information on its products, nutrition, and its support of physical activity programs. A click on the "corporate links" button also gives access to the company's "Corporate Responsibility" program, which proudly proclaims that Coca-Cola is "more than a beverage company" because it is a "corporate citizen of the world."

A screenshot of Coca-Cola's Corporate Responsibility program is illustrated in figure 8.1 and is accurate as of October 2006 (see following page).

Within the parameters of its programs, Coca-Cola has quite literally developed a mountain of material for consumers to digest and most could be forgiven for skipping the most superficial levels of this section of the site. Those who persevere, however, will be confronted by an array of different initiatives that seek to underpin Coca-Cola's assertion that it is an upstanding constituent of the world's most prominent commercial organizations.

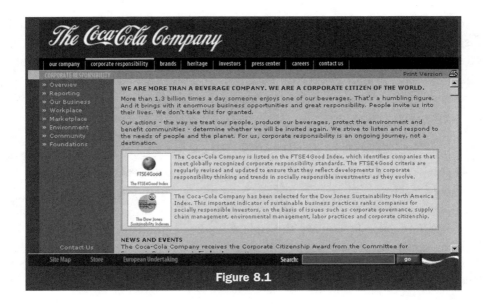

Figure 8.1

In cutting to the chase, Coca-Cola claims on its Web site that in 2005, the Coca-Cola Foundation gave $76 million (approximately 1.14 percent of sales) to community initiatives and programs all over the world, an increase of 13 percent over its level of contributions in 2004. In detailing where the money went, the company cites its active involvement in projects. Two examples are Kenya's "Watershed," which is designed to improve the provision and purification of water, and the "Little Red Schoolhouse" in the Philippines, which hopes to increase the standard of education reached by children living in rural areas.

In making such a depth of presentation and by locating it within a number of non-oppressive and discreet locations on *Coca-cola.com*, Coca-Cola's "Corporate Responsibility" and "Commitment to Wellness" policies are both indicative and representative of a modest but account-able outlook on where the business should stand in terms of meeting the level of expectation set by the global community. This perception is underpinned by the Web site's subtle use of video and imagery, which although it is actively designed to support Coca-Cola's cause-related themes, is both selective and unobtrusive in how it is portrayed. In using this approach, the company gives the impression that although it is well aware of its global obligations, it doesn't feel the need to proac-tively sell its altruism to the extent that it appears duplicitous.

Microsoft

Microsoft is ranked number two by Interbrand, and just like Coca-Cola, it keeps its corporate citizenship program away from the direct gaze of the homepage, which means that it can only be accessed by those who are either specifically looking for it or by users wishing to find out more about Microsoft as a company.

A screenshot of Microsoft's Corporate Citizenship overview as of October 2006 is illustrated in figure 8.2:

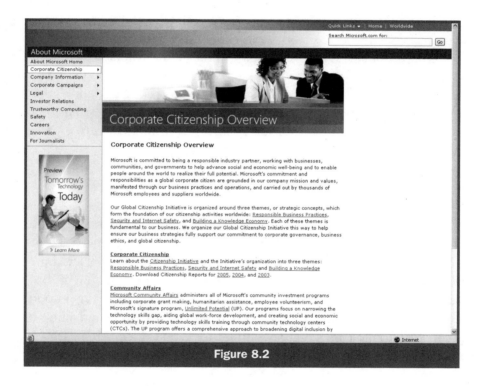

Figure 8.2

In executing a strategy that is by no means dissimilar to its Atlanta-based peer, Microsoft also appears to practice a self-effacing approach to the concept of communicating its corporate code of ethics.

In focusing on three major areas (responsible business practices, security and internet safety, and building a knowledge economy), Microsoft is striving to galvanize its businesses toward behaving both ethically and conscientiously in terms of improving its contribution to the global community. Microsoft recognizes its role in the technological revolution, but it also believes that as a global market leader it should be setting the benchmark for responsible behavior within the knowledge economy.

Aside from the above, Microsoft operates an extensive "Community Affairs Program," which is specifically aimed at improving the levels of technological awareness and increasing the amount of access to available skills and infrastructure for both non-profit organizations and underprivileged communities all around the world. In doing so, Microsoft can point to beneficiaries of its generosity in every single continent and in a host of countries that range from Vietnam to Venezuela, as well as in economies both rich and poor.

Perhaps not surprisingly, in establishing such a global network of appreciative recipients, Microsoft has assured itself of some positive PR with regard to its stance on community involvement throughout the developed world. Because it hasn't openly sought to draw attention to its endeavors, the company has also portrayed itself as sincere in its approach and driven up its brand strength accordingly.

IBM

IBM is ranked number three in Interbrand's most valuable brands list. It has revenues approaching $100 billion and employs more than 320,000 people in offices all over the world. Despite these impressive facts, however, you will be hard-pressed to find a straightforward example of IBM's cause-related marketing content when visiting the company's main portal of *IBM.com*, as the material is widespread and is hidden behind a number of very unassuming links that lie within the section titled "About IBM."

Although at first glance the subject matter may appear to be somewhat fragmented, IBM has a very good reason for adopting this approach. This is because rather than evangelize one or two initiatives that might serve as strong endorsements of the company's socially responsible culture, IBM has attempted to weave both the concept of philanthropy and its duty of care toward the global community throughout everything it touches—and as you can imagine, that's quite a lot!

The end result is a veritable library's worth of information and initiatives, as IBM goes to great lengths to convince us that it is the real deal in corporate citizenship. Indeed, regardless of whether you're looking to learn how IBM manages its global supply chain, what it does in the community, how it allocates its venture capital, or what its policy is for improving the environment, *IBM.com* provides page upon page of facts and figures and a list of global projects that run as long as your arm. By way of illustrating the sheer depth of material that is contained within the confines of IBM's cause-related Web proposition, a screenshot of just one area, "Community Relations," is illustrated in figure 8.3 and is accurate as of October 2006.

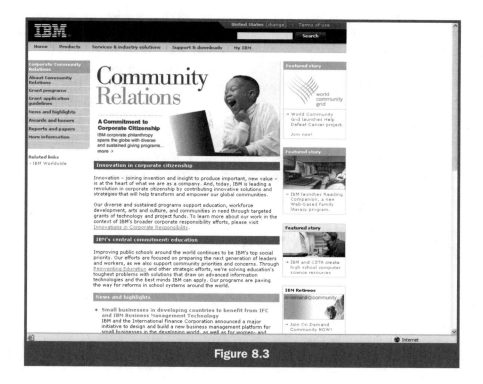

Figure 8.3

As you can see from the information contained in figure 8.3, IBM has a lot going on when it comes to contributing to the betterment of the communities in which it is involved. Notwithstanding the company's work in this area, however, it is only when one stops to consider that "Community Relations" is only one element of IBM's cause-related culture and that exactly the same depth of detail is present in such sections as corporate responsibility, global procurement, diversity and environment, that the gravity attached to IBM's commitment toward improving the lives of the people who inhabit this planet can subsequently be appreciated.

GE

GE, or General Electric, should you wish to give it its Sunday name, is ranked number four within Interbrand's most valuable brands list and is the first of our examples to include a couple of links to some of its cause-related material directly from its homepage.

Just like the previously discussed organizations, GE uses its Web site to provide potential stakeholders with a lot of information relating to company culture and, of course, its attitude toward the concept of corporate citizenship. Take the "Ecomagination" section, for instance, where GE has gone to the trouble of designing an excellent portal from which to evangelize its commitment to the environment.

Coming complete with a living, breathing message from the company's CEO, Jeff Immelt, Ecomagination is a first-rate example of blending culture, information, and of course, technology in order to enhance brand value. Aside from Immelt's introductory message, Ecomagination has a dedicated video "guide" that is constantly on hand to help Web users appreciate the merits of GE's efforts at improving the world in which we live, as well as being brim-full of traditional

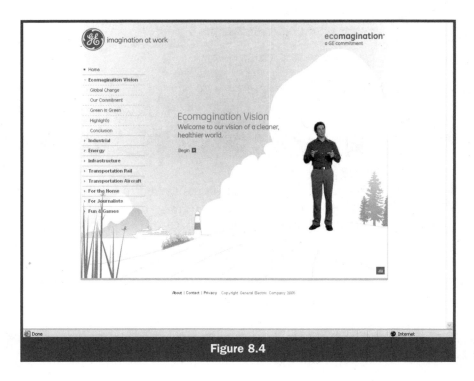

Figure 8.4

content that highlights the extent of the projects and initiatives that GE has developed in response to its environmentally friendly strategy. A screenshot of GE's Ecomagination portal, complete with its video guide, is illustrated in figure 8.4 (previous page).

In addition to its superb Ecomagination section, GE has a comprehensive section relating to its position on corporate citizenship. Beginning with a letter from Immelt and covering such sensitive issues as globalization and human rights, GE is proud to point to community donations that totaled $215 million during 2005, of which $50 million was cash and the remainder delivered by way of GE's products and services.

Intel

Ranked number five in Interbrand's most valuable brands list, Intel is a world leader in the manufacture of computer-related technology, such as chipsets, processors, and motherboards.

Intel focuses its cause-related marketing strategy on the two principal areas of corporate responsibility and community relations. Just like its predecessors on the Interbrand list, it provides a wealth of information on its Web site that gives the distinct impression that Intel's care for the global community is a theme that's interwoven into the company's corporate culture. To illustrate this point, a screenshot of Intel's Corporate Responsibility Web page taken in October 2006 is shown in figure 8.5 on the following page.

Although there are many examples of Intel's desire to improve its corporate citizenship, I would cite two of the strongest as the company's "Teach to the Future" program, which, since its launch in 2000, has trained 3 million teachers in thirty-five countries on the benefits of using technology in the classroom and the "World Ahead Program," which aims to invest $1 billion over the next five years in order to improve the levels of technological accessibility and subsequent connectivity within many of the world's poorer populations. In addition to these initiatives, Intel can point to a number of projects that are regularly undertaken by employees from around the world, as well as its "Computer Clubhouse Network," which aims to provide kids from less fortunate backgrounds with access to professional software and technology that they can use "to create computer-based projects inspired by their own ideas" (4).

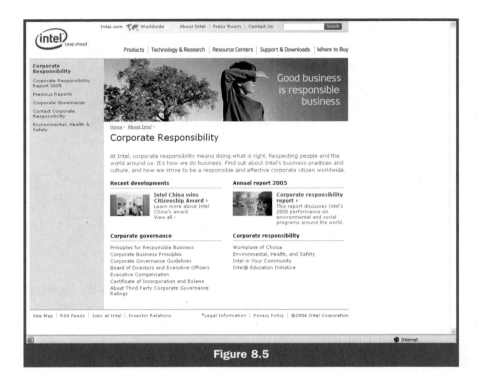

Figure 8.5

Add to all of this stuff a very well-put-together and extremely detailed policy on environmental health and safety, a series of commitments on climate and conservation, student grant schemes, research programs, and a very clear strategy on improving the level of technology that exists within the healthcare industry, and it becomes very easy to feel warm and fuzzy about Intel as a brand. But then that's the general idea, isn't it?

Conclusions and Common Denominators

When taking a step back to try and assess the synergies between the Web-based cause-related marketing strategies of Coca-Cola, Microsoft, IBM, GE, and Intel, it's easy to identify some very simple parallels.

In the first instance, it's clear from both the depth of content and the amount of time and resources that each and every business has ploughed into its positioning toward corporate citizenship that all of our involuntary respondents have made a significant commitment and contribution to the welfare of the global community. Indeed, such is the extent that they have embraced their corporate code of ethics, that they would probably take great exception to having their Web sites dissected for the purposes of some vulgar analogy concerning the concept of cause-related marketing and would most likely prefer to be seen as pioneers of corporate change. To that end, they are actively seeking to evolve each facet of their organizational cultures in order to complement those behaviors that are widely perceived as base elements for any multinational and its associated duty of care and documenting their progress on the Internet.

In addition to these observations and as a direct consequence of each organization seeking to align its culture to its corporate code of ethics, not one of the businesses we have discussed openly feels the need to evangelize either its contribution or its commitment to the planet on which we live directly from its homepage. Instead, they feel quite clearly that in order to further develop their work within the fields of corporate citizenship and community relations, they should adopt and progress a series of open-ended and holistic programs that are completely transparent and measurable, so that they can continue to evolve their work in each area.

By adopting this approach and by keeping their Web presences subtle, Coca-Cola, Microsoft, IBM, GE, and Intel are very much seen as businesses that quietly go about their task of fulfilling their roles as pillars of corporate society and that are more than happy to stand up and be counted when the day of reckoning comes. In addition, and because they have a fully integrated strategy, they are highly unlikely to be seen as quick-witted profiteers that are desperate to make a quick buck from one good cause or another. They have committed for the long term—and they are happy to be seen as such.

Charity Begins at Home

If the examples above are indicative of companies that have really got the street smarts when it comes to ensuring that their Internet behavior is absolutely reflective of their desired philanthropic cultures, what about those businesses that haven't quite reached that level of excellence as yet?

Earlier on in this chapter, I mentioned Barbara Brenner from the BCA and her passionate desire to ensure that when it comes to evangelizing the amount of work that some corporations purport to carry out on behalf of a charity or a nonprofit organization, some would do well to remember that a cause is for life, not just for Christmas. In other words, if the most plausible approach as demonstrated by our top five brands is to pick a theme and stick to it, can some companies be construed as a little bit opportunistic if they appear to latch on to a cause for just a short period of time?

In attempting to answer this question, let's take a look at BCA's pink ribbon campaign, which carries particular resonance not just because it represents the specific area of work in which Brenner is involved but also because I am writing this chapter during the month of October.

For a number of years now, autumn in the northern hemisphere has traditionally been the month when supporters of the Breast Cancer Awareness Campaign start handing out pink ribbons in the hope of raising money for one of the world's most deserving charities.

Cancer is an awful disease and is not only tragic for the many thousands of people who have been forced to endure its consequences directly but also for the friends and families of loved ones, who quite often have to carry the additional burdens of responsibility and grief while a companion or relative undergoes treatment. Because of its prevalence, almost everyone knows someone who has been affected by cancer and, to that end, many people are willingly prepared to put their hands in their pockets whenever they are asked to "give generously."

Barbara Brenner herself was a victim of breast cancer and was diagnosed with the disease when she was just forty-one years old back in 1993. Previously a partner in a San Francisco law firm, Brenner is now seen as a "tireless activist" and is a frequent campaigner on behalf of the BCA. In 1998, the BCA became "the only national breast cancer organization that expressly refuses to accept funding from pharmaceutical or cancer treatment companies, or companies that pollute the environment" (5).

While in no way decrying the work of the pink ribbon campaign, Brenner has been extremely vocal in her advice to consumers who buy branded products that are directly associated with the cause. In essence, Brenner believes that rather than blindly buying the goods consumers should always seek to question exactly what percentage or dollar value of a sale from a product that's linked to the pink ribbon campaign actually finds its way to the charity concerned. To help get her point across, Brenner and her colleagues within the BCA launched a project called "Think Before You Pink," which of course, has its very own Web site (6).

From its home in cyberspace, the Think Before You Pink project is actively able to communicate both its guidance and its counsel to anyone who may be interested in buying a product that's linked to the pink ribbon campaign. To that end, Brenner and her colleagues have painstakingly collated a substantial amount of information concerning the level of donations that the pink ribbon campaign receives and conversely, the amount of positive PR that some businesses generate by way of their association with the cause—and some of the facts and figures that the BCA has published may astound you.

Take for example, the industrial giant 3M, which is quoted on the Think Before You Pink Web site as follows:

> In a 2005 PR Week article, 3M touted that its 2004 breast cancer awareness effort, involving a 70-foot-tall ribbon made of Post-it Notes in Times Square, reached more than 3 million people and increased sales 80% over expectations. The article reports that 3M spent $500,000 on the marketing campaign (no actual numbers on profits were released), but only gave a little over half of that amount ($300,000) to the cause.

Another business that is questioned in terms of its strategy is Ralph Lauren and its associated Pink Pony brand:

> Many companies are ambiguous about the amount they donate from each purchase. For example, Ralph Lauren's Pink Pony products range in price from $10 to $598, yet the only information given to consumers is that "a portion of the proceeds from Pink Pony products benefits the Pink Pony Fund for Cancer Care and Prevention." The consumer has no way of knowing how much money from each product is actually being donated.

By way of illustrating the gravity that Ralph Lauren places on its Pink Pony campaign, a screenshot of its Web site taken in October 2006 is illustrated as follows:

Figure 8.6

In terms of trying to help consumers understand exactly how much money is being donated by each business that participates in the pink ribbon campaign, the Think Before You Pink project has published a list of organizations on its Web site along with their respective commitments under the banner "Parade of Pink."

Although the Parade of Pink has a disclaimer at the top of the page which is careful not to endorse or criticize the companies involved, it is difficult not to question the levels of generosity employed by a number of the list's constituents, or indeed the amount of publicity that some organizations are attempting to generate by way of being associated with the unassuming pink ribbon.

After all is said and done, of course, it really comes down to the consumers themselves to decide which good causes they should be supporting and how they would like to do so—and that includes the purchasing of branded goods and services. With that in mind, Barbara Brenner and her colleagues at the BCA are simply trying to educate people into making the right choices based upon the principles of informed debate and education.

Notwithstanding the above, perhaps what is most interesting is that despite the amount of activity surrounding the pink ribbon campaign during its most visible time of the year, it didn't appear once within any of the Web sites of the five most valuable brands. Obviously, this could be due to a number of different reasons, such as the possibility of initiatives taking place at a local level or the fact that the organizations concerned have simply committed themselves elsewhere. It would be fair to say, however, that whatever the rationale, there is a very marked difference between the ideologies of corporate citizenship as practiced by some of the world's most valuable brands and the basic concept of cause-related marketing and, of course, how both philosophies translate themselves on the Web. The former can be seen to be very cultural in its approach and insist upon the engagement of the entire organization, whereas the latter could quite often be construed as somewhat opportunistic if not executed with a degree of ethics and philanthropy. As a result of this dichotomy, organizations need to think and choose very carefully before embarking on the journey of improving their self-worth by helping with the betterment of all on planet Earth—and of course, before evangelizing their involvement on the Internet.

As far as the output of this argument is concerned, I guess I will leave the last word to Barbara Brenner, who, when asked whether or not some of the supporters of the pink ribbon campaign, such as companies involved in the manufacture of pharmaceuticals and cosmetics, actually contributed to the causes of breast cancer, replied by giving the somewhat encapsulating statement (7):

If you care about women's lives, you clean up your products or take the pink ribbon off them.

As far as I'm concerned, this just about says it all.

The Giving Mall

Giving malls have been around since the late 1990s and have continued to gather momentum along with both the surge in popularity of the cause-related marketing concept and the ever-increasing adoption rates of the World Wide Web.

Essentially, a giving mall is nothing more than an online portal that acts as a consolidated host for a range of different e-tailers—in essence, it's a shopping mall in cyberspace. Unlike most of its counterparts, however, the giving mall predicates much of its success on not just its ability to introduce shoppers to e-tailers but to ensure that a percentage of the proceeds from every transaction go directly to a good cause that's nominated by the shopper.

The benefits of a giving mall, as far as the e-tailer is concerned, are that it can open up a company's online trading capability to a larger target market, and at the same time generate some valuable cause-related and brand-based PR. The benefits to the shopper are that he can still buy the goods he wants while contributing to either one or a number of his favorite charities. The benefits to a cause are that once it becomes registered with a giving mall, it can instantly be enabled to tap into a wider source of revenue and evangelize its ethics to a much larger audience. The benefit to the giving mall is that more often than not it makes money by attracting more and more e-tailers by virtue of its customer base.

Like everything else on the Internet, the plausibility and longevity of giving malls can range from one extreme to another, as do the names of the parties involved. One of the longest running giving malls resides at the Web address of *iGive.com*, which, since its inception in 1997, has generated and distributed nearly $2 million to a total of 30,000 charitable causes (8).

In line with evangelizing such brand-driven partners as Barnes & Noble, eBay, and Land's End, *iGive.com* states that its mission is "to enable the economic power of individuals to benefit their chosen communities." To that end, *iGive.com* is completely transparent about its policies and its partners, which now includes more than 400 online stores and a range of donation levels per transaction of somewhere between almost nothing up to a maximum of 26 percent. The total donation to each good cause can range from just a few dollars to the kind of substantial sum that really makes a difference. For those of you hell-bent on the detail as to the machinations behind the organization, *iGive.com* explains how it works as follows (9):

When we say 12.5% or 8% or 10% to your cause next to a merchant at the Mall, each and every penny goes directly to your favorite cause. No administrative costs, no fees, nothing—100 percent to your cause. iGive.com is paid a sales commission (over and above the charitable contribution percentage) when our members make purchases, allowing us to continue to expand our services. Also, many merchants pay us to advertise on our Web site.

A screenshot of *iGive.com*'s homepage is illustrated in figure 8.7:

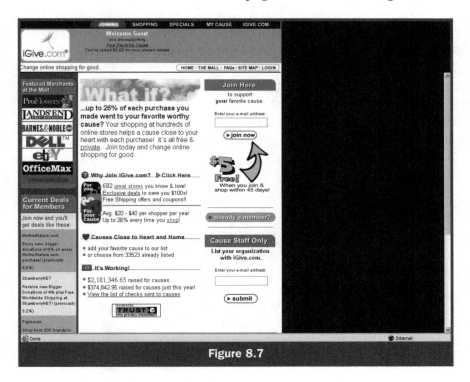

Figure 8.7

Aside from *iGive.com*, there are many more examples of giving malls on the Internet, with some of the more popular portals including *charitymall.com*, *mycause.com*, and *greatergood.com*. With that in mind, how can a brand be sure that it's aligning itself with the right one?

Unfortunately, the answer to that question is not particularly straightforward as apart from the obvious commercial implications, there is also a risk that a brand could find itself aligned with some unfortunate adverse publicity. As an example, let's have a look at PETA, which stands for "People for the Ethical Treatment of Animals" and is listed as a cause at both *iGive.com* and *mycause.com*.

Founded in 1980 and with more than a million members world-wide, PETA is the largest animal rights organization in the world and receives annual donations of close to £30 million. Stating part of its mission as being "dedicated to establishing and protecting the rights of all animals," PETA is an extremely active campaigner against the use of animals for either research or entertainment and by its own admission, takes an "uncompromising" stance.

Now, having read up to this stage in the book, it really shouldn't surprise you what's coming next—that's right, thanks to the global gateway known as the World Wide Web, PETA has an anti-site that cheerfully resides at the domain of *petakillsanimals.com* (10).

Created by the Center for Consumer Freedom (11), the owners of the PETA anti-site believe they have a duty to inform the general public as to what they feel is the "truth" behind PETA and, to that end, list a number of damning arguments on a Web page entitled "7 Things You Didn't Know about PETA" (12). These are just a sample of the points that are covered:

- PETA has euthanized more than 14,500 domestic animals at its Norfolk, Virginia, HQ in a little more than seven years and in 2005 killed 90 percent of the animals that it collected from members of the public (12).
- In 2001, PETA made a donation to a body that was certified by the FBI as a "domestic terrorist" group and has also made donations to the Animal Liberation Front (ALF)—cited by the FBI in 2002 as presenting a "serious terrorist threat" and responsible for a number of crimes within the USA (13).
- PETA has repeatedly attacked organizations such as the American Cancer Society because it supports animal-based research that may one day result in the discovery of a cure for the disease.

With this example of PETA in mind, the immediate argument that presents itself is that if a brand associates itself with a giving mall, how can it be sure that the proceeds from a transaction involving the sale of one of its products will not contribute to a cause that it may prefer not to support? The short answer to this, of course, is that it can't—just as Burberry couldn't be sure that its manufacturing and distribution of items such as checkered baseball caps would not appeal to an undesirable market segment.

No doubt the many giving malls on the Web would beg to differ, as most will not actually list a cause on their Web site until it has been authenticated. The truth is, however, that no one except for the giving malls themselves really understands the robustness of the authentication process and with some Web sites such as *mycause.com* carrying a database of more than 275,000 nonprofit organizations, there surely must be room for error.

Notwithstanding this argument, however, giving malls look like they will be around for a while, and there is certainly no shortage of readily recognizable brands and organizations that are more than happy to be associated with them. Indeed, aside from the examples of Dell, Barnes & Noble, Staples, and Land's End that can be found at *iGive.com*, the likes of Amazon, American Express, and Expedia can be found at *mycause.com*, with more of the same residing at *greatergood.com*.

With that in mind, and as with the discussion of the pink ribbon campaign, it really is up to consumers to decide what they want to do with their cash and where they want to spend it. Likewise, it is up to a brand to decide exactly what it wants to be associated with and, of course, how it should do so. The moral of the story, however, is there for all to see—thanks to the Internet, innocent consumers now have a degree of transparency over brand behavior that has been hitherto unheard of and, as a result, they may just be receiving more conduits of influence than some businesses give them credit for.

The Web's Contribution

One of the common threads within this book has been that when a new idea appears or a viable commercial opportunity is recognized, the Internet finds a way of getting itself in on the act either as a direct communications medium or as the platform for a new and emerging technology. Bearing that point in mind, we will spend the last section in this chapter taking a brief look at how the Web is being used to further the cause-related marketing concept, outside of the parameters discussed so far.

The Halo Awards

The Halo Awards are something of a spinoff from the Cause Marketing Forum (14), which was founded in 2002 "to help companies and nonprofits do well by doing good." Membership in the Cause Marketing Forum is open to businesses, individuals, and nonprofit organizations, and the annual subscriptions range from $150 to $1,000, depending on the class of membership chosen. Once on board, subscribers can look forward to anything and everything, from tele-classes and workshops to the open exchange of research information.

The Halo Awards themselves have been in existence since 2003 and are designed to enable organizations to earn recognition for their cause-related efforts in the shape of several categorized "gongs." Award winners are usually presented with their prize at a gala event (the 2006 winners received their accolades at a lunch in New York's Marriott Marquis Hotel) and in the past have included such organizations as Home Depot, Yoplait, and the Susan G. Komen Breast Cancer Foundation.

Now call me old-fashioned if you will, but what I find really strange about the concept of the Halo Awards is why on earth people would crave such recognition in the first place if they were genuinely committed to a cause for the right reasons?

Perhaps the answer is apparent on the Halo Awards homepage (15), a screenshot of which is attached in figure 8.8 on the opposite page.

So let's be clear here. "A well crafted cause marketing campaign is a thing of beauty because it can make the cash register ring for its corporate sponsor" and "move consumers to act out of a desire to do good." From these statements, then, should we take it as gospel that acting out of a sense of responsibility toward the global community and the environment as a result of recognizing the roles that for-profit organizations play within the social spectrum and subsequently choosing not to crow about it wouldn't qualify a company for a Halo Award? Well, bang go the chances of the five major brands that we covered earlier in this chapter—although I don't suppose they'll lose much sleep over it!

Now, please don't misunderstand me here, as I'm not saying that there's no place for such concepts as the Halo Awards. On the contrary, I personally would like to see the tireless work carried out by many companies and organizations, both for-profit and nonprofit,

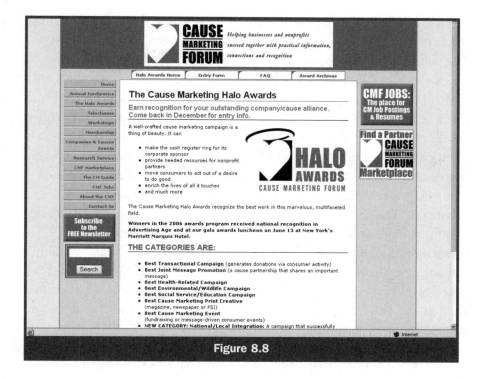

Figure 8.8

recognized wherever possible. That said, I would also like to see such businesses recognized for all the right reasons and not just because they were motivated by the desire for cold, hard cash.

Personally, I feel that the statements made by the Cause Marketing Forum encapsulate the differences between cause-related marketing and corporate citizenship entirely, in that while one can be seen as cultural, behavioral, and as having a positive influence on overall brand value, while the other could easily be construed as opportunistic, cynical, and exploitative—and I will leave it with you to define which one is which!

Web-Based Applications

As more and more businesses start to get serious about the concept of philanthropy, so do their programs and initiatives. With such a wide range of available options, it should come as no surprise that some companies struggle to fully integrate their programs within the overall fabric of the organization.

Although there are several ways of addressing this issue, galvanizing the power of the World Wide Web has become an increasingly attractive solution because of its depth and breadth of fluidity and, of course, its flexibility. This is where organizations such as 4charity systems (16) come in:

The concept that was to become 4charity systems was originally developed by a group of Stanford University students who, in the spring of 1998, built a Web site that enabled their colleagues and classmates to buy books from *Amazon.com* while simultaneously contributing a percentage of the purchase price toward the Special Olympics. The idea subsequently turned itself into a for-profit organization in 1999 and in 2004 was acquired by the Inovaware Corporation. Today, 4charity systems is actively involved in "making philanthropy easy" and specializes in the field of enabling Internet-based applications to "automate a company's philanthropic programs," such as the collection of donations, the reconciliation of accounts, and the authentication of nonprofit organizations.

A nonprofit organization that's not too dissimilar to 4charity systems is MissionFish (17), which is a service of the Points of Light Foundation (18)—a large-scale network of volunteers who "help to solve serious social problems in thousands of communities."

Specializing in the field of "creating innovative technology-based solutions that help nonprofits find new, efficient sources of unrestricted funding," (19) MissionFish provides the software for eBay's "Giving Works" program. As a result of its partnership with MissionFish, eBay has given the opportunity for the millions of people who sell items on its Web site each day to donate to their favorite cause on a "per transaction" basis. In turn, MissionFish authenticates each cause before listing it on its database and then provides the seller with a receipt for his donation after each auction has closed.

Per-Click Donations

These types of Web sites are interesting affairs and simply involve the user clicking on a button in order to trigger a donation from the sponsor. For instance, visitors to *thehungersite.com* (20) can help donate cups of food just by clicking on a button that takes them to a page full of advertisements. The Hunger Site also publishes its level of donations and states that, in 2005, its respondents funded more than 2,500 tons of staple food that was subsequently delivered to the starving.

Before you get too carried away with the results, however, and start hurriedly clicking away for the benefit of all mankind, it is worth bearing in mind that the Hunger Site is an offshoot of *CharityUSA.com*—a for-profit organization that also owns and operates the similar domains of *thebreastcancersite.com*, *theanimalrescuesite.com*, and the *childlhealthsite.com*.

Another Web site with a big perspective on charity is that of the Internet search engine, *Everyclick.com* (21). Launched in 2005, Everyclick states that it will donate 50 percent of its gross revenue to charity, meaning that users of its service can raise money for a cause without it costing them a penny. As of October 2006, Everyclick estimated that up to 20,000 people were using its service each day and that they were raising upward of £1,000 in the process (22).

Direct Donations

Another, and perhaps more traditional, way of using the Internet to contribute to a good cause is simply to make an online donation either directly to the charity concerned by way of using its Web site or through a third party. Examples of organizations that allow for online donations include the UK's National Society for the Prevention of Cruelty to Children (NSPCC), Cancer Research UK (23), and the U.S.-based National Breast Cancer Foundation (24). Examples of organizations that will process donations to charities free of charge include the Alliance and Leicester Bank (25) and *justgive.org* (26), which is a nonprofit U.S.-based portal that can facilitate online donations for up to 1,000 listed charities.

In terms of assessing the Internet's ability to raise money directly for good causes, it is estimated that more than $20 million was raised online in little more than a week following the Asian tsunami disaster over Christmas 2004 (27).

• • •

Key Points

The key points to remember from this chapter are as follows:

- Larger brands and organizations have evolved the cause-related marketing concept into that of corporate citizenship and attempted to build the ideology into their organizational cultures while documenting their progress on the Web.
- If a cause-related marketing strategy is poorly conceived, inadequately communicated, or ineffectively implemented, it can have a negative effect on the brand that it was originally designed to enhance. Given the amount of readily available information that exists on the Web, organizations should think through their strategies carefully before embarking on a cause-related path.
- Giving malls have surged in popularity and are often used by major brands and e-tailers as an Internet distribution channel—some are better than others, however, and great care should be taken before a partner is selected.
- The Internet has spawned many potential nonprofit and for-profit partners that can assist major brands and organizations in the development of their cause-related marketing strategies. The Web can also be used to manage key processes and transactions on behalf of a philanthropic program, either within or outside of the host organization.

ENDNOTES

1. http://brandchannel.com/features_effect.asp?pf_id=43
2. http://promomagazine.com/othertactics/marketing_cause_effect/
3. http://www.intel.com/education/icc/
4. www.bcaction.org/Pages/LearnAboutUs/AbouttheStaff.html
5. www.finfacts.com/brands.htm
6. www.thinkbeforeyoupink.org/
7. www.montrealmirror.com/2004/092304/front.html
8. www.prwatch.org/node/4965
9. www.igive.com/html/faqs2.cfm
10. http://petakillsanimals.com/petaKillsAnimals.cfm
11. www.consumerfreedom.com/
12. http://petakillsanimals.com/article_detail.cfm?article=134

13. *www.fbi.gov/congress/congress02/jarboe021202.htm*
14. *www.causemarketingforum.com/default.asp*
15. *www.causemarketingforum.com/page.asp?ID=79*
16. *www.4charity.com*
17. *www.pointsoflight.org/about/mediacenter/releases/2006/08-10.cfm*
18. *www.missionfish.org*
19. *www.pointsoflight.org/*
20. *www.thehungersite.com*
21. *www.everyclick.com/*
22. *www.fundraising.co.uk/blogs/newswire/2006/10/02/everyclickcom-challenges-Internet-users-to-change-the-way-they-search-during-national-giving-week/*
23. *www.nspcc.org.uk/*
24. *www.cancerresearchuk.org/*
25. *www.nationalbreastcancer.org/*
26. *www.billpayment.co.uk/charitypay/home.asp*
27. *www.justgive.org/index.html*
28. *www.banktech.com/showArticle.jhtml?articleID=56900373*

9

The Emotionally Intelligent Web Site

There is always something ridiculous about the emotions
of people whom one has ceased to love.
—OSCAR WILDE

SO HERE WE ARE AT THE VERY LAST CHAPTER OF THE
book—and it's here that we will attempt to pull together everything
that we have learned so far in order to try and identify just exactly
what constitutes a perfectly branded Web site. Before doing so, however, let's just have a quick recap of what we have covered and see
where it all fits in:

In chapter 1, we talked about the stuff that makes the Internet
work and focused in particular on the areas of domain names and
search engines. In chapter 2, we started looking at color schemes and
page designs and how they immediately start stimulating a series of
emotional responses as our brains begin to decode the information.
Chapter 3 covered the bare basics of the homepage as far as content
was concerned, such as links to the About Us, Products and Services,
and Contact Us sections, and in chapter 4 we covered segmentation
and positioning. After that, in chapter 5 we discussed promotional
techniques before talking in chapter 6 about the ways in which technology has enhanced the levels of functionality that we currently see
on the Web. In chapter 7, we hosted the luxury brand debate and the

concept of online shopping, and in chapter 8 we talked about cause-related marketing and how it is often portrayed and perceived on the Internet today.

In this chapter, I'm going to focus on the concept of emotional response. In doing so, I will try and convince you that as time moves on, the more successful branded Web sites will be those that maximize their emotional returns against all of the key criteria that we have discussed within this book. In getting started, I have attempted to separate the key points from each chapter and have listed the main concepts and attributes that a Web site can be measured against, complete with some questions regarding the types of emotional responses that may be generated, in table 9.1 as shown on the opposite page.

By looking at some of the main concepts and attributes that we have covered so far within this book in tabular form, and in asking just a few simple questions in terms of how that information may be perceived by a user when surfing a branded Web site, it should now be relatively easy to see that there is an inextricable link between the site itself and the emotional responses that it invokes within the mind of the user. By way of assimilating this perspective, just cast your mind back to some of the good and bad Web sites that you have visited on the Internet and ask yourself how they made you feel. Was your experience with them satisfying, were you impressed and did you find exactly what you were looking for, or were you constantly lost and frustrated by a perpetual feeling of incongruity?

Because I passionately believe that there is such a direct link between a branded Web site and the emotions that it generates within the mind of a user, I feel that there is a huge opportunity for development in that area. To that end, I would like to share my prediction with you that as we move into the future, more and more corporately branded Web sites will be engineered and developed with the goal of becoming emotionally intelligent and that, just like the brands they represent, they will be built with their own type of unique DNA. In other words, not only will they be capable of augmenting and reflecting a user's emotional triggers in line with a proprietary brand, but they will also be capable of tuning themselves to an individual's emotional preferences to such an extent that stimulating those positive triggers will be almost second nature.

TABLE 9.1		
Concept	Attributes	Emotional response?
Location	Choice of domain name, search engine visibility	Was the Web site easy or difficult to find?
Design	First impressions and brand recognition, color scheme, linearity of design, prospects for navigation	Are the first impressions good or bad/in keeping with the brand or not?
Basic communication, content, and material	About Us, Contact Us, Products and Services, Company History	Is the Web site immediately informative and communicative or vague and ambiguous?
Segmentation and positioning	Type or types of segmentation— country/department/product/ taste, appropriate positioning, depth and breadth of connec- tivity, reflective of the brand	Does the Web site cater to the right audience; is it targeting the right markets; is it clear in terms of approach and reflective of the brand or brands it represents?
Promotion	Value-added content—free downloads, clubs and commun- ities, online vouchers and coupons, interactive content	Does the Web site encourage and retain traffic flow by pro- viding engaging and value-added material?
Functionality	Account access, information exchange, engage with products/ services links to ERP platform	Can the user interactively engage with the site to carry out basic tasks in keeping with the brand?
Online shopping	Direct or indirect through a cyber-distributor—depth and breadth of product availability	Can the user buy the brand's products on the Internet?
Corporate citizenship	Cause-related or citizenship driven—opportunistic or cultural	Does the Web site convey the right sense of philanthropy and enhance its brand as a result?

Now let's just reflect on that for a while. Is it really possible to build and develop a Web site that can influence the emotions of users to such an extent that they constantly feel good about both it and the brand it represents? Well, I believe it is—and I also believe that several companies have started to make it happen already.

If this sounds like a crazy idea to you then just stop and think about some of the customization that you have already encountered on the Web and one or two of the better sites that we have discussed within this book. Aside from establishing the right type of cultural feel and developing an intuitive model for navigation, a site like Amazon can automatically hit you with some favorable genres of literature and music whenever you start browsing its catalogue. In addition, it can make recommendations to you that are based on your previous purchases and navigational behavior. L'Oreal enables its online visitors to customize their experience based on whether they're consumers, scientists, journalists, or job seekers and modifies its content accordingly. Add to this some of the other Web-enabled functionality, such as cookies that facilitate your instant recognition whenever you log on to a Web page, and the various selections and check boxes that exist when setting up your user preferences or account details on a site that you may use for banking or paying utility bills and you don't have to be a nuclear physicist to see where it's all going. The journey toward brand customization in cyberspace is already well advanced, and the key to it all is artificial emotional intelligence—a unique environment where a Web site can both stimulate and react to your preferences based on your online behavior.

So in accepting that it might just be possible to build an emotionally intelligent Web site and that some companies are already well down the track in that regard by way of developing their Web propositions, let's now take a look at the concept of emotional intelligence itself before exploring just a few of the forms it can take when applied to the Internet.

What Is Emotional Intelligence?

Like any other ideology, there is no shortage of theories and definitions as to what emotional intelligence actually does and does not constitute. For the purposes of this book, however, I have detailed just a few of the more applicable explanations as follows.

Professors Victor Dulewicz and Malcolm Higgs (1)—"Achieving one's goals through the ability to manage one's own feelings and emotions, to be sensitive to, and influence, other key people, and to balance one's motives and drives with conscientious and ethical behavior."

Robert Cooper and Ayman Sawaf (2)—"Emotional intelligence requires that we learn to acknowledge and understand feelings—in ourselves and others—and that we appropriately respond to them, effectively applying the information and energy of emotions in our daily life and work."

Wikipedia.org (3)—"Emotional Intelligence, also called EI and often measured as an Emotional Intelligence Quotient or EQ, describes an ability, capacity, or skill to perceive, assess, and manage the emotions of one's self, of others, and of groups. However, being a relatively new area, the definition of emotional intelligence is still in a state of flux."

So there you have it, emotional intelligence (or EI as I will refer to it hereafter) is essentially being able to demonstrate an empathetic sense of emotional awareness both in ourselves and others in order to gain influence over an environment, a person, or a situation—preferably in an ethical way. (So that rules out most of the fun at the office Christmas party!)

All joking aside, it should be pretty obvious that possessing the ability to practice EI effectively can open up many possibilities for those who invest the time and effort. For example, how many times have you heard someone described as "letting their heart rule their head" or found yourself in a position where you decided to dig your heels in during an argument, even though you knew it made no rational sense? Imagine, therefore, how successful you could be in life if you could pragmatically control your own emotions and influence those of other people. Imagine how persuasive and compelling you could be—and imagine how mesmeric a branded Web site could be if it were designed to achieve the same thing.

Because EI is such a relatively new concept, it is still the subject of much debate and in many ways, the arguments that revolve around it are not too dissimilar from those that center on the best ways in which to segment a market (which we talked about briefly in chapter 4).

For instance, some of the skeptics with regard to EI, who believe that it is no real substitute for absolute intelligence, prefer to advocate the purely transactional methods of measuring brain power that are mainly used to quantify IQ. Others, however, believe that the levels of cerebral activity that are associated with a range of human emotions are simply too big to ignore and that their ability to influence the decision-making process should never be discounted. With this in mind, therefore, to arbitrarily rule out the concept of EI and its potential value to digital branding on the basis that it sounds irrational would probably be irrational in itself—particularly given the psychological lengths to which most brand strategies go in order to leave a marked impression on our minds.

By way of encapsulating the argument for the concept of EI as compared with IQ or when simply comparing the power of intelligence with the power of emotion, I would like to refer to a quote by Dr. Daniel Goleman, who said (4):

Intelligence comes to nothing when the emotions hold sway; passions overcome reason time and again.

Dr. Goleman is seen as one of the leading lights with regard to EI. In his 1996 book *Emotional Intelligence—Why It Can Matter More than IQ*, he argued that "our emotions play a much greater role in thought, decision making and individual success than is commonly acknowledged (5)."

Goleman also believes that there are five clear emotional competencies, which are listed as follows:

1. *The ability to identify and name one's emotional states and to understand the link between emotions, thought and action.*
2. *The capacity to manage one's emotional states—to control emotions or to shift undesirable emotional states to more adequate ones.*
3. *The ability to enter into emotional states (at will) associated with a drive to achieve and be successful.*
4. *The capacity to read, be sensitive to, and influence other people's emotions.*
5. *The ability to enter and sustain satisfactory interpersonal relationships.*

So if Dr. Goleman is right and our emotions do actually play a much greater role in the process of decision making than most people give them credit for, just imagine the potential for improving brand value on the Web if emotions could be first established and then subsequently controlled and influenced online.

Having put forward the case for the concept of EI, one of the key arguments with regard to its sustainability is whether or not it is a skill that can be learned and extended or whether it has a finite capacity. There is also significant debate around whether or not it can be measured—for example, by way of a mechanism that will return an EQ (emotional intelligence quotient) that can subsequently be improved upon. Because of these issues, EI is not without its critics and it is important to bear that in mind. Nevertheless, I believe it has significant credence and I foresee a great future for businesses that can apply it to positive effect on the Web.

Despite its potential drawbacks, EI is gaining more and more credibility within the corporate sector and there is no shortage of success stories doing the rounds regarding organizations that have adopted the ideology in one way or another. Take L'Oreal, for example, which claims to have enjoyed a dramatic improvement in sales as a result of switching its recruitment strategy from that of a modern conformist position to that of a business placing greater importance on the emotional qualities of applicants (6).

Likewise, Dr. Cary Cherniss, a specialist in the field of EI, details nineteen examples (including that of L'Oreal) of how applying EI can bump up a company's bottom line on the Web site of the EI Consortium (7)—a body whose mission is to "aid the advancement of research and practice related to emotional intelligence in organizations."

So as the adoption of EI gathers speed within the corporate sector, is it really irrational to make the assumption that one day we might just see an emotionally intelligent Web site? Certainly not in my view—and here is why I think that way.

EI and the Branded Web Site

Throughout the pages of this book, I have continually harped about the importance of a Web site's ability to connect with people on a number of different emotional levels—and to do so very quickly. My reasons for this are that I absolutely believe that if a Web site can establish a set of emotional states that are truly reflective of the qualities that are found within a particular brand, it can also subsequently influence those emotions to reach a desired outcome—and just imagine how powerful a Web proposition like that could be.

By way of underpinning this theory as well as my belief that Web sites could, at some point in the future, be constructed to reflect a number of the characteristics associated with the concept of EI, I asked Dr. Goleman whether he felt that it was possible to create an online branded environment that could simulate the facets associated with the theory. In his reply, he said that:

It makes sense that a Web site could map key traits of emotional intelligence, particularly in its responsivity to users.

To that end, let's revisit Dr. Goleman's five emotional competencies and see whether it really is possible to apply them in cyberspace:

1. *The ability to identify and name one's emotional states and to understand the link between emotions, thought, and action*—In terms of a branded Web site, it is actually quite easy to identify it with an emotional state based squarely upon the elements that I have listed in this book. For example, when you are browsing a Web site, does it appear uplifting or is it rather depressing? Are its colors loud and brash or subtle and conservative? Is it full of technological wizardry, or is it predominantly one-dimensional? Is it in line with your preconceived impressions of a brand, or is it way out of line?

Given the flexibility that exists around Web site design and, of course, the facility to change and update both content and material more or less in perpetuity, there is absolutely no reason why a Web site can't start to identify with a range of emotional states. Indeed, because it is also possible to tailor individual sections of a Web site to suit a particular audience (for instance, kids' sections, press and media, consumers, or distributors), it is conceivable that a Web site can represent more than one emotional state at any given time—depending upon the navigational behavior of the user.

2. *The capacity to manage one's emotional states—to control emotions or to shift undesirable emotional states to more adequate ones*—While on the surface of it, this may appear somewhat difficult for a Web site to achieve it is possible for a Web site to enter into either an appropriate or inappropriate emotional state based on its primary and secondary content. For example, no doubt many of you will recall the example of Tommy Hilfiger in chapter 3 and his associated vehement denials of impropriety when accused of making racial slurs. What impression did that leave you with?

As another example, consider how many times you have picked up a newspaper and reacted either positively or negatively to a headline based upon your own perception. After 9/11, for instance, the image of the "Falling Man" (8) invoked a myriad of emotions all around the globe—both positive and negative. Can you remember what yours were and what would your thoughts be if you saw the image on a Web site?

The importance of content and material are critical in terms of establishing the emotional state of a branded Web site because although in most cases they are secondary to the color scheme and layout, they are only just so. In other words, if the initial impression of a site is favorable, a user is likely to take time to browse, which means that the site has been given some additional opportunities to influence the mind of a visitor. If first impressions are unfavorable, however, it's likely that the user will just be another statistic.

3. *The ability to enter into emotional states (at will) associated with a drive to achieve and be successful*—This particular emotional competency is interesting because to make it live and breathe on the Internet, a Web site must demonstrate the ability to interact with the user in such a way that it can tailor its content and material accordingly. To that end, more and more Web sites are now being developed with Java-based technology within the primary viewing area, which changes its content every few seconds until a user sees something he's interested in and subsequently reacts. Examples of such material could be the sequential presentation of a number of environmental variables like major news events, seasonality, industry-related occurrences (such as changes in legislation or market price movements), a selection of products and services, and organizational news flow.

By presenting its users with a range of choices such as those above, a Web site can then direct any given person to the specific site area to which it feels he is best suited—then it can really go to work on building credibility.

4. *The capacity to read, be sensitive to, and influence other people's emotions*—Provided that a Web site has managed to get its act together with points 1, 2, and 3 and is both sensitive and interactive to the ways in which a user chooses to navigate, there is no real reason why this emotional competency cannot be achieved on the Web. As mentioned previously in this chapter, for example, Amazon is already more than capable of providing its users with purchase recommendations based on past history and navigational behavior, so why can't more Web sites behave in a similar way? Is it really inconceivable, for instance, to anticipate that audio greetings complete with individual advertisements that state a person's name are too far over the horizon, given the technology we saw during Budweiser's "Giving Lip" campaign?

Furthermore, why not augment the material and enhance the user experience with things like streaming video, the facility to order some samples of products, improved levels of functionality, or the opportunity to engage with a brand's corporate citizenship program? All of these things can influence emotions and if done correctly, could result in an exponential rise in brand value provided the user leaves the Web site feeling uplifted and fulfilled.

5. *The ability to enter and sustain satisfactory interpersonal relationships*—This is probably my favorite of all of Dr. Goleman's emotional competencies because its success is predicated on the credibility of the previous four points. Indeed, if the previous emotional competencies are satisfied, there is a very good chance that users will return to a Web site again and again, drawn both out of loyalty and the desire to continually interact with the content and material on show.

In this regard, the advent of online clubs and communities has proven to be just one way of ensuring that users return to a Web site repeatedly. Add to that some of the other engaging and interactive content that we have discussed within this book and couple it with some compelling material and the bonds that can be associated with a brand in the middle of cyberspace will become stronger with each passing day.

The Web Site Emotional Intelligence Model

Having just spent some time reviewing the potential for Web sites to behave in an emotionally intelligent way, based on such things as their layout, content, material, presentation, and functionality, let's now run through an exercise to see whether it's all making sense.

I now want you to start drawing together everything that we have discussed so far within the framework of information that was presented within table 9.1 and then start applying it to a very simple model, after first reading through some guidelines

The purpose of this exercise is to try to ascertain how good, bad, or indifferent a particular Web site has been in terms of managing and influencing your emotions. The better Web sites tend to strike a very strong set of emotional chords within the minds of users who visit them. They portray the right culture and increase a brand's value by providing a range of uplifting, engaging, and informative connections with a brand that cannot be replicated on a single platform elsewhere.

The poorer Web sites, on the other hand, erode brand value by being nothing more than banal representations of what a brand should stand for, with second-rate content and inadequate designs.

Although there are no hard-and-fast rules as to how you complete this model, you do need to bear in mind that it's all about *your* perception—and after all, why shouldn't it be? You are entitled to your own point of view, so get ready to express it!

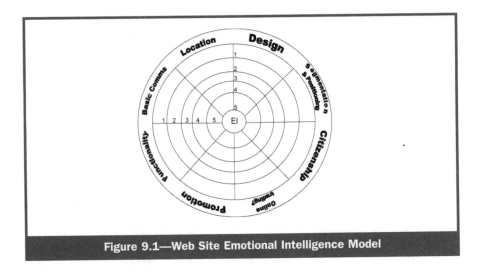

Figure 9.1—Web Site Emotional Intelligence Model

In terms of completing the model, all I want you to do is simply start looking at a branded Web site (and you may even want to start with one of the Web sites that I have talked about in this book). Then, using the knowledge that you have gained, start scoring it according to both the criteria within the model itself and the extent that you feel that Web site emotionally connects with you.

For example, if you think a Web site was very easy to find because it ranks highly on a search engine's response list, uses its brand name as a domain, and is frequently evangelized within an organization's traditional marketing methods, you may want to score it with a 4 or a 5 under the heading "Location." Similarly, if you were immediately engaged by the homepage because the layout was easy to follow, and the color schemes and images were absolutely in tune with the brand and triggered some associated recall, you may want to score it highly under "Design."

Conversely, if you were not particularly impressed with the immediate messages of the site, it failed to give you enough basic information, or it left you feeling unfulfilled, you will probably score it as a 1 or a 2 under the heading of "Basic Comms." Likewise, if you felt that the site didn't make good use of the Web's available technology and that it failed to deliver an engaging and interactive experience from a functional perspective, you will probably give it a low score under the heading of "Functionality."

Once you get the hang of it, just continue working through all of the headings as you surf the site in question and either refer to the information within table 9.1 or within the relevant chapters of this book if you suddenly find yourself devoid of ideas. Don't worry too much about the section titled "Online Trading" either, as not all of the Web sites you'll look at will need to have that facility attached to them—of course, if a particular Web site doesn't and you feel that it should, you will probably want to score it accordingly!

When you have finished reviewing your site and settled on your final score (and feel free to spend either as much or as little time on this as you like—although it will probably be your first impressions that set the tone), just take a step back and ponder the results for a minute or two.

All things being equal, you should see some sort of synergy between the emotional perception that you had of the Web site you were looking at and the way you have scored it on the model. Obviously, the closer all of the points are on the model to the bull's-eye marked "EI," the more (artificially) emotionally intelligent the Web site is, the better it has managed your emotions, and the more favorable your perception will be. Conversely, the further your scoring is away from the bull's-eye, the stronger the likelihood that your brush with the site will not be a particularly memorable one.

In extending this debate a little (and for those of you who might not have either the time or the inclination to review a site yourself), I have used the Web site Emotional Intelligence Model to score the online offerings of both Nabisco and L'Oreal in figures 9.2 and 9.3, respectively.

As you can see (and I am sure this comes as no surprise), my opinion of Nabisco's Web proposition is less than favorable in almost every department, primarily because with the exception of its domain name (which can still be a bit confusing due to its referral as *Nabisco.com* and *Nabiscoworld.com*), I have almost no idea as to just exactly what it is that Nabisco is trying to achieve on the Web. Indeed, from the very first click I found its messages confusing, its layout well below average, and its commitment to corporate citizenship completely nonexistent. Indeed, had it not been for the vast selection of online games that Nabisco has to offer (hence the scores in promotion and functionality), the Web site could well have been a whitewash. That said, how would you score Nabisco and how would you rate its level of EI? Did it strike the right chords with you—or would you agree with my observations?

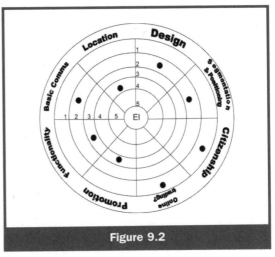

Figure 9.2

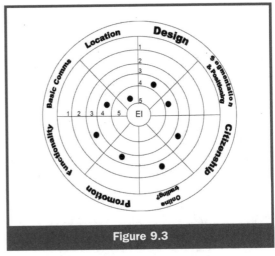

Figure 9.3

Moving on from the example of Nabisco, let's now take a look at *L'Oreal.com*, which is an altogether much more sophisticated and empathetic affair.

As you can see from the illustration in figure 9.3, I scored L'Oreal very highly with regard to its design, location, basic communication, and segmentation and positioning. Notwithstanding those points, however, and despite the Web site's impressive array of imagery, I still feel that it could have done a bit more with the Web's functionality in terms of online promotion and it would also have been nice to have direct access to an online shopping facility. But given that L'Oreal can easily be classed as a luxury brand, perhaps this is no big surprise.

What are your thoughts on *L'Oreal.com*, and how would you score its Web site? Would it be similar to my appraisal or would it be completely different?

By far the most important thing to remember when looking at the examples of Nabisco and L'Oreal is that as far as I (as a consumer) am concerned, perception is reality and as such, it will now take a great deal of time for me to change my opinions of the two brands in question. On the one hand, I see L'Oreal as a progressive and dynamic organization that is clear about what it stands for and is completely in touch with its public—Nabisco, on the other hand, I see as something different.

Hopefully, this little cameo and the use of a somewhat rudimentary model has helped crystallize in your minds the importance and potential of using a Web site to generate a predetermined emotional response. The difference between the examples of Nabisco and L'Oreal online are substantial, and emotionally this should also be reflected in your opinions of the brands.

The Emotional Impact of a Branded Web Site

At this stage, it is probably prudent to stress that my belief that branded Web sites should be graded and measured in terms of their perceived level of artificial emotional intelligence could well be seen as a rebellious break from protocol, as historically most Web sites have mainly been judged by slightly more tangible means.

For example, around the turn of the millennium, Forrester Research, quite probably the primary source of most people's information when it comes to technological statistics and Web-based innovation, released the results of a study that related to the "Factors Driving Repeat Visits to Web Sites." The results of the Forrester study can be found on the Internet with very little effort—indeed, the digital branding consultancy Imirage even has them published within the confines of its site (9). For those without immediate Web access, however, I will list them as follows in table 9.2:

TABLE 9.2 FACTORS DRIVING REPEAT VISITS TO WEB SITES			
High Quality of Content	75%	Cutting-Edge Technology	12%
Ease of Use	66%	Games	12%
Quick to Download	58%	Purchasing Capability	11%
Updated Frequently	54%	Customizable Content	10%
Coupons and Incentives	14%	Chat and Bulletin Boards	10%
Favorite Brands	13%	Other	4%

Source: Forrester Research

From the results of the Forrester study, it could be argued that it is quite easy to discount my theory of branded Web sites evolving into artificially intelligent portals due to the low scores attributed to "Customizable Content" and "Chat and BBS."

Before doing so, however, I would urge you to think of a number of the arguments that we have discussed within this book and, in particular, the phenomenal growth in Internet adoption rates that has taken place within the last few years, the increasing availability of the Web to an international audience, the surge in online shopping, and the dramatic increase in popularity of Internet-based communities. Put all of that together with the highest scoring factors in the Forrester study, such as "High Quality of Content" (which could easily be substituted for such things as positioning and promotion) and "Ease of Use" (which can once again be substituted for design or functionality) and I think that you'll agree that times have moved on.

Indeed, in my opinion it is this dynamic fluidity that gives the Web its greatest appeal as there is no other single branding platform like it in the world. Gone are the days when the Internet was simply a hangout for techies and Net-nerds with nothing better to do—and gone, too, are the days of the one-dimensional online proposition that simply acted as a single-page flyer. Today, the Web is host to a multinational and multicultural community, and it is more vibrant and interactive than at any time before. Its possibilities are now quite literally endless, as are its abilities to influence a range of human emotions in little more than the blink of an eye.

In support of this view, you will no doubt recall the results of the study carried out by Gitte Lindgaard that we discussed in chapter 2 and her belief that users begin to form impressions of a Web site's visual appeal within 50 milliseconds (1/20th of a second) of logging on.

In a subsequent interview with *Websiteoptimization.com,* Lindgaard's study was discussed in terms of how it initiated the process of what is commonly known as the "Halo Effect" and how the minds of Web users subsequently became shaped by their immediate emotional response and not by cognitive thought (10):

> *The speed at which users form value judgments of Web pages pre-cludes much cognitive thought. The users tested had an emotional reaction to home pages that they could not control. This pre-cognitive "affective reaction" is a physiological response to what they see on the screen—a gut reaction. This carry over of first impressions to other attributes of products is sometimes called the "halo effect," or cognitive "confirmation bias" where users search for confirming evidence and ignore evidence contrary to their initial impression. People want to be right, and tend to look for clues that validate their initial hypothesis.*

Lindgaard then went on to say:

> *. . . the strong impact of the visual appeal of the site seemed to draw attention away from usability problems. This suggests that aesthetics, or visual appeal, factors may be detected first and that these could influence how users judge subsequent experience. . . . Hence, even if a Web site is highly usable and provides very useful information pre-sented in a logical arrangement, this may fail to impress a user whose first impression of the site was negative.*

Dr. Lindgaard's belief that a user bases his or her immediate impression of a Web site on emotion instead of reasoning is not one she holds in isolation. Indeed, her views are also indicative of the thoughts of Dr. B.J. Fogg, an experimental psychologist who teaches persuasive technology at Stanford University. As far back as 2003, when Dr. Fogg was carrying out research on the emotional credence of corporate Web sites, he commented (11):

There clearly is an interplay between our emotional reaction to a Webpage, and our conscious thought process. "Consumers apply both holistic (emotional) and analytic (cognitive) judgment in the decision to buy a product". So that feeling you evoke in users through a "clean, professional design" can have a halo effect on their buying judgments.

So not only does the research of Drs. Lindgaard and Fogg suggest an immediate emotional reaction to a Web page based upon its primary visual appeal, it also suggests that a favorable initial response may well contribute to a halo effect that can be carried over into many other areas of a site. Conversely, a negative initial response may well render the site as useful as a handbrake on a canoe.

Imagine, therefore, just how powerful a Web proposition could be if it reinforced those initial, positive thoughts and feelings at every point of engagement. Imagine, indeed, an online environment that created an interactive window to organizational culture and to absolute brand loyalty, where every user felt an intimate affinity and resonance with each of the emotional qualities that pervade it.

Given the research of Drs. Lindgaard and Fogg and, of course, the thoughts of Dr. Daniel Goleman, I would hope that you are now convinced that an inextricable set of emotional links exists between a Web site and the brand that it represents. I would also hope that you are convinced of the World Wide Web's potential for increasing brand value—and for eroding it.

Of course, given the amount of psychological research that goes into a brand development program, perhaps none of the emotional connections that we have uncovered in this chapter should come as a real surprise; for decades, most advertising campaigns have predicated their success on the ability to strike the right chords within the mind of a consumer. As I have said several times within this book, however, the Internet is different from traditional communications channels because it's both functional and interactive, and it enables a user to become intimate with a brand in ways that have never before been possible—and therein lies a world of opportunity for businesses that dare to be bold.

The Internet is also still evolving, whereas many traditional channels have been standing still for decades. In addition, demands for improvements in mobility and connectivity have driven an incredible surge in the adoption of Net-ready PDAs, which, together with the growth in wireless hotspots and Internet cafés, has given birth to a society that need never be away from the Web for long. At its current rate of speed, most people could be forgiven for wondering where it's all going to end—will things eventually settle down, or will the world be transformed into a digital society where nothing is achieved unless it is connected to an Internet gateway?

The Evolution of a Branded Web Site

Given that the last five to eight years have seen so many changes with regard to the digital branding concept, what does the future hold by way of Web development and what should we expect to see within the next few years?

My view on this issue, as I have already pointed out, is that because we are witnessing such a paradigm shift in terms of the Web's availability and appeal, I subsequently expect to see more customization and a much more emotionally focused style of Internet marketing—in essence, a style that focuses on brand culture.

As an example, just consider my family for a second. At one end of the scale, I have a nine-year-old daughter, who has been actively surfing the Net (under supervision, of course) since she was six years old. Having done so, she is now well versed in the online offerings of Disney, Bratz, and Nickleodeon and is also starting to ask about the dreaded world of Internet chat. At the other end of the age range, I have an eighty-five-year-old father-in-law who often cruises the Web in order to book flights and make travel arrangements when visiting his extended family. When he's online, he checks out the news from the BBC, calls us via Skype (which is extremely handy given that he's in Glasgow and we are in Sydney), and has become no stranger to the homepages of airlines such as British Airways, BMI, and Flybe.

So given the increasing diversity in the Internet's demographics, how can a branded Web site make sure that it caters for all ages and cultures by way of its online material, and how should it be looking to position itself?

In many ways, Forrester Research has already attempted to answer these questions by recognizing, and reacting to, the next stage of the

Internet's evolution. Because it predicates its business on identifying and "focusing on the business implications of technology change" (12), Forrester Research tends not to be very far from the mark when forecasting what lies ahead.

For instance, in October 2006, Forrester's Consumer Forum took place in Chicago under the mantle "Humanizing the Digital Experience." The purpose of the forum was to highlight a number of the challenges facing many of today's consumer-oriented businesses, given society's dependence on digital technology.

During the event, Christine Spivey Overby, principal analyst at Forrester Research, addressed a number of delegates under the conference theme, and in identifying a significant change in the demographic that's engaged with the World Wide Web, expressed that henceforth the Internet should be a much more user-friendly environment as it's now become mainstream and is no longer the sole domain of the technologically blessed. In defining her belief, Overby said (13):

> We're at a point where mainstream consumers are coming online and they're not going to put up with the same technology hassles.

In conceptualizing where she felt the future of digital marketing would go, she said (14):

> Everyone who wants to interact with the brand should be able to, while connecting with relevance. Marketers should ask three questions: First, what makes digital experiences more compelling—available to all, meaningful to one? Next, how do you design and support the humanized digital experience? Finally, what's the return on investment of digital experiences?

By way of determining an answer to Spivey Overby's question of "how do you design and support the humanized digital experience?" Forrester ran a series of blogs as part of its promotion of the Consumer Forum (15) and invited a number of industry professionals to contribute. In one such column, Christopher Carfi, the author of The Social Customer Manifesto Blog (16) and co-founder of the Cerado sales consultancy (17), crafted his response as follows (18):

What is a humanized digital experience?
An interaction in which the human benefits are more visible than
*   the technology*
Emotional
Tactile
We feel part of the community

The building blocks of a humanized digital experience:
Useful
. . . offers value
Relevant
Reliable
Functional

Not long after posting his views on the Forrester Blog, Carfi also used his social customer blog to review a keynote presentation given by Marissa Mayer, Google's vice president of search products and user experience (19), who was speaking at Harvard's Cyberposium on November 11, 2006. During her presentation, Mayer cited Google's future strategy as having four major strands:

- More content
- Easier computing
- Personalization
- Better search

Within each point, Mayer then went on to detail some of the key initiatives that Google was pursuing and under "personalization" listed such objectives as:

- Implicit search . . . bring interesting content without asking for it
- Personalized homepage . . . make it your own
- Gadgets, API to create, able to syndicate (can add to own homepage)
- Google notebook . . . research tool
- Custom search engine

As you can see from Mayer's articulation of Google's Internet strategy, Google is looking to focus on improving its range of content and material while also improving its functionality to facilitate a much easier ride for the user—and it's also looking to customize itself in as many ways as it can in order to make its Web experience absolutely unique.

I have no doubt that Google will be successful in executing its plans and in developing a much more customized online proposition. I also have no doubt that many other businesses will follow its lead and, as a result, help make the Internet an even more dynamic and engaging environment than it is today.

Of course, the benefits of adopting such a strategy for any type of business with marketing on its mind are more or less blindingly obvious—a greater dependence on the brand, an increasing desire to log on, a deeper sense of organizational engagement, and a positive impression of the brand's cultural qualities, to name but a few. That will not be all, however, as the more an individual becomes dependent upon his daily fix of digital branding, the more difficult it will be to displace his loyalties—such is the influence of emotional response.

Perhaps this will mean that Web sites such as *Ba.com*, the homepage of British Airways, will start producing online content for kids as part of its "Skyflyer" program in order to reflect the care and attention that it shows for children in the air. It may also mean that many of the world's online banking portals start tailoring their content by age range, too, to appear more attractive to aspiring investors. The possibilities are endless for organizations that are capable of thinking holistically, and that can only be viewed as a positive when considering such things as the digital branding concept and technological innovation.

Web 2.0

The technology at the forefront of the new generation of branded Web sites will undoubtedly be driven by Web 2.0—the imminent next stage in the Internet's evolution.

The concept of Web 2.0 was started just a few years ago by a relatively small group of people who collectively focused on the development of the Web as a multipurpose platform. Such has been the pace of adoption, however, that Web 2.0 now has its very own "summit" (20) and attracts a great deal of interest from many organizations that share a vested interest in developing the Internet's potential. Because of this, attendance at the Web 2.0 summit is by invitation only.

Essentially, the evolution of Web 2.0 concentrates on the Web's ability to develop as a multifunctional platform by improving the ways in which it harnesses and shares information, galvanizes and enriches the user experience, and increases its levels of user participation. By way of helping people understand just what Web 2.0 represents, Tim O'Reilly, founder and CEO of O'Reilly Media and a previous host of the Web 2.0 conference, has published an excellent paper on his Web page (21).

Although there are still a great many views as to just exactly what Web 2.0 will deliver, the common school of thought is that it will substantially change the ways in which the Internet is perceived. For instance, when I spoke to Gitte Lindgaard about how she saw the Web evolving from a branding perspective, she told me:

> *The Internet will definitely become more multi-sensory as it evolves over time. It also has to cater for people who are blind and deaf, not to mention a rapidly ageing population. To do this, it needs to start incorporating such things as hand-held controllers and touch screens that vibrate or react responsively. This technology already exists and it could well become widely used in the future.*

So just imagine what this might bring: the ability to carry out a virtual test-drive of a new car perhaps or the facilitation of online shopping for the audibly impaired?

Two examples of Web sites that are deemed to possess a number of the qualities required to satisfy the requirements of Web 2.0 are *Flickr.com* (22) and *del.icio.us* (23). While the former is a site for sharing photographs and images, the latter is a site for the "social sharing of bookmarks." The key advantage of both of these sites is that users can access their data and material wherever they are in the world without accessing their own machine and that they can share their stuff with the entire Internet community. I will leave it to you to decide which one might be the next YouTube!

Of course, there are many other examples of Web sites that possess the qualities associated with Web 2.0, but from a pure-play branding perspective many of the large corporations have yet to catch on. So who knows what we might see in the future when the larger corporations wake up. Perhaps the personalization and self-managed, user-based content that is currently associated with Web sites like Flickr will become an invaluable component to many of the big-name brands within the next couple of years.

Whatever the future may bring as far as the Net is concerned, I hope you embrace it with open arms. The World Wide Web is a wonderful place, and it just might be the final frontier. It has made some people fortunes, and it has lost others millions. It can also be the making, or breaking, of a brand. In the midst of all this change, however, one thing is certain: The sites that emotionally connect with people have the best chance of success.

• • •

Key Points

The key points to remember from this chapter are as follows:

- Branded Web sites generate a series of emotional responses.
- It is possible to construct a Web site to take advantage of emotional states and influence desired outcomes.
- In the future, more and more Web sites will be designed to be emotionally responsive and will be capable of personalizing content to an extremely high degree.

ENDNOTES

1. *http://hrfundablog.blogspot.com/2005_05_01_archive.html*
2. *http://competencyandei.com/Definition-of-emotional-intelligence*
3. *http://en.wikipedia.org/wiki/Emotional_intelligence*
4. *http://thewellspring.com/Cat/Adult_books/Emotional_Intelligence.html*
5. *www.danielgoleman.info/purchase.html*
6. *www.allaboutmedicalsales.com/articles/emotional_intelligence_ mb_110602.htm*
7. *www.eiconsortium.org/research/business_case_for_ei.htm*
8. *www.esquire.com/features/articles/2003/030903_mfe_falling_1.html*
9. *www.imirage.com/default.aspx?pageid=152*
10. *www.Websiteoptimization.com/speed/tweak/blink/*
11. *www.Webpronews.com/topnews/topnews/wpn-60- 20060303YouCantDrinkAnUglySitePretty.html*

12. *www.forrester.com/FactSheet*

13. *www.dmnews.com/cms/dm-news/Internet-marketing/38740.html*

14. Ibid.

15. *http://blogs.forrester.com/consumerforum/*

16. *www.socialcustomer.com/*

17. *www.cerado.com/*

18. *http://blogs.forrester.com/consumerforum/2006/10/index.html*

19. *www.socialcustomer.com/2006/11/googles_maria_m.html*

20. *www.Web2con.com/*

21. *www.oreillynet.com/pub/a/oreilly/tim/news/2005/09/30/what-is-Web-20.html*

22. *www.flickr.com/*

23. *http://del.icio.us/*

Epilogue

DURING THE INTRODUCTION TO THIS BOOK, I SAID THAT I
sincerely hoped you would find it both informative and entertaining—
with any luck in that regard, it will have fulfilled your expectations. I
also hope that it has helped you look at the ways in which you now
perceive branded Web sites. Perhaps in the future when you log on,
you will do so with a more critical eye.

These days, there is really no excuse for a poorly designed and
managed online proposition. We have more technology available than
we've ever had before, and we have access to a greater target audience
than we have ever known.

In the five to six years that I have been reviewing sites for brandchannel, I have seen some fantastic examples of branded portals.
Indeed, during the writing of this book, I was particularly impressed
with GE and IBM, not to mention those good old soldiers of Coca-
Cola and Disney. Unfortunately, however, I have also seen some rather
poor representations of brands that deserve better and I am sure that
as you surf the Web you will find them too.

Notwithstanding the perpetual evolution that is taking place
around us with regard to the World Wide Web and the remarkable

technological advancements that have been made, we should all bear in mind that brand strategies are created by people, for people, and there is no substitute for that.

In closing this book, therefore, I would simply like to say that it is clear from the content that exists on the Internet now that there are some very special people in the world today, with talents far greater than mine. Take the team at Java, for instance, or, indeed, the man who gave birth to Flash technology, Jonathan Gay. Add to that some of the brand strategists, marketers, product developers, and Web designers who have made it their mission in life to produce both compelling and engaging material and I think you'll agree that the world would be somewhat morose without them.

With that last thought in mind, I would like to thank each and every one of them for their efforts so far and, of course, in helping to make the Internet what it is today. I've had a real blast over the last few years reviewing the outputs of their endeavors—and I look forward to seeing a lot more of their work in the future.

Glossary

ACSI: American Customer Satisfaction Index

Anorak: A train-spotting techie

B2B: Business to business

B2C: Business to consumer

BBC: British Broadcasting Corporation

Bitmap: Digital image file

Boston Grid: Marketing model designed by the Boston Consulting Group

Bundoo: Thick dense reeds and weed grass—most prevalent on Ranfurley Castle Golf Course

Charles Laughton: Famous for playing Quasimodo in the 1939 classic *The Hunchback of Notre Dame*

DNS: Domain Name System

GIF: Graphic interchange format—very low-resolution, animated graphics that are often used in "banner" creation

HTML: Hypertext markup language

ICANN: Internet Corporation for Assigned Names and Numbers

IP: Internet protocol

ISP: Internet service provider

Layout: The navigational design of a Web page

MENSA: The High IQ Society

Net Nerd: See Web Head

Pixel: The smallest picture element—single dot or square

Porter's 5 Forces: Market model designed by global strategy expert Michael Porter

PPL: Phonographic Performance LTD

Raster Graphics: Illustration of an image made up of pixels

RSS: Really Simple Syndication

Techie: A bearded, Nike-wearing individual, usually found in a darkened room

UDRP: Uniform domain names dispute resolution policy

URL: Uniform resource locator

Vector Graphics Technology: The production and illustration of mathematically created images

VOIP: Voice over Internet protocol

Web Head: Someone who spends almost every available minute playing with the Internet

XML: Extensible markup language

SEO: Search engine optimization

Index

Books from Allworth Press

Allworth Press is an imprint of Allworth Communications, Inc. Selected titles are listed below.

Brandjam: Humanizing Brands Through Emotional Design
by Marc Gobé (Hardcover, 6¼ × 9¼, 288 pages, $24.95)

Emotional Branding: The New Paradigm for Connecting Brands to People
by Marc Gobé (Hardcover, 6¼ × 9¼, 352 pages, $24.95)

Citizen Brand: 10 Commandments for Transforming Brands in a Consumer Democracy
by Marc Gobé (Hardcover, 5½ × 8½, 256 pages, $24.95)

Branding for Nonprofits: Developing Identity with Integrity
by D.K. Holland (paperback, 6 × 9, 208 pages, $19.95)

The Real Business of Web Design
by John Waters (paperback, 6 × 9, 256 pages, $19.95)

Design Management: Using Design to Build Brand Value and Corporate Innovation
by Brigitte Borja de Mozota (paperback, 6 × 9, 288 pages, $24.95)

Creating the Perfect Design Brief: How to Manage Design for Strategic Advantage
by Peter Phillips (paperback, 6 × 9, 224 pages, $19.95)

The Copyright Guide: A Friendly Handbook to Protecting and Profiting from Copyrights, Third Edition
by Lee Wilson (paperback, 6 × 9, 256 pages, $19.95)

Fair Use, Free Use, and Use by Permission: How to Handle Copyrights in All Media
by Lee Wilson (paperback, 6 × 9, 256 pages, $24.95)

The Trademark Guide: A Friendly Handbook for Protecting and Profiting from Trademarks, Second Edition
by Lee Wilson (paperback, 6 × 9, 256 pages, $19.95)